ILLUSTRATED BIBLE MAPS

Illustrated Bible Maps

Published by Rose Publishing
An imprint of Tyndale House Ministries
Carol Stream, Illinois
rose-publishing.com

ISBN 979-8-4005-0251-4

Library of Congress Cataloging-in-Publication Data

Names: Tyndale House Publishers, editor.
Title: Illustrated Bible maps.
Description: Carol Stream, Illinois : Rose Publishing, [2025] | Includes index. | Summary: "Bible maps, illustrations, and photographs showing when and where events in the Bible happened"-- Provided by publisher.
Identifiers: LCCN 2024062201 (print) | LCCN 2024062202 (ebook) | ISBN 9798400502514 (paperback) | ISBN 9798400502538 (epub)
Subjects: LCSH: Bible--Geography. | Bible--History of Biblical events. | Bible--Geography--Maps. | Bible--History of Biblical events--Maps.
Classification: LCC BS630 .I55 2025 (print) | LCC BS630 (ebook) | DDC 220.9/1--dc23/eng/20250215
LC record available at https://lccn.loc.gov/2024062201
LC ebook record available at https://lccn.loc.gov/2024062202

Printed in the United States of America
April 2025, 1st printing

CONTENTS

THE BEGINNING

The book of Genesis recounts God's grace in the beginning of human history and in the lives of Israel's ancestors. This first book of the Old Testament introduces themes that weave throughout the Bible—themes such as blessings and curses; righteousness and sinfulness; God's sovereignty and human rebellion; and the ongoing struggle between good and evil that has characterized humanity ever since the garden of Eden.

Starting with Adam and Eve, God created humans in his image and gave them stewardship over the earth. When the first couple rebelled against their Maker, they and their descendants fell under the curse of sin and death. But God, in his grace, still provided for their needs, and the human race multiplied.

While the curse continued to hang over the fallen world, God chose a certain family whom he would use to bring salvation and blessing to all the nations of the earth. God established an eternal covenant with Abraham and his descendants.

Even though Abraham's family sometimes proved themselves unworthy of their covenant blessings, God kept his commitment. We can see throughout the stories in Genesis that the Lord of the universe will move heaven and earth to bring about his plan. His promises are great, and he is fully able to bring them into fruition at his appointed time. To participate in God's plan has always required faith—faith like Abraham's, to follow God's calling, because, as the writer of Hebrews says, "It is impossible to please God without faith" (Heb. 11:6).

GENESIS

Genesis is a book of beginnings—of the universe and humanity; of sin and its catastrophic effects; and of the formation of God's chosen people. Genesis traces God's promised blessings from Abraham and Sarah through their descendants: the twelve sons of Jacob (Israel). Genesis is foundational to the biblical narrative, because most other books of the Bible draw from its contents.

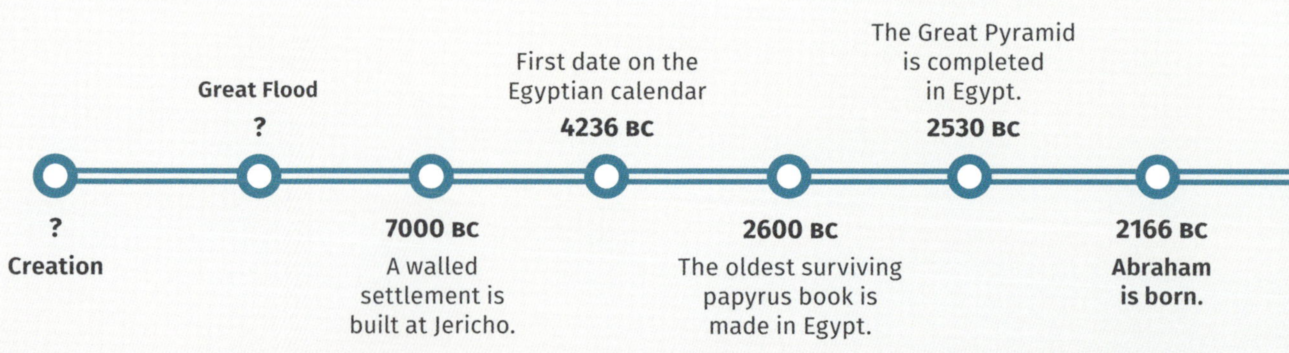

TURKEY
Fertile Crescent
SYRIA
Canaan
IRAQ
Tigris River
Euphrates River
Ur
IRAN
EGYPT
SAUDI ARABIA

The earliest events of biblical history took place in a large region known as the Fertile Crescent, which included the relatively lush land around the Tigris and Euphrates rivers. Abraham and Sarah's journeys took them throughout the Fertile Crescent, from Ur to Canaan—and for a short time to Egypt.

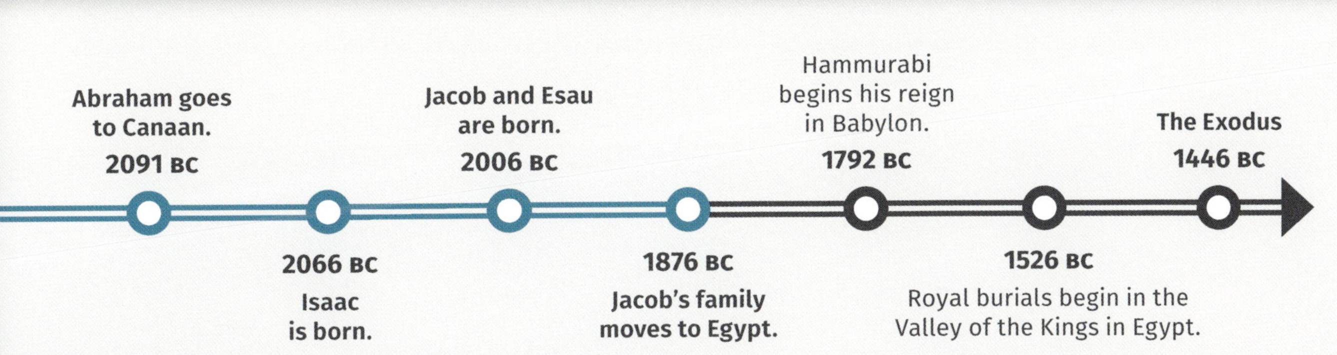

God's Good Creation

God transformed chaos into the present ordered universe. In the first three days of creation, he separated light and dark, water and sky, sea and land. In the next three days, he populated each realm: sun, moon, and stars in the heavens; birds in the air and fish in the seas; animals and humans on the land. The seventh day stood apart as God's day of rest, which would provide a weekly pattern for human activity and Sabbath rest (Ex. 20:8–11). When God looked upon the created order, he declared it all "very good!" (Gen. 1:31).

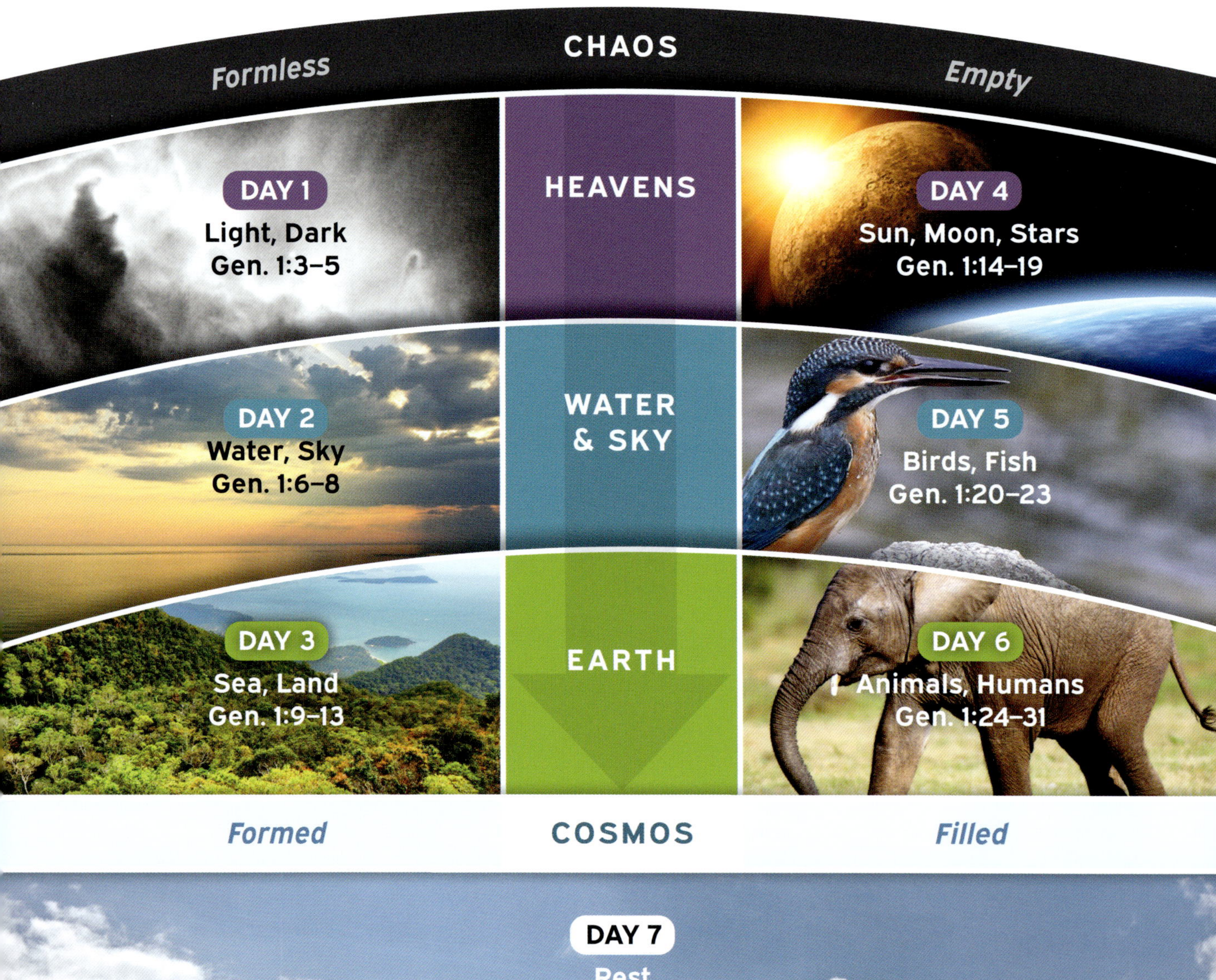

Adam and Eve in the Garden

God created the first couple, Adam and Eve, to populate and govern the earth (Gen. 1:26–31). Adam and Eve lived in the garden of Eden in a state of innocence. But when they violated God's one prohibition of eating from the tree of the knowledge of good and evil, everything changed. Immediately, they felt shame and hid from their Creator (Gen. 3:1–8). Though God expelled them from Eden, making them live out their days in a fallen world, he still provided for them and gave them children (Gen. 3:21; 4:1).

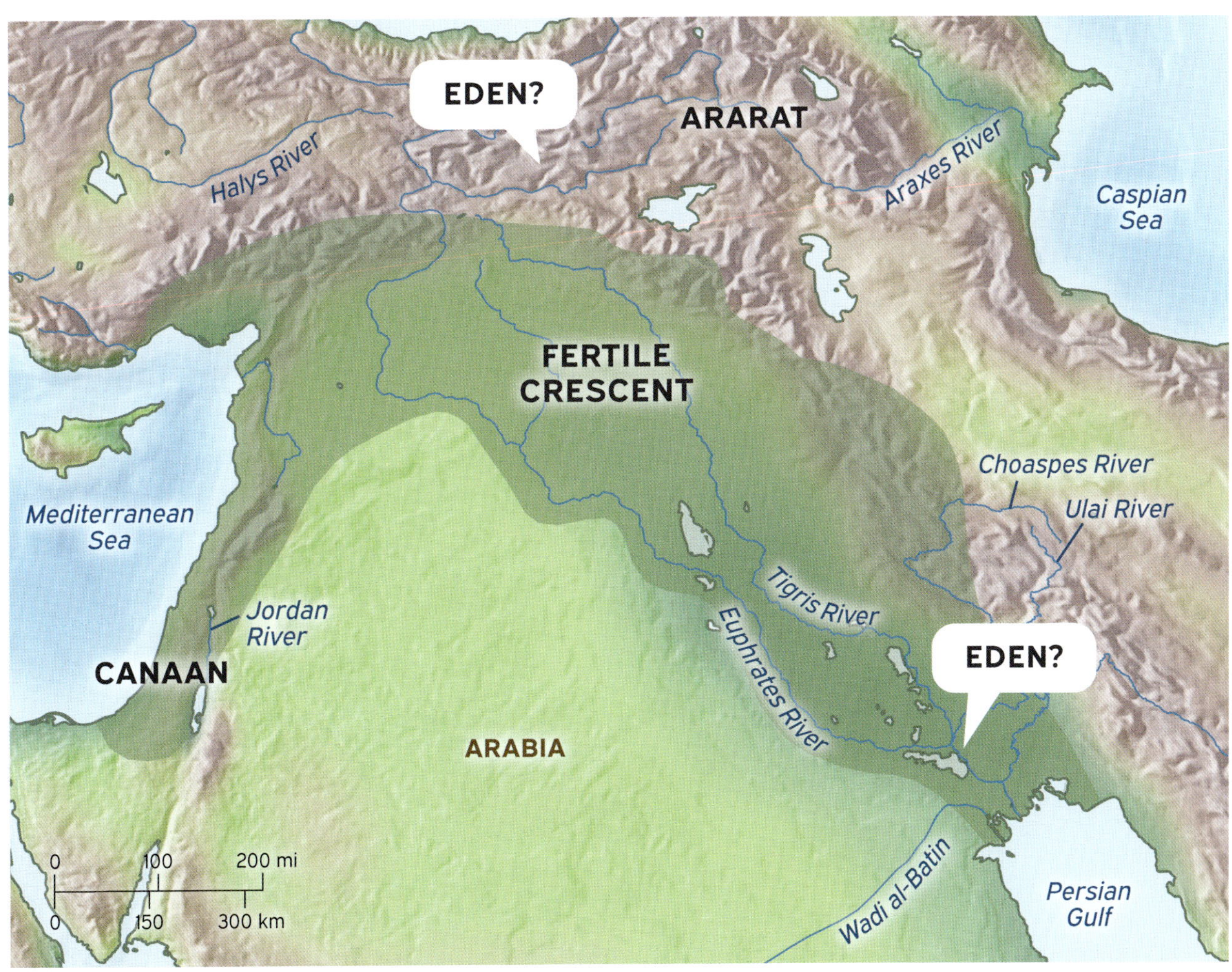

Where Was Eden?

Eden was the general location in which the garden was placed, not the garden itself. The term *eden* may mean "plain," "delight," or "fertility." Though no one knows Eden's exact location, it is described as being "in the east" (Gen. 2:8), that is, east of Canaan, the Israelites' later homeland. Genesis 2:10–14 indicates that four rivers flowed from Eden: Pishon and Gihon (both unidentified) and the great Tigris and Euphrates. Eden might have been located near the mountains of Ararat (eastern Turkey today) or in the marshy delta near the Persian Gulf. Possibilities for the four rivers exist in either location.

The Great Flood

Over time, humans multiplied and filled the earth, but sinful thoughts and actions multiplied with them. Genesis tells us that God regretted what had become of his beautiful creation, and he chose to destroy it in a great flood and to begin again with one righteous man, Noah, and his family. At God's direction, Noah built an ark to save his family and "every kind of animal" (Gen. 7:14). The rain lasted forty days, but the floodwaters which covered the earth took much longer to recede. After a year inside the ark, Noah and his family opened the door of the ark and exited onto dry land. God made a covenant with Noah and all creation that never again would he send such a flood as judgment upon the world. The sign of this covenant would be the rainbow in the sky (Gen. 9:8–17).

> **"The water covered even the highest mountains on the earth, rising more than twenty-two feet above the highest peaks."**
>
> GENESIS 7:19–20

Mount Ararat

Where Was Noah's Ark?

Genesis tells us that the ark rested "on the mountains of Ararat" (Gen. 8:4). These mountains may be the same mountain range that is located southeast of the Black Sea near Lake Van and that spreads across parts of Turkey, Armenia, and Iran. A "Mount Ararat" is located in eastern Turkey, with its peak reaching nearly 17,000 feet (5,200 m) above sea level, and it has been the site of much speculation about whether it holds the remains of Noah's ark, though Genesis does not specify a particular mountain.

Places in Genesis

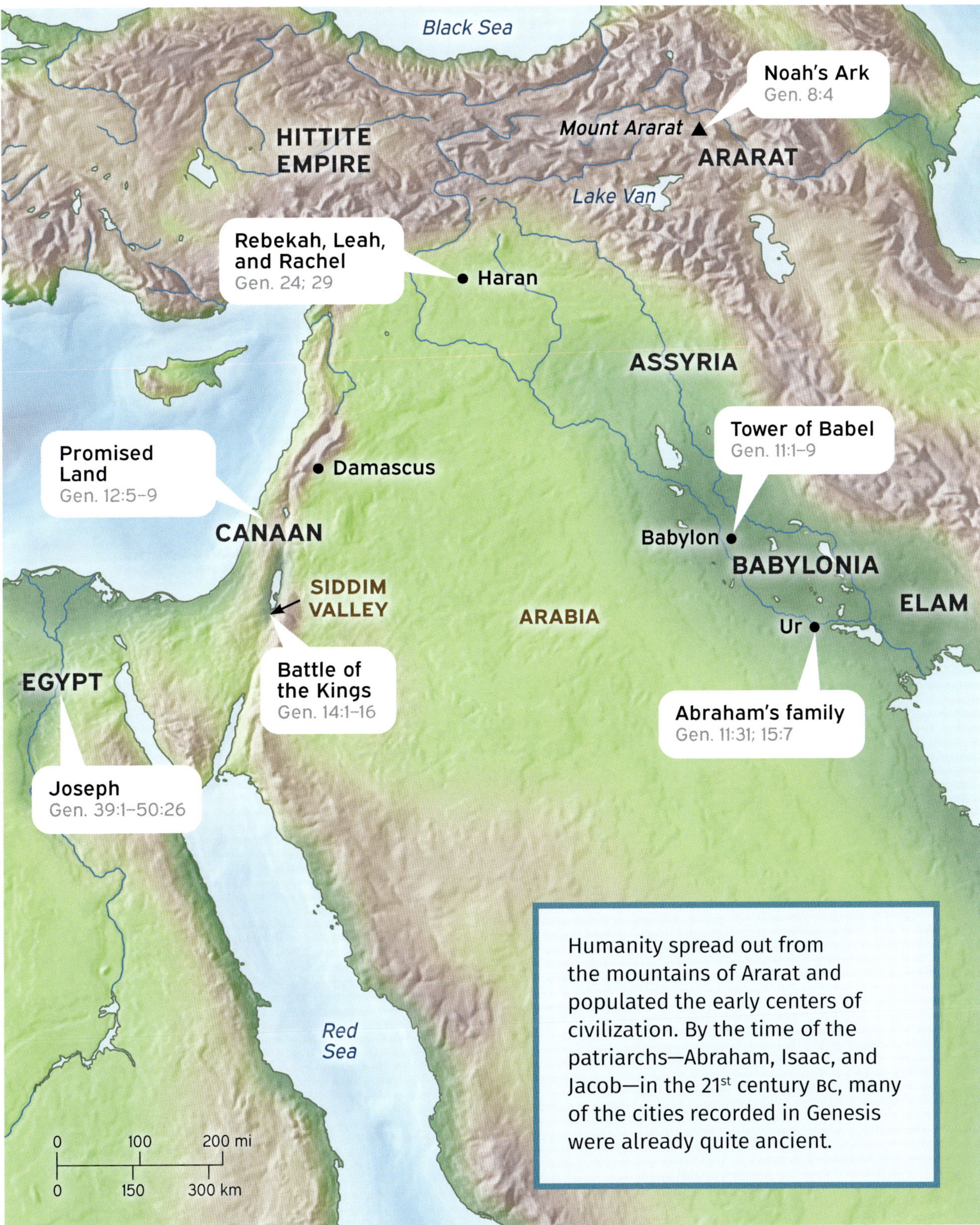

Humanity spread out from the mountains of Ararat and populated the early centers of civilization. By the time of the patriarchs—Abraham, Isaac, and Jacob—in the 21st century BC, many of the cities recorded in Genesis were already quite ancient.

Reconstructed Ziggurat of Ur in southern Iraq

The Tower of Babel (Gen. 11:1–9)

The Tower of Babel may have resembled ancient ziggurats. These buildings, found in the major cities of Mesopotamia, consisted of several platforms, each smaller than the one below it. The top platform held a small temple dedicated to the builder's or the city's god. Ziggurats were intended to serve as pathways reaching up to the gods. The Tower of Babel may have been similar in construction to—though considerably larger than—the Ziggurat of Ur, which dates back to the 21st century BC.

Table of Nations

Over half of the names listed in Genesis 10:1–32 are identifiable ancient peoples, whose broad areas of settlement are shown on the map. Arrows indicate general lines of descent of Noah's three sons: Shem, Ham, and Japheth.

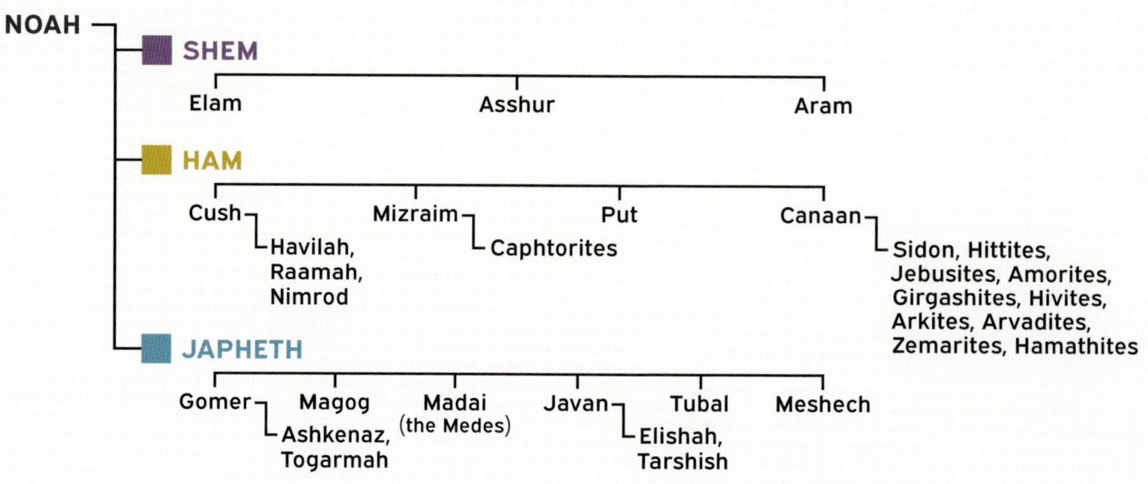

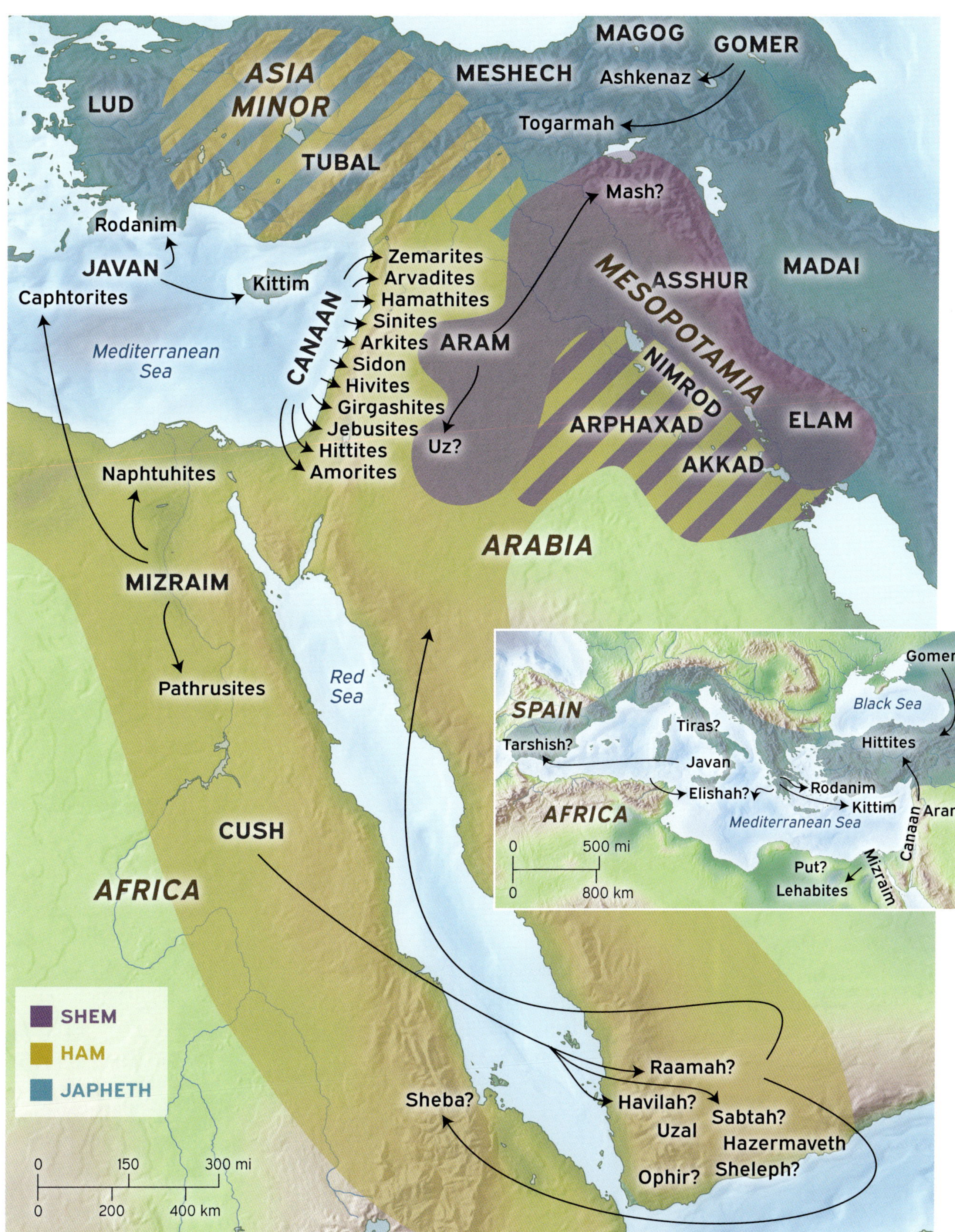
MAGOG
GOMER
MESHECH
Ashkenaz
ASIA MINOR
LUD
Togarmah
TUBAL
Mash?
Rodanim
JAVAN
Kittim
Caphtorites
Zemarites
Arvadites
Hamathites
Sinites
Arkites
Sidon
Hivites
Girgashites
Jebusites
Hittites
Amorites
CANAAN
ARAM
Uz?
MESOPOTAMIA
ASSHUR
MADAI
NIMROD
ARPHAXAD
ELAM
AKKAD
Mediterranean Sea
Naphtuhites
MIZRAIM
ARABIA
Pathrusites
Red Sea
CUSH
AFRICA
Gomer
Black Sea
SPAIN
Tiras?
Tarshish?
Hittites
Javan
Rodanim
Elishah?
Kittim
Aram
AFRICA
Mediterranean Sea
Canaan
0 500 mi
0 800 km
Put?
Lehabites
Mizraim
SHEM
HAM
JAPHETH
Raamah?
Sheba?
Havilah?
Sabtah?
Uzal
Hazermaveth
Ophir?
Sheleph?
0 150 300 mi
0 200 400 km

The Call of Abraham

Abram's family was from Ur of the Chaldeans, but Abram's father, Terah, moved the family to Haran. That, however, was not the home God had planned for Abram. God called Abram to go to a land that God would show him (Gen. 12:1). In faith, Abram obeyed, and he, his wife Sarai, and his nephew Lot migrated to Canaan (Heb. 11:8). God changed Abram's and Sarai's names to Abraham ("father of many") and Sarah ("princess"). God's covenant with Abraham included promises of land and numerous descendants. Though Abraham and Sarah were childless, God fulfilled his promise by giving them a son, Isaac; thus, Abraham became the patriarch of God's chosen people.

The Standard of Ur (2500 BC) depicting spoils of war

UR

Ur of the Chaldeans was an important city in southern Mesopotamia (in modern-day Iraq). The city had a complex system of government and trade, as well as a writing system that was used for issuing receipts, making contracts, and drafting other legal documents. The city contained streets, drains, two-story houses, a temple tower (ziggurat), and roads linking it to other major cities.

"Beehive" homes in Haran, a style of housing dating to 2000 BC

HARAN

Haran means "caravan." Ancient commercial routes converged in Haran, making it a bustling site for trade. The city was also known for its worship of the moon god, Sin. Terah's name is related to the word for moon in Hebrew, and his family appears to have worshiped such gods (Josh. 24:2–3). Haran is located near the border of Syria and Turkey today.

Flocks grazing in the Judean desert

CANAAN

Canaan in the Old Testament is the land west of the Jordan River. Canaan's economy depended on farming and herding sheep, goats, and camels. In Canaan, Abraham and his family lived a semi-nomadic lifestyle, relocating to different places to find food and water for their flocks (Gen. 20:1; 21:34; 26:1).

Where Were the Hittites?

Canaan lay between the Egyptian Empire to the south and the Hittite Empire to the north. The Hittite Empire had its center in Anatolia (modern-day Turkey), with its capital at Hattusha, but at times the empire extended over a much larger area without definite boundaries because it included many dependent city-states. The Hittites had a strong presence in Canaan, as seen in the story of Abraham purchasing a burial site for Sarah from Hittites in Hebron (Gen. 23:1–20).

Abraham in Canaan

Abraham, Sarah, and Lot probably entered Canaan by following the King's Highway—an ancient and well-traveled route that ran just east of Canaan. By this time, some Canaanite settlements—Jericho and Megiddo, for example—had already been established for centuries. Abraham and his family traveled southward through Canaan, building altars to the Lord, and the Lord renewed his promise: "I will give this land to your descendants" (Gen. 12:7).

> **"Abram traveled through the land as far as Shechem. There he set up camp beside the oak of Moreh.... Abram built an altar there and dedicated it to the LORD, who had appeared to him. After that, Abram traveled south and set up camp in the hill country, with Bethel to the west and Ai to the east. There he built another altar.... Then Abram continued traveling south by stages toward the Negev."**
>
> GENESIS 12:6–9

What Were Altars For?

The first recorded altar was built by Noah (Gen. 8:20–21), though Cain and Abel gave the first offerings (Gen. 4:3–4). The patriarchs built numerous altars to designate sacred sites of divine revelation or personal claims to land. As places of sacrifice, altars were the most common image of worship in the ancient world. Altars were made of stone, earth, brick, or metal and wood. Their table-like form allowed smoke to rise unhindered. The typical altar was on a raised platform accessed by a ramp or stairway, elevating sacrificial worship heavenward.

Altar built by Abraham, Isaac, or Jacob
Abraham's entry into Canaan
Lot's route to Sodom
Hazor
Sea of Galilee
Ashteroth-karnaim
Mount Carmel
Mount Tabor
Megiddo
Ham?
Mount Gilboa
Jordan River
The King's Highway
Mediterranean Sea
Mount Ebal
Mount Gerizim
Oak of Moreh
Joppa
CANAAN
Bethel
Ai
Jericho
Mount Moriah
Kiriathaim
Oaks of Mamre
PHILISTIA
Dead Sea
Hebron
Gerar?
Beersheba
Gomorrah?
Kir-hareseth
Sodom?
NEGEV
Zoar
Beer-lahai-roi?
To EGYPT
0
25 mi
0
25 km

Jacob's Escape

Even from birth, twins Jacob and Esau struggled against each other, with Jacob often getting the upper hand. With his mother's help, Jacob deceived his father, Isaac, into blessing him instead of Esau. Fearing his brother's revenge, Jacob moved to his grandfather Abraham's old homeland, Haran in Paddan-aram. There, Jacob married sisters Leah and Rachel, though it was only Rachel he had wanted. Over time, Jacob and his father-in-law, Laban—who had already proven himself as deceitful as Jacob (Gen. 29:15–30)—had a falling out, and God told Jacob to return to Canaan (Gen. 31:1–3).

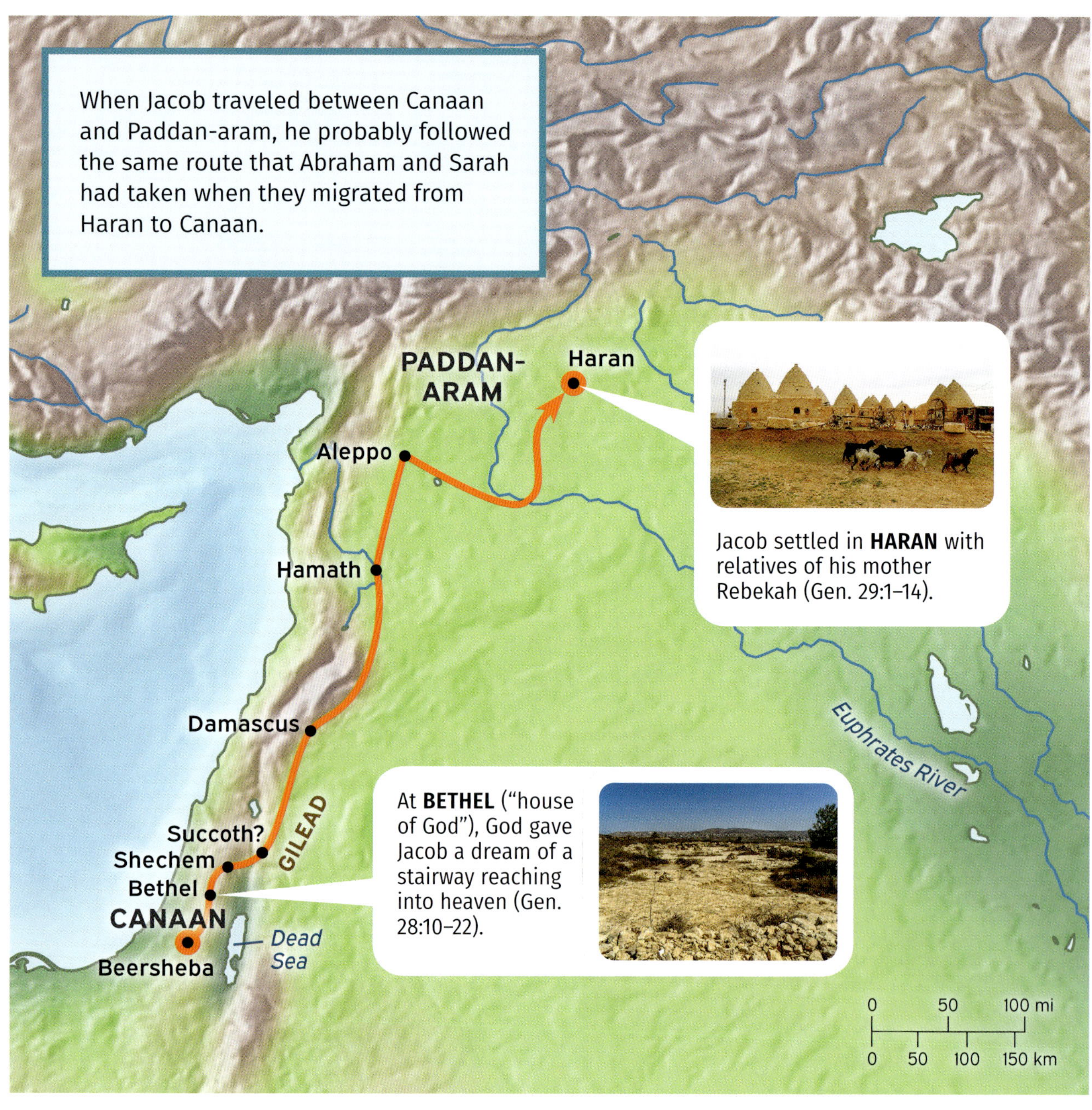

Jacob's Return

Going back to Canaan meant facing his estranged brother, Esau. As Esau and his four hundred men were on their way to intercept Jacob's caravan, Jacob quickly sought God's protection and sent gifts to pacify his brother. When Esau arrived, Jacob was not met with revenge but with forgiveness. The two were reconciled, though Jacob did not follow Esau back to Edom but rather went on to Canaan (Gen. 33). No matter where Jacob lived throughout his lifetime, the covenantal promises that God had made to Abraham clearly followed Jacob: His life was spared, his wealth increased, and his family grew.

Jacob and Esau were reunited near the Jabbok River, before Jacob left to settle near **SHECHEM** (Gen. 33:1–20).

Jacob was near the **JABBOK RIVER** when he wrested with God at Peniel ("face of God"), where God changed his name to Israel ("struggles with God") (Gen. 32:22–30).

Joseph in Egypt

While most of the events involving the families of Genesis—Isaac, Rebekah, Jacob, Leah, and Rachel—take place in Canaan or in Abraham's former homeland of Haran in Paddan-aram, the story of Joseph at the end of Genesis is different. Joseph's story is set primarily in Egypt. Joseph's father, Jacob (Abraham's grandson), had twelve sons who would become the ancestral patriarchs of the tribes of Israel. Joseph was Jacob's eleventh son, and Joseph's ten older brothers were so jealous of him that they sold him to passing merchants who took him to Egypt. But God was with Joseph in Egypt. Joseph prospered and rose from being a slave to becoming the second-highest ruler in the empire. Eventually, his family was reconciled with him in Egypt.

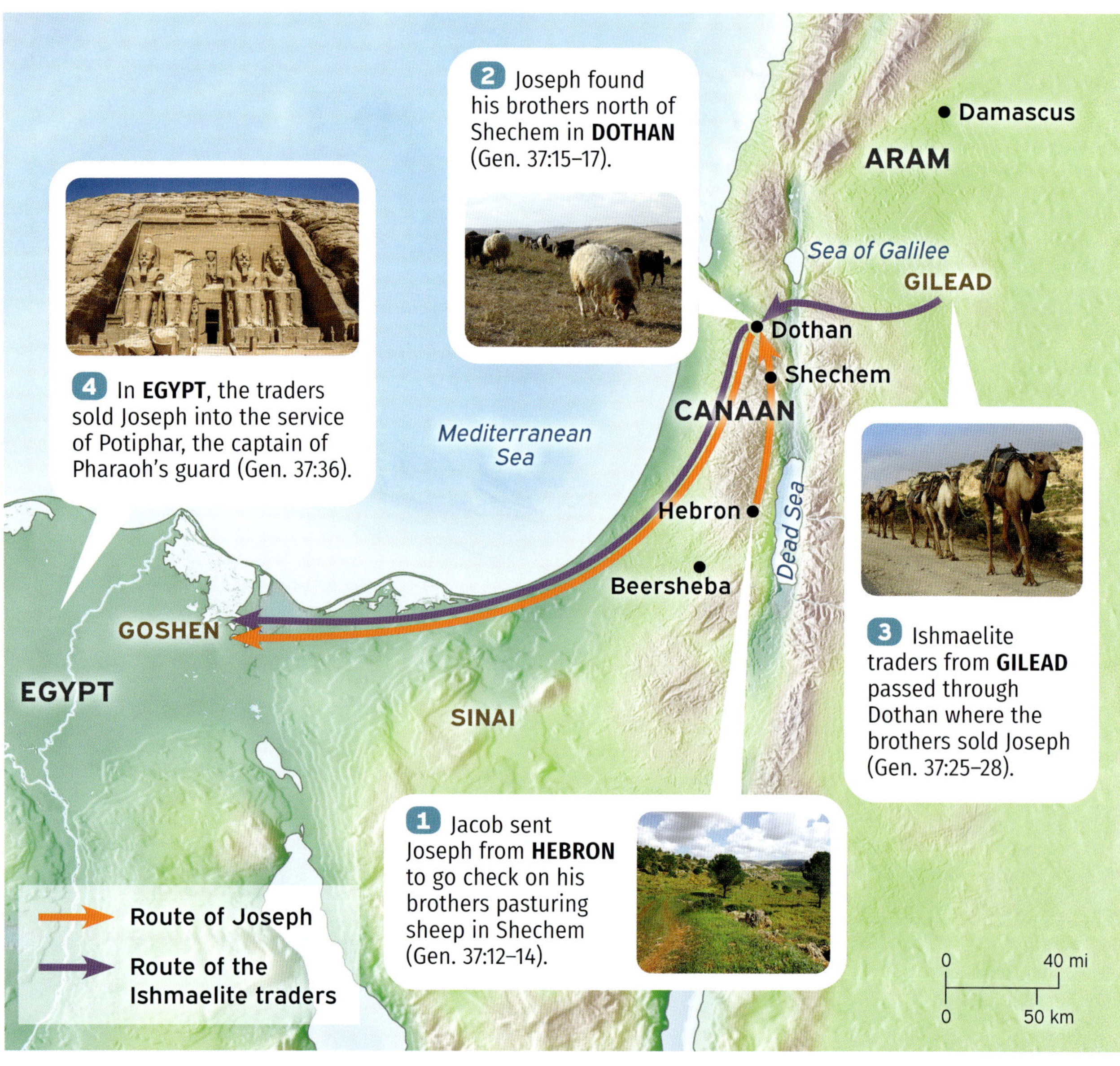

Jacob had twelve sons and one daughter from four different wives. The descendants of these sons would become the twelve tribes of Israel, whom Moses would lead out of Egypt four centuries later.

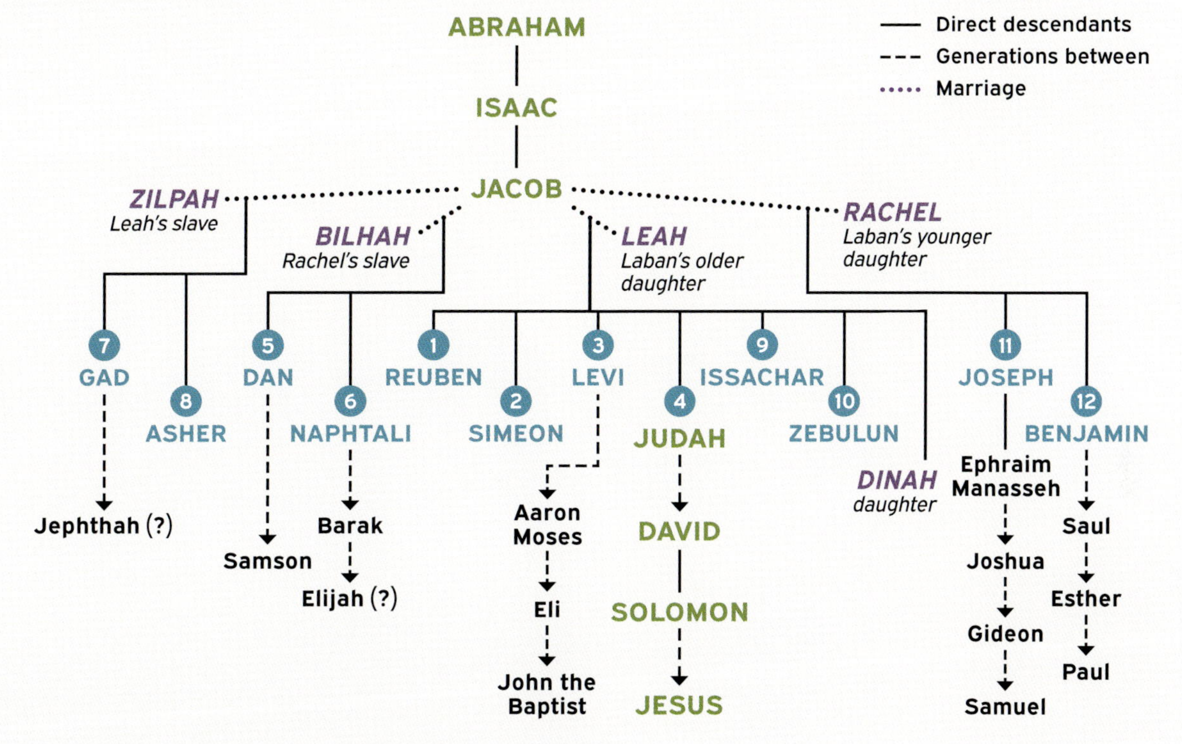

Where Did Jacob's Family Settle?

At Joseph's urging, Joseph's father and siblings and their families settled in Goshen to wait out the severe famine (Gen. 45:10–11). Famines were a frequent occurrence in the ancient Near East. (Abraham had also taken refuge in Egypt during a famine; Gen. 12:10.) Goshen, the fertile region of the Nile Delta in the northeast corner of Egypt, must have been a very welcome respite for Jacob's family from Canaan, where "the famine continued to ravage the land" (Gen. 43:1). Jacob's descendants lived in Egypt far longer than the seven-year famine in Joseph's day. The descendants of Jacob's twelve sons prospered and eventually "filled the land" of Goshen (Ex. 1:1–7). The book of Genesis ends with God's chosen family not in the promised land but in Egypt.

Sinai Mountains

THE EXODUS

By the end of Genesis, God's chosen family had grown from Abraham and Sarah to a fourth generation consisting of seventy family members who traveled from Canaan to Egypt to escape a famine. In Egypt, Joseph (Abraham's great-grandson) used his prominent position to provide for his family as they settled in the region of Goshen in the lush Nile Delta.

But at some point after the death of Joseph, a pharaoh came to power who had no regard for Joseph's legacy in Egypt. This pharaoh feared the growing population of Hebrews (the descendants of Jacob's family). So the pharaoh enslaved them and worked them ruthlessly. The people cried out to God for help, and he heard them, and he used a man named Moses to bring them out of Egypt and lead them to their ancestral homeland, the land God had promised to Abraham, Isaac, and Jacob.

This exodus from Egypt occurred sometime between 1450 and 1250 BC, when Egypt was arguably the greatest military and cultural power in the world. It was during this golden era of Egyptian power that the Hebrew slaves departed Egypt. God did not sneak his people out during a time of Egyptian weakness; he led them out when the pharaoh was strong, demonstrating that any earthly ruler and any man-made god was no match for the one true Lord.

EXODUS THROUGH DEUTERONOMY

Exodus is about God rescuing his people from slavery in Egypt and providing for them in the wilderness. Leviticus deals primarily with the duties of the tribe of Levi, especially the sacrifices, holy days, and ceremonies involving the tabernacle. Numbers (named after the two censuses in the book) records the Israelites' decades-long wanderings through the wilderness. Deuteronomy consists of the sermons Moses gave on the edge of the promised land to the younger generation who would enter Canaan.

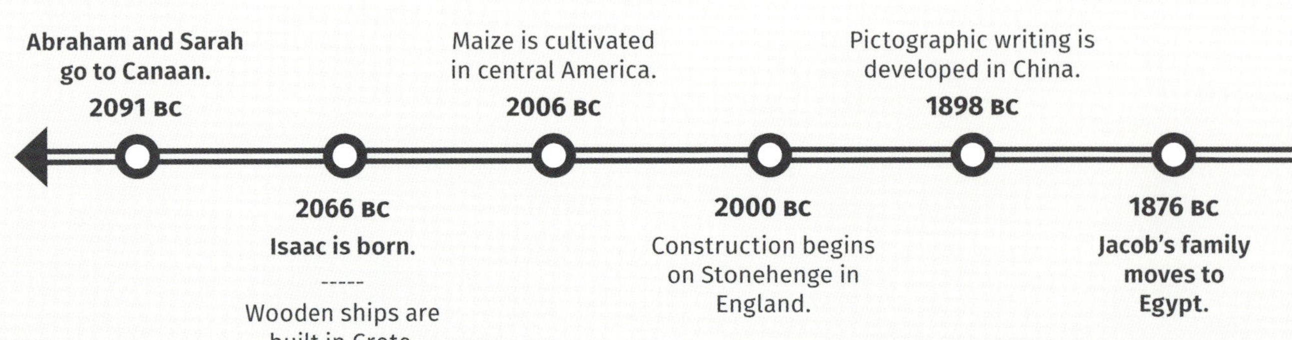

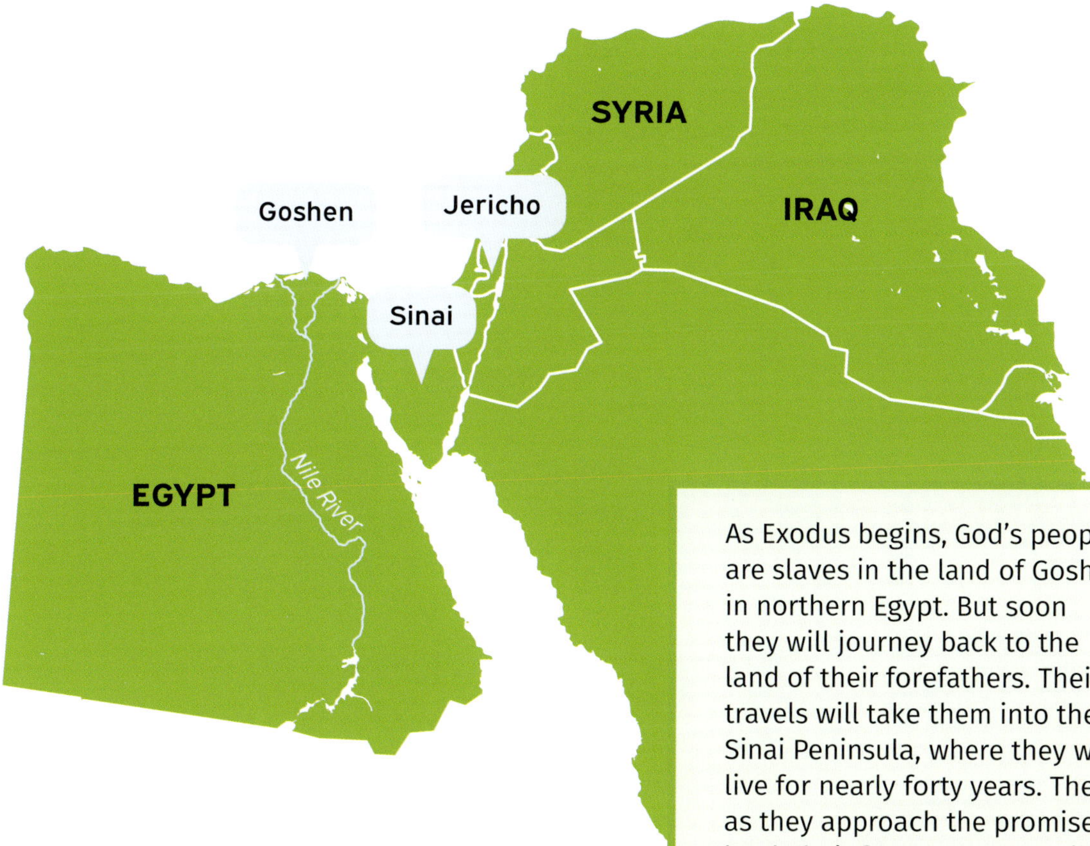

SYRIA

IRAQ

Goshen

Jericho

Sinai

EGYPT

Nile River

As Exodus begins, God's people are slaves in the land of Goshen in northern Egypt. But soon they will journey back to the land of their forefathers. Their travels will take them into the Sinai Peninsula, where they will live for nearly forty years. Then, as they approach the promised land, their first encounter will be with a city called Jericho.

This timeline reflects the traditional early date for the exodus.

The Geography of Ancient Egypt

GIFTS OF THE NILE: In the rich soil along the Nile River, farmers raised barley, wheat, onions, leeks, lentils, dates, figs, grapes, flax, castor beans, and sesame. The land along the river also supported cattle, sheep, goats, pigs, donkeys, and horses.

THE PYRAMIDS, built nearly 1,000 years before Israel arrived, are iconic symbols of ancient Egypt's culture, with its exalted pharaoh, servile populace, and intense desire for security in the afterlife.

ZOAN AND MEMPHIS were administrative centers (Num. 13:22; Ps. 78:12; Isa. 19:13).

THEBES was the chief city of Upper Egypt; nearby was the Valley of Kings, where many pharaohs were buried during and after the time of Moses. Thebes was later conquered by the Assyrians (Ezek. 30:14–16; Nah. 3:8).

Ten Terrifying Plagues

Born to Hebrew slaves and rescued as a baby from the Nile River, Moses was raised by Pharaoh's daughter. As a young man he fled far from Egypt and settled in Midian. But years later, from a burning bush on a mountainside, God called Moses back to Egypt. Moses and his brother, Aaron, confronted Pharaoh to let the Hebrews leave. But the hard heart of Pharaoh did not budge, even after God sent nine plagues upon the land of Egypt. Only after the tenth plague—the death of firstborn sons—did Pharaoh relent.

The Nile River

Egypt has been called the "gift of the Nile," and no other river has been so vital to the history of the nation through which it flowed. To the ancient Egyptians, it was simply "the river." The river's annual floods brought new fertile soil for crops, and its waters provided food from its abundance of fish and waterfowl, as well as fresh water for drinking and cleaning.

In the book of Exodus, the Nile, a source of life, becomes a place of death for Hebrew infants when the murderous pharaoh orders male newborns to be thrown into its waters (Ex. 1:22). Is it any wonder that the first plague God sent upon Egypt was to deprive the people of their river by turning its waters into blood?

The Exodus and the Wilderness

Mediterranean Sea

Nile River Delta

GOSHEN

Zoan

Rameses

Migdol

Way to the Land of the Philistines

SHUR DESERT

Pithom

Way to Shur

ISRAEL'S JOURNEY BEGAN IN RAMESES, in Goshen (Ex. 12:37), where they had lived since the time of Joseph (Gen. 47:1–12). It was a fruitful land, but it had become a place of unbearable oppression.

Marah?

PHARAOH AND HIS ARMY CHASED ISRAEL to the edge of the Red Sea, where they were trapped until the Lord made a way for them through the waters (Ex. 14:5–15:21).

Exodus

Elim?

Red Sea (Gulf of Suez)

SIN DESERT

SINAI PENINSULA

EGYPT

GOD PROVIDED MANNA to sustain Israel in the wilderness (Ex. 16). This bread from heaven continued until they entered the promised land (Josh. 5:10–12).

Rephidim?

GOD MET ISRAEL AT MOUNT SINAI, where he established his covenant with the nation. There Moses received the Ten Commandments and much of the law (Ex. 20–Num. 10).

Mount Sinai? (Jebel Musa)

Leviticus

TWELVE SPIES EXPLORED CANAAN and returned to Kadesh-barnea with a report of good things and strong people. Lacking faith, Israel refused to enter the land (Num. 13–14).

MOSES DIED ON MOUNT NEBO, near Israel's camp on the plains of Moab, after seeing the promised land (Deut. 34).

EDOM REFUSED ISRAEL PASSAGE through their territory, so Israel was forced to take a long journey around it (Num. 20:14–21).

THE TABERNACLE was the place of God's presence with Israel throughout their journeys (Ex. 40:34–38). It was designed, constructed, and first set up while Israel was camping at Mount Sinai (Ex. 25–40).

CANAAN
Acacia Grove
Deuteronomy
Jericho
Gaza
Beersheba
Dead Sea
Dibon
Arnon River
NEGEV
MOAB
Mount Hor?
Zered Brook
Kadesh-barnea
Punon
EDOM
Mount Hor?
Jotbathah
WILDERNESS OF PARAN
Ezion-geber
Numbers
Hazeroth?
MIDIAN
Red Sea (Gulf of Aqaba)
Red Sea

The Covenant at Sinai

After bringing the Israelites across the parted sea and putting an end to Pharaoh's pursuit once and for all, God led his people through the wilderness to a mountain in Sinai. There at Mount Sinai, God and his people entered into a covenant. Through Moses, God gave his people the Ten Commandments, laws for the Israelite community, and detailed instructions for building the tabernacle.

The traditional Mount Sinai, called Jebel Musa ("Mountain of Moses"), is in southern Sinai and rises approximately 7,500 feet (2,285 m) above sea level. Jebel Musa has served as the attested location of Mount Sinai since the late fourth century AD, with a monastery built there in the sixth century to protect the traditional site of the burning bush.

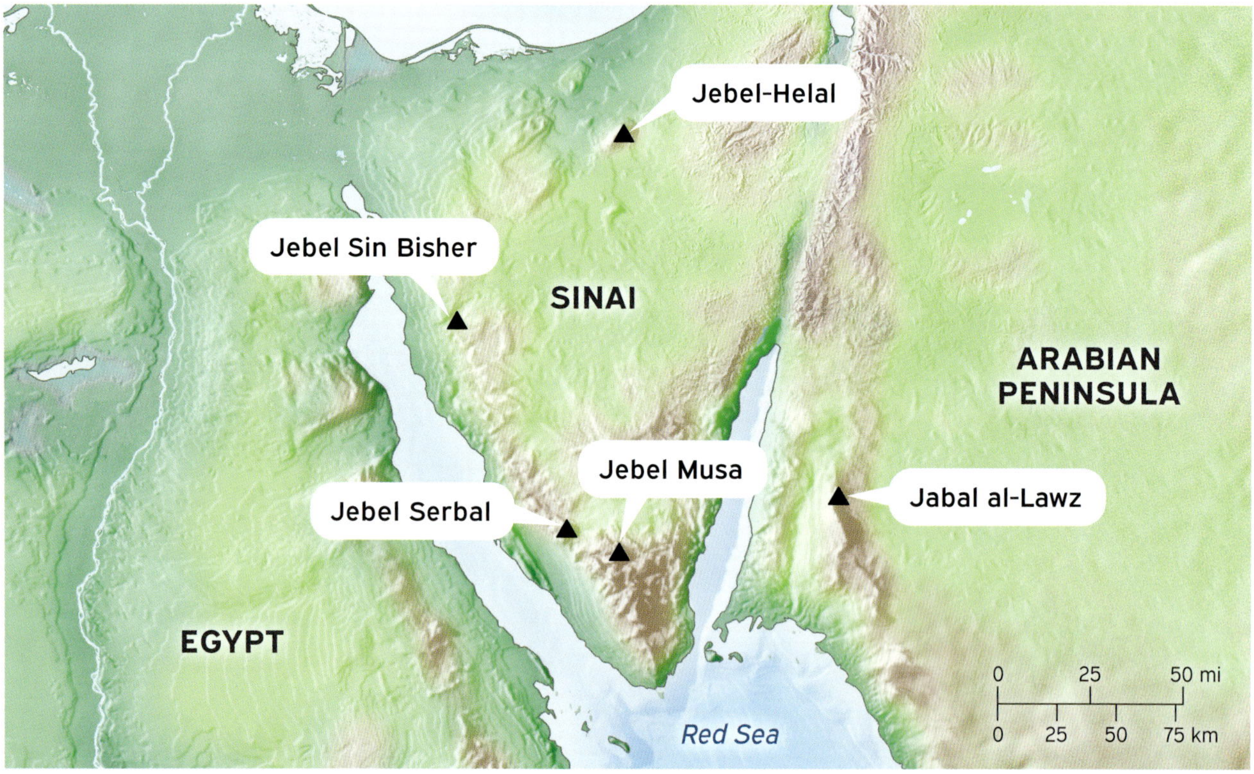

Jebel-Helal
Jebel Sin Bisher
SINAI
ARABIAN PENINSULA
Jebel Musa
Jebel Serbal
Jabal al-Lawz
EGYPT
Red Sea
0 25 50 mi
0 25 50 75 km

Where Was Mount Sinai?

Since no one knows the precise route the Israelites took through Sinai, several locations for Mount Sinai have been proposed. These include four sites in the Sinai Peninsula and one in present-day Saudi Arabia.

God's Presence through the Tabernacle

Exodus 35–40 describes the construction of the tabernacle and its sacred items. The tabernacle was a mobile sanctuary of God's presence with his people as they sojourned in the wilderness. Its most sacred item was the ark of the covenant, which contained the tablets of the Ten Commandments representing God's covenant with Israel. The tabernacle was the place where the priests and the people made sacrifices and offerings in worship of the Lord.

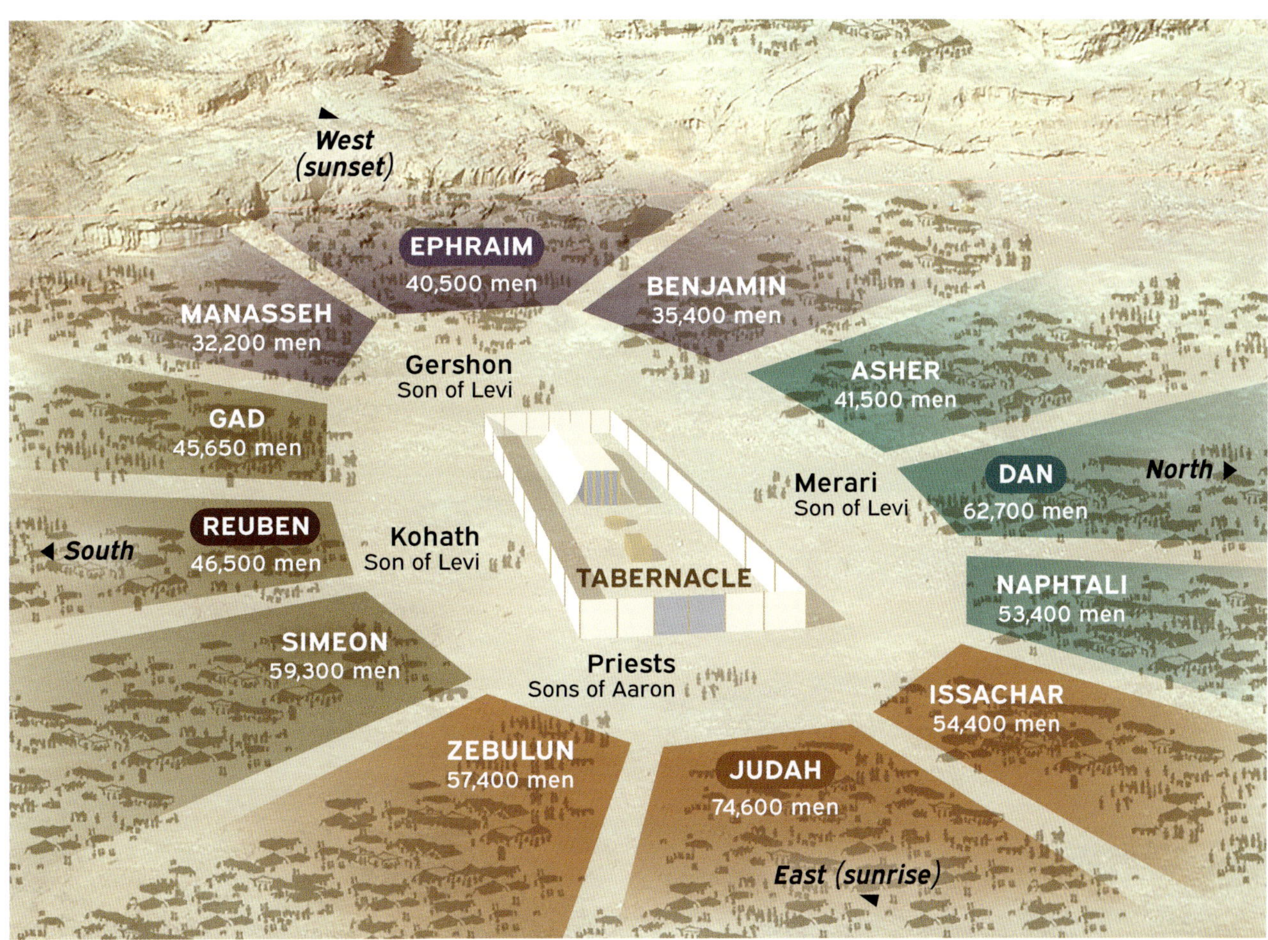

The Tabernacle at the Center of the Camp

The twelve military tribes of Israel camped in groups of three on each side of the tabernacle. Each of the groups camped under the banner of the leading tribe of the group: Judah for the tribes on the east, Reuben on the south, Ephraim on the west, and Dan on the north. The priestly tribe of Levi camped nearest the tabernacle, with the Levitical families on each side. This arrangement ensured the protection of the tribe of Levi and also the tabernacle and the ark of the covenant that were in their care. The figures in this illustration reflect the size of each tribe according to the first census in the book of Numbers (Num. 1–2).

Route of the Twelve Spies

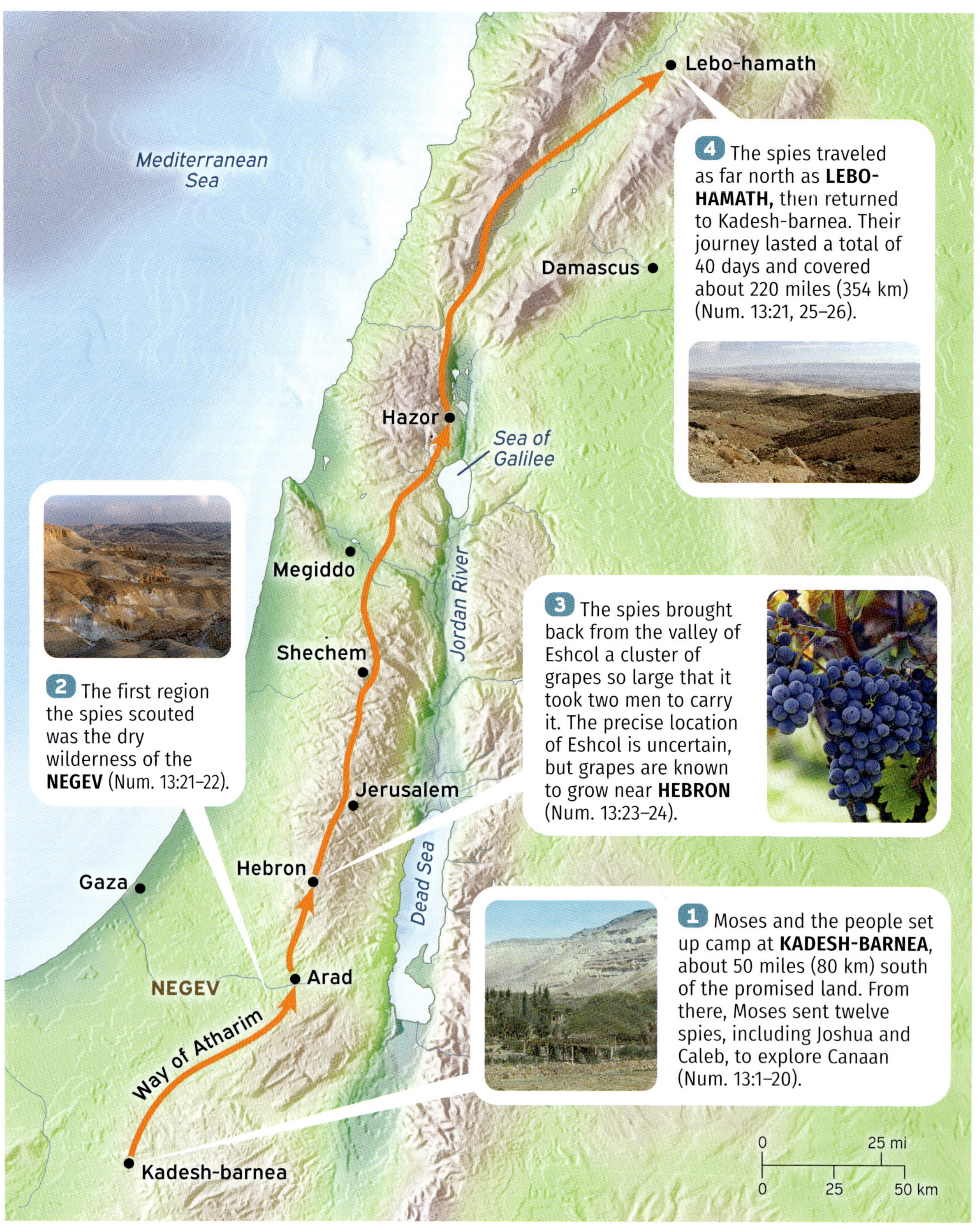

The Edge of the Promised Land

When the spies returned from Canaan, ten of the twelve claimed that the land was harsh and the inhabitants were strong, and Israel's courage faltered (Num. 13:27–14:10). The people remained in the wilderness, wandering for decades. Once that fearful generation passed away, Moses and the next generation traveled to the border of Canaan, just east of the Jordan River. This generation would take hold of the land God promised to their forefathers. The Israelites camped on the plains of Moab, where Moses gave his farewell address (the sermons recorded in the book of Deuteronomy). When he finished exhorting the people to seek and obey the Lord, Moses climbed Pisgah Peak, viewed the promised land, and then died at 120 years old.

> **"Moses went up to Mount Nebo from the plains of Moab and climbed Pisgah Peak, which is across from Jericho. And the LORD showed him the whole land."**
>
> DEUTERONOMY 34:1

Pisgah is a section of the Abarim mountain range, east of the Jordan River. This range's most prominent peak is Mount Nebo. Virtually the whole land west of the Jordan River can be seen from this vantage point.

Mount Tabor

THE LAND

The account of Israel's priests and soldiers walking around Jericho until its walls came tumbling down is one of the most famous stories in the Bible. Joshua had served as Moses's apprentice, so when God appointed him as Israel's next leader, Joshua was ready. He brought the Israelites across the Jordan River to the walls of Jericho and led them in military campaigns across Canaan.

As the Israelites began to settle in the land, Joshua divided the territory among Israel's tribes, a fulfillment of God's covenant with Abraham, Isaac, and Jacob. The patriarchs had traversed the land as nomads, but now their descendants lived in the land as beneficiaries of God's faithfulness to his promises.

After Joshua, a time of social disorder occurred, known as the era of judges. As generations passed, the tribes of Israel entangled themselves with their pagan neighbors and worshiped local deities. So the Lord raised up charismatic leaders, called judges, from among his people to free them from oppression and lead them back to worshiping the one true God—the God who had rescued their ancestors from Egypt centuries earlier.

The turbulent era of judges sets the stage for what comes next in the Bible: the era of kings. Following a horrific story of civil war between the Israelite tribes, the book of Judges concludes with this statement: "In those days Israel had no king; all the people did whatever seemed right in their own eyes" (Judg. 21:25).

JOSHUA, JUDGES, AND RUTH

The book of Joshua narrates the battles of the Israelites' entry into Canaan and records Joshua's division of the land among the tribes. The book of Judges covers a dark period of violence between the Israelites and their neighbors. The book of Ruth is a short story about two women, Ruth and Naomi, whose lives are restored after experiencing famine, widowhood, and poverty during the era of judges.

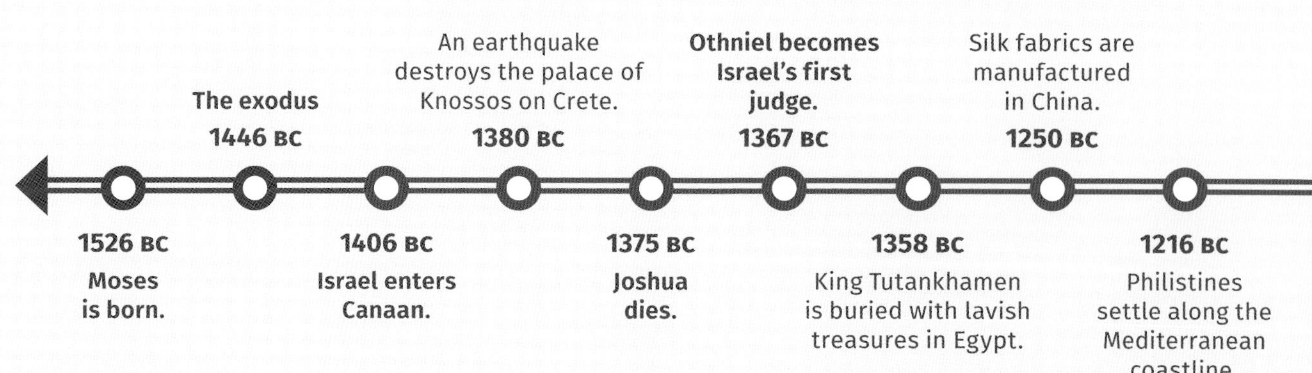

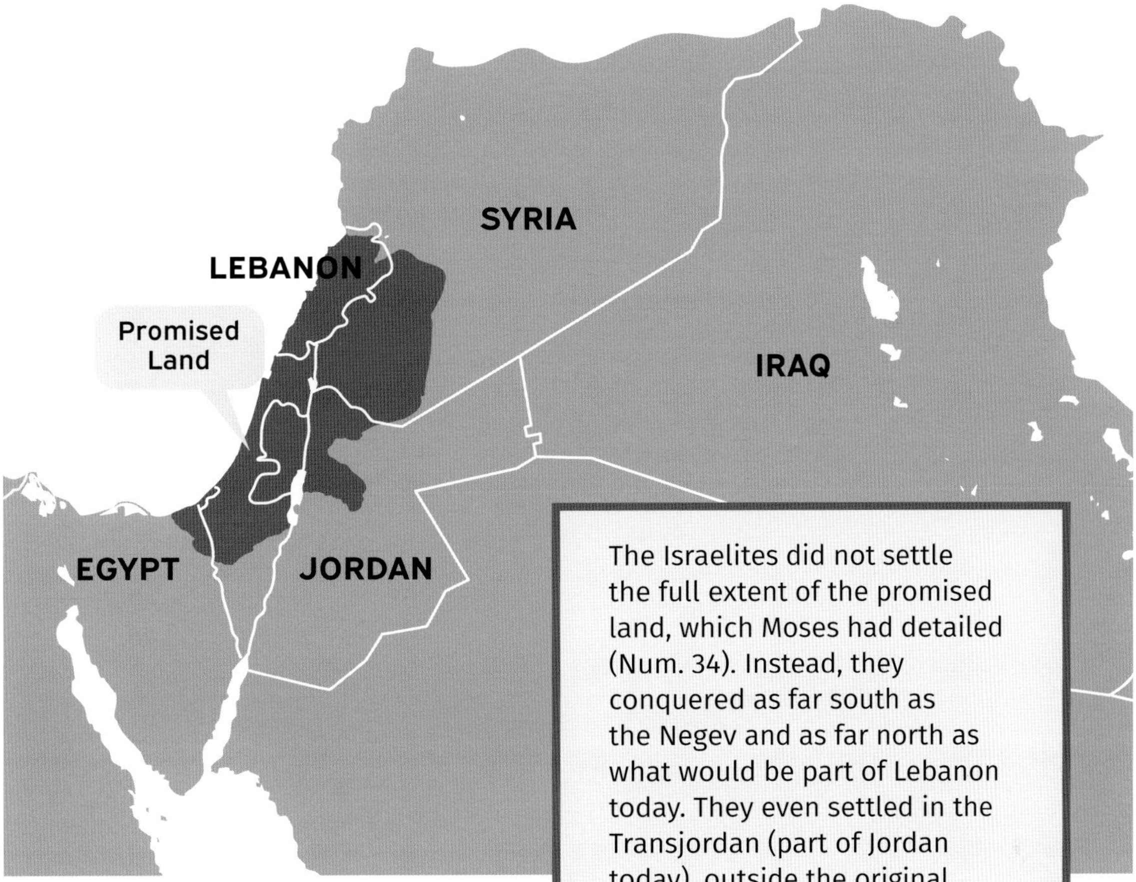

SYRIA

LEBANON

Promised Land

IRAQ

EGYPT

JORDAN

The Israelites did not settle the full extent of the promised land, which Moses had detailed (Num. 34). Instead, they conquered as far south as the Negev and as far north as what would be part of Lebanon today. They even settled in the Transjordan (part of Jordan today), outside the original promised land borders.

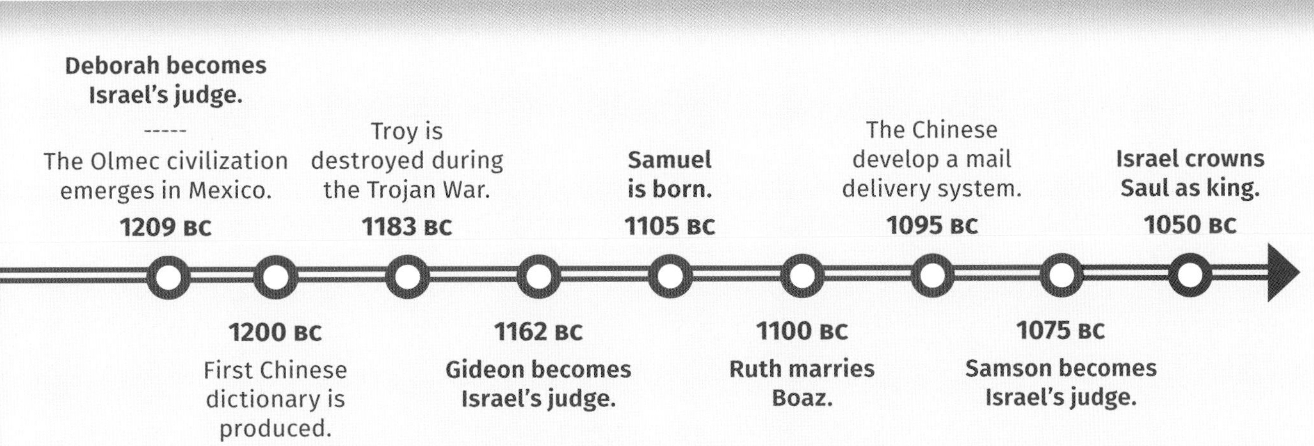

Dates for the judges are uncertain. The era of judges is about 350 years when using the early date for the exodus (1446 BC).

Joshua

After the exodus, Joshua successfully led Israel's warriors when Amalek attacked God's people (Ex. 17:8–13). Shortly thereafter, Joshua was among the twelve men Moses sent to scout the promised land. Joshua and Caleb were the only spies who urged Israel to occupy Canaan immediately; and they were the only two from their generation whom God permitted to enter the promised land nearly four decades later (Num. 13:16; 14:30). God directed Moses to designate Joshua as his successor (Num. 27:15–23). After Moses died, Joshua rallied the people and led the young nation in the conquest of Canaan.

Israel Enters Canaan

From Israel's camp at Acacia Grove, two spies went to Jericho where Rahab hid them. They then went into the hill country (probably near Bethel) before returning to camp to give their report (Josh. 2). The Israelites left Acacia Grove and crossed the Jordan River in a miracle reminiscent of the crossing of the Red Sea. They stopped at Gilgal where Joshua chose twelve stones from the Jordan River to build an altar as a memorial to God's mighty works (Josh. 4:19–24). They then attacked Jericho and Ai.

Dead Sea and Jordan River

The City of Jericho

Jericho was the first city the Israelites conquered when they invaded Canaan. Despite Joshua's curse (Josh. 6:26), the city was rebuilt and destroyed several times over the centuries (1 Kings 16:34). In fact, in the first century AD, it was in Jericho that Jesus healed blind Bartimaeus and brought salvation to Zacchaeus (Mark 10:46–52; Luke 19:1–10).

Mediterranean Sea
Mount Carmel
Sea of Galilee
GALILEE
Jordan River
COASTAL PLAIN
HILL COUNTRY
JORDAN RIVER VALLEY
TRANSJORDAN
Jericho
Dead Sea
NEGEV

Ancient Canaan was subdivided by geographical features into four narrow north-south strips:

- To the east of the Jordan River was the plateau of **Transjordan**, the area "across the Jordan."
- Westward from the Transjordan, the land drops steeply into the deep **Jordan River valley**, which reaches down to the shores of the Dead Sea, the lowest dry land on earth.
- The central **hill country** runs from the mountains and hills of Galilee in the north to the Negev in the south.
- The **coastal plain** lies along the Mediterranean Sea, interrupted near its northern end by the ridge of Mount Carmel that juts into the sea.

Renewing the Covenant

After their victories over Jericho and Ai, the Israelites traveled north to Shechem. There at Mounts Ebal and Gerizim, Joshua followed the instructions given in the law by pronouncing the blessings and curses of the covenant (Josh. 8:30–35; Deut. 11:29–32; 27:12–13). Years later, when the conquest was finished and the tribes settled in their allotted territories, Joshua and the people again renewed the covenant at Shechem, and Joshua gave the people a final charge to faithfully serve the Lord (Josh. 24).

> **"Choose today whom you will serve. Would you prefer the gods your ancestors served beyond the Euphrates? Or will it be the gods of the Amorites in whose land you now live? But as for me and my family, we will serve the LORD."**
>
> JOSHUA 24:15

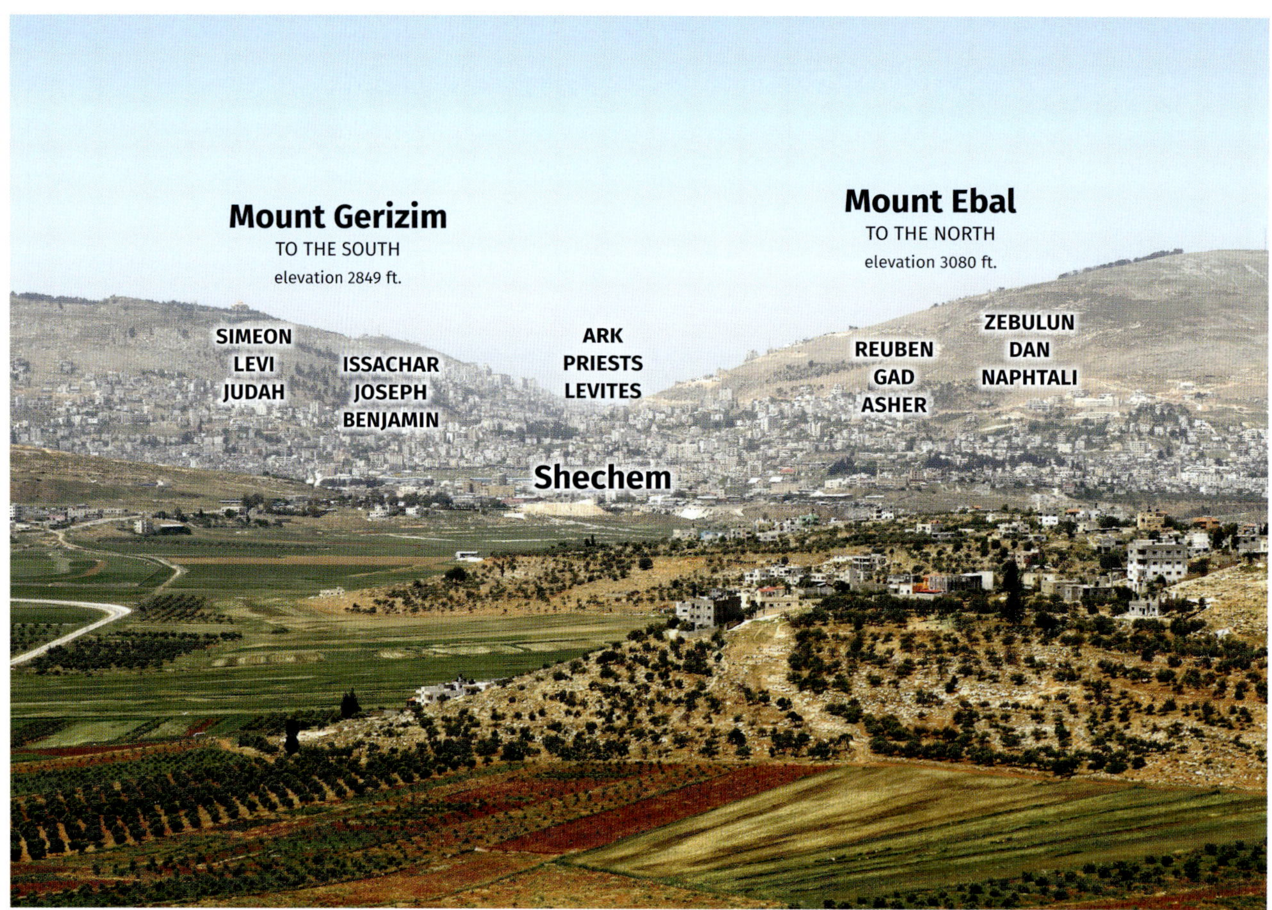

Shechem was strategically located at the entrance to the pass between Mount Ebal and Mount Gerizim, where it could control several key roads through the central hill country. In time, Shechem became one of Israel's cities of refuge and, after King Solomon, it became the first capital of the Northern Kingdom of Israel (1 Kings 12:25).

The Conquest of Canaan

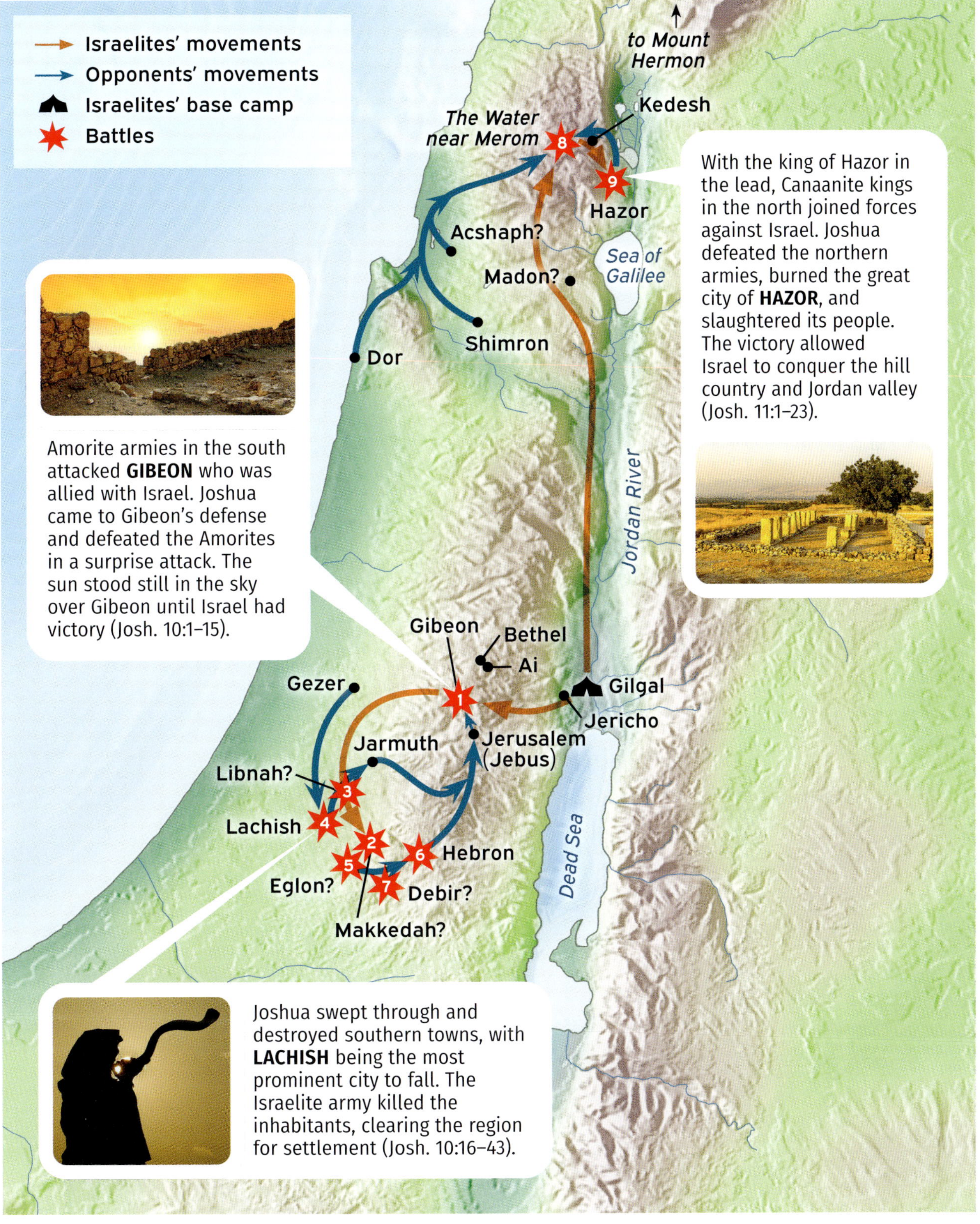

Amorite armies in the south attacked **GIBEON** who was allied with Israel. Joshua came to Gibeon's defense and defeated the Amorites in a surprise attack. The sun stood still in the sky over Gibeon until Israel had victory (Josh. 10:1–15).

With the king of Hazor in the lead, Canaanite kings in the north joined forces against Israel. Joshua defeated the northern armies, burned the great city of **HAZOR**, and slaughtered its people. The victory allowed Israel to conquer the hill country and Jordan valley (Josh. 11:1–23).

Joshua swept through and destroyed southern towns, with **LACHISH** being the most prominent city to fall. The Israelite army killed the inhabitants, clearing the region for settlement (Josh. 10:16–43).

Allotment of the Land

Joshua divided Canaan among the twelve tribes of Israel and gave the tribe of Levi forty-eight cities scattered throughout the territories. Much of the land, however, remained unconquered. In time, the Philistines came to control the whole Mediterranean seaboard. The tribe of Dan could not take possession of their allotment, so they eventually moved north, settling near the northern border of Israel's territory (Josh. 19:47).

Cities of Refuge

God established the cities of refuge to prevent cycles of revenge from destroying communities (Josh. 20). These six cities were under the jurisdiction of the Levites and served as safe havens for those who had accidentally killed someone. If the fugitive was convicted of murder, he would be turned over to the avenger and receive his due punishment. But if he was found innocent, he would be granted asylum and would remain in the city of refuge (Num. 35:9–32).

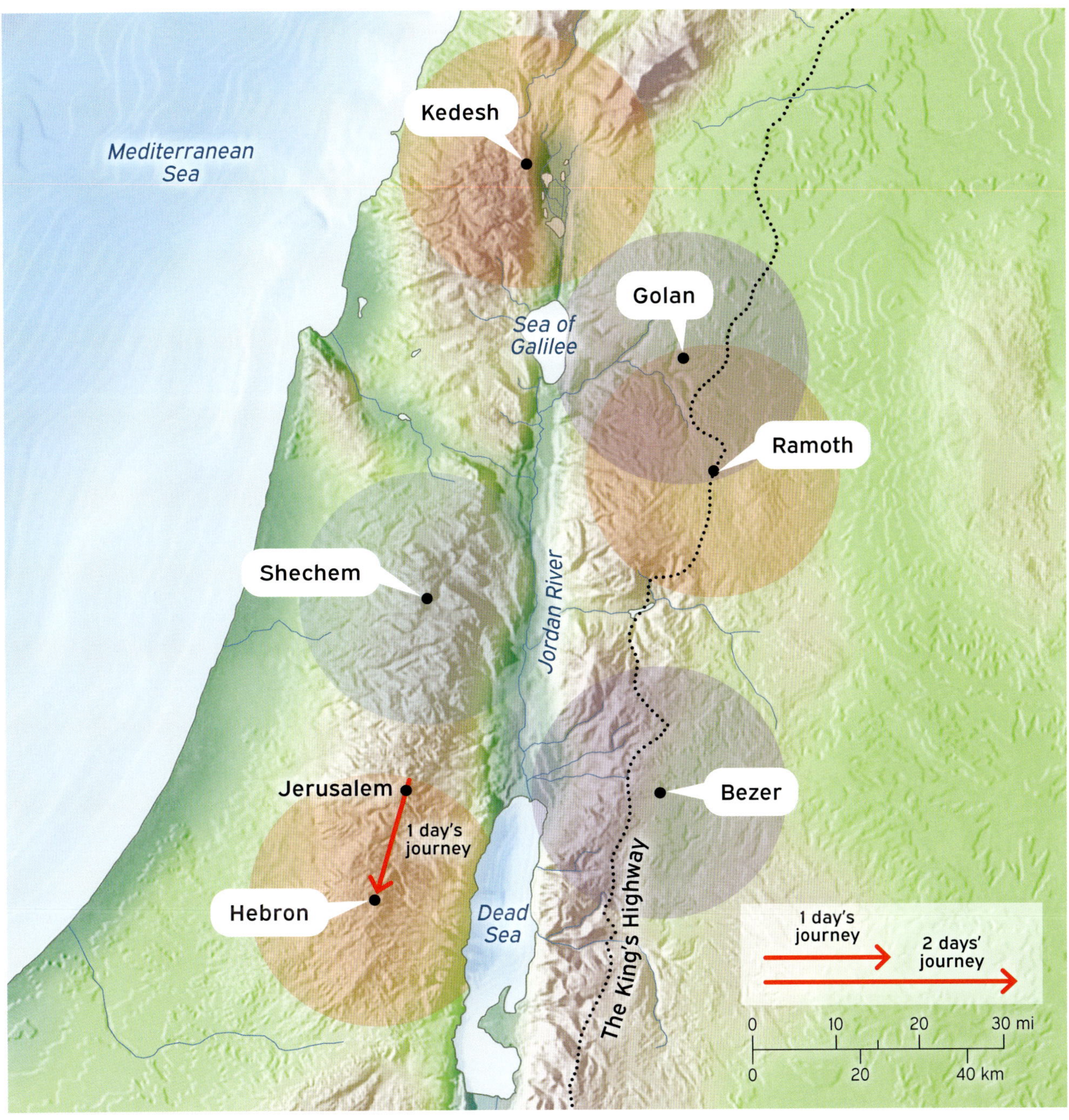

The Era of Judges

Following Joshua's death, the Israelites began to lose faith and started serving the gods of the Canaanites. Growing political fragmentation among the tribes of Israel allowed nearby nations to gain enough strength to oppress God's people. Philistines, Moabites, Ammonites, and others launched attacks against the tribes. So God's Spirit empowered charismatic figures, or judges, to lead the Israelites to victory over their oppressors and to reestablish peace. But their peace was not permanent. In time, the people would forsake the Lord once again, and the cycle would start over.

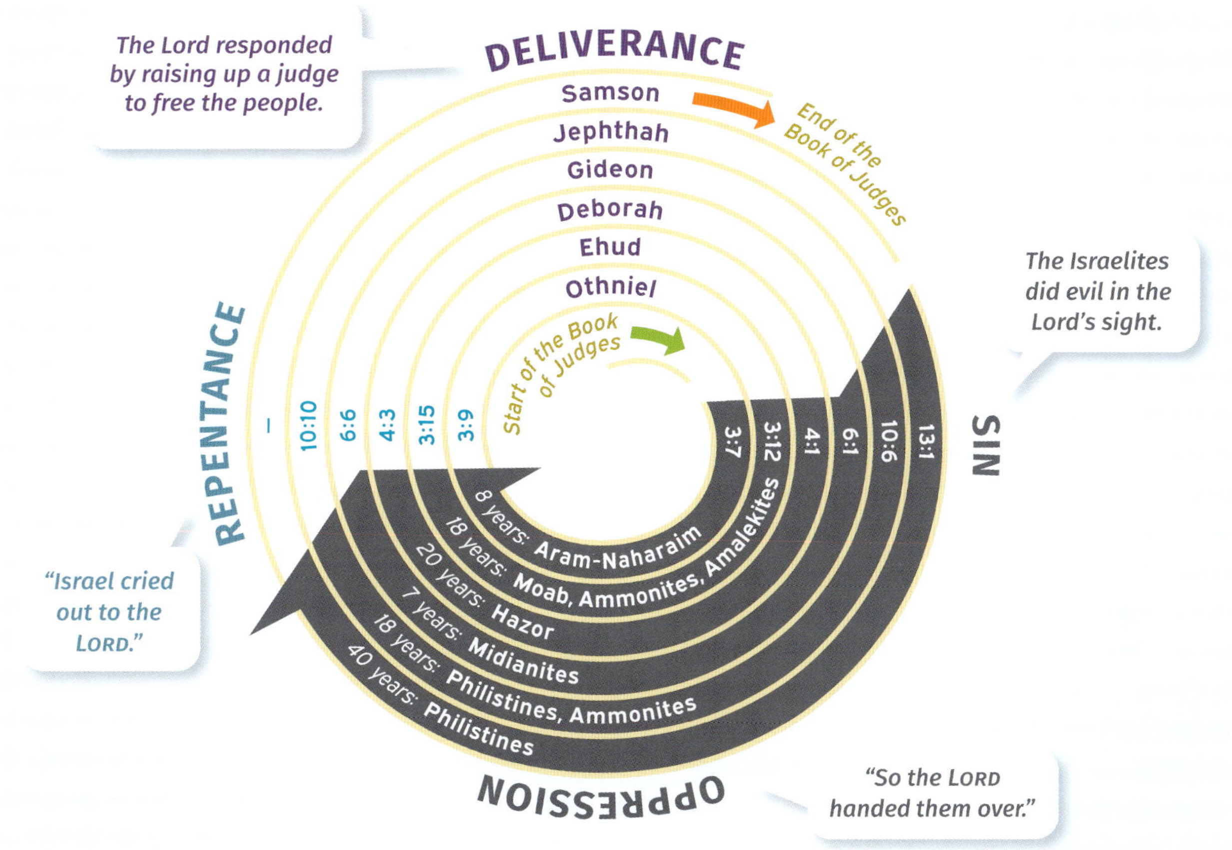

OTHNIEL, the first judge and a nephew of Caleb, conquered Debir (Judg. 1:11–14; 3:7–11).

EHUD, a left-handed Benjamite, assassinated King Elgon of Moab near Gilgal (Judg. 3:12–30).

SHAMGAR, possibly from Beth-anath, killed six hundred Philistines with an oxgoad (Judg. 3:31).

DEBORAH, who judged from between Ramah and Bethel, accompanied Barak in battle against the Canaanites (Judg. 4:1–5:31).

GIDEON, a farmer from Ophrah, led a small army to defeat the Midianite raiders (Judg. 6:1–8:32).

TOLA, from Shamir, led Israel for over two decades (Judg. 10:1–2).

JAIR, a judge whose thirty sons owned thirty towns in Gilead, was buried in Kamon in Gilead (Judg. 10:3–5).

JEPHTHAH of Gilead defeated the Ammonites, but at the expense of his only child, a daughter (Judg. 10:6–12:7).

IBZAN, from Bethlehem, had thirty sons and thirty daughters who married outside their clan (Judg. 12:8–10).

ELON, from the tribe of Zebulun, led Israel for ten years (Judg. 12:11–12).

ABDON, a judge from Pirathon, had forty sons and thirty grandsons (Judg. 12:13–15).

SAMSON, born in Zorah, had unusual physical strength, which he used in his feud with the Philistines (Judg. 13:1–16:31).

Deborah, the Prophet and Judge

As a prophet, Deborah received divine revelations; as a judge, she arbitrated legal disputes. She lived possibly a century and half after Joshua. This was a period of increasing moral depravity, spiritual blindness, and political fracturing. The Israelites were doing "evil in the LORD's sight" (Judg. 4:1), so God turned them over to an oppressor, King Jabin of Hazor, for twenty years. Then, Israel "cried out to the LORD for help" (Judg. 4:3). Through Deborah, God called Barak to fight Sisera, the commander of King Jabin's army. But Barak did not rcceive God's call with enthusiasm. Instead, he set a condition: Deborah must go with him. She agreed but with a cost: The glory for the victory would not go to Barak but to a woman.

Barak defeated Sisera's army with its nine hundred iron chariots, but the glory went to Jael who killed Sisera by her own hand and a tent peg, fulfilling Deborah's prophecy (Judg. 4:17–22).

Mount Tabor

The Battle at Mount Tabor

Deborah went with Barak to Kedesh, and Barak stationed his forces on Mount Tabor. Sisera's army marched from near Hazor and were passing Mount Tabor on their way to the Kishon River when Barak attacked (Judg. 4:9–14). Sisera's forces fled south toward Taanach, only to be intercepted and crushed by the armies of the tribes of Ephraim, Benjamin, and Manasseh (Judg. 5:13–21). Sisera himself fled north toward the oak at Zaanannim, where he fatefully encountered Jael (Judg. 4:11, 17).

Gideon's Calling

God chose Gideon, a relatively unknown farmer, to fight against the Midianites who were plundering Israelite villages (Judg. 6:14–16). Gideon was slow to believe his divine calling, requiring miraculous signs as confirmation. But the Spirit of God came upon him, and Gideon raised an army. No recruiter had greater success than Gideon, as 32,000 men responded to his call. God, though, directed him to pare down the number of men to 300. Gideon led his small army against an overwhelming Midianite force and defeated them! Later, Gideon, weak in faith and dependent upon visible signs, made a gold ephod which Israel began to worship (Judg. 8:27). Israel enjoyed peace during Gideon's day, but his lack of faithfulness bore bitter fruit after his death (Judg. 8:33–9:5).

The Midianites were semi-nomadic tribes who lived in the Arabian Peninsula east of the Gulf of Aqaba, stretching as far north as the Transjordan. The Midianites Gideon faced were marauding bands, far from their homeland, who raided northern Israelite towns, leaving their victims to starve (Judg. 6:1–6).

Gideon's Victory

After the Lord reduced Gideon's army to 300 men at the Spring of Harod, they gathered on Mount Gilead (possibly Gilboa) overlooking the Midianite camp in the valley below. Gideon and his men attacked and chased the Midianites past Succoth and Peniel, where Gideon killed the Midianite kings near Jogbehah. On his return, Gideon punished the leaders of Succoth and slaughtered the men of Peniel for their refusal to feed his army (Judg. 7:1–8:21).

Samson, the Strong and Weak Judge

Dedicated to the Lord at birth and endowed with extraordinary physical strength, Samson fulfilled his calling to rescue Israel from Philistine oppression—but he did so from selfish and vengeful motives. Nonetheless, in situation after situation, God enabled him to bring harm to the Philistines. Samson's final act of vengeance against the Philistines came as their captive. With his eyes gouged out, Samson pushed down the pillars of their temple, killing three thousand assembled Philistines as well as himself.

The Story of Ruth

The events in the book of Ruth took place in the latter part of the era of judges, possibly around 1100 BC. Whereas the book of Judges records violent, momentous events, the book of Ruth shows an ordinary side of life; it's a story about a family trying to make ends meet. In the ancient Near East, a few years of low rainfall could cause severe famine, the kind which opens the story of Ruth. Ruth was the widowed Moabite daughter-in-law of Naomi, a widowed Israelite. Together, these women endured poverty and hard labor, with Ruth gleaning in the fields. But they devised a plan to secure their future. Ruth married a kind, honorable, and wealthy landowner, Boaz, who redeemed Naomi's family land. The book of Ruth closes with a genealogy in which the reader learns that Ruth and Boaz are ancestors of King David.

Moab

Because of a famine, Elimelech and Naomi, along with their two sons, took a drastic step and relocated from their home in Bethlehem to the land of Moab, east of the Dead Sea (Ruth 1:1–2). The Israelites despised the Moabites, calling them a cursed race (Deut. 23:3–6)—something which makes the Moabite Ruth all the more interesting as the faithful protagonist of the story and the ancestor of both King David and Jesus Christ (Ruth 4:17; Matt. 1:5–16).

Old City Walls of Jerusalem

THE KINGDOM

Moses had predicted that the people of Israel would one day ask for a king to reign over them (Deut. 17:14–20). Throughout the turbulent days of the judges, Israel's tribes lacked unity. So by the time of Samuel in the eleventh century BC, the Israelites were looking for a strong ruler to protect them from both internal and external threats.

Samuel was born to Hannah, a godly woman who dedicated her firstborn son to serve in God's tabernacle. Samuel grew up to become both a national prophet and the last judge in the era of judges.

God had spelled out the requirements for a king but also warned of the evils associated with human rulers (1 Sam. 8:10–22). Nonetheless, the people insisted on a king. Over Samuel's lifetime, he anointed two kings, and Israel transitioned from a tribal coalition to a monarchy.

Three successive kings—Saul, David, and Solomon—ruled over Israel for more than a century. Saul's reign was characterized by jealousy and revenge. But David's kingdom—though it had its troubles—succeeded where Saul's had failed. Under Solomon, Israel experienced a time of national peace and prosperity.

Centuries later, one of David's descendants would become the sovereign and eternal King of the whole world: Jesus, the ultimate heir to the throne (John 7:42; Rev. 5:5).

SAMUEL, KINGS, AND CHRONICLES

The two-part books of Samuel, Kings, and Chronicles cover more than 500 years of Israel's history. They record genealogies, epic battles, and the rise and fall of many kings. The parts that tell the history of the united kingdom of Israel under Saul, David, and Solomon can be found in 1 and 2 Samuel, 1 Chronicles, and the early chapters of 1 Kings and 2 Chronicles. The remainder of the books covers the period of the divided kingdom after Solomon.

1406 BC Israel enters Canaan.

1075–1040 BC The prophet Samuel leads Israel.

1050 BC Saul becomes the first king of Israel.

1020 BC David defeats Goliath.

1011–971 BC David reigns as king.

1000 BC Classical paganism develops in Greece.

1000 BC Mayan dynasties rule in Central America.

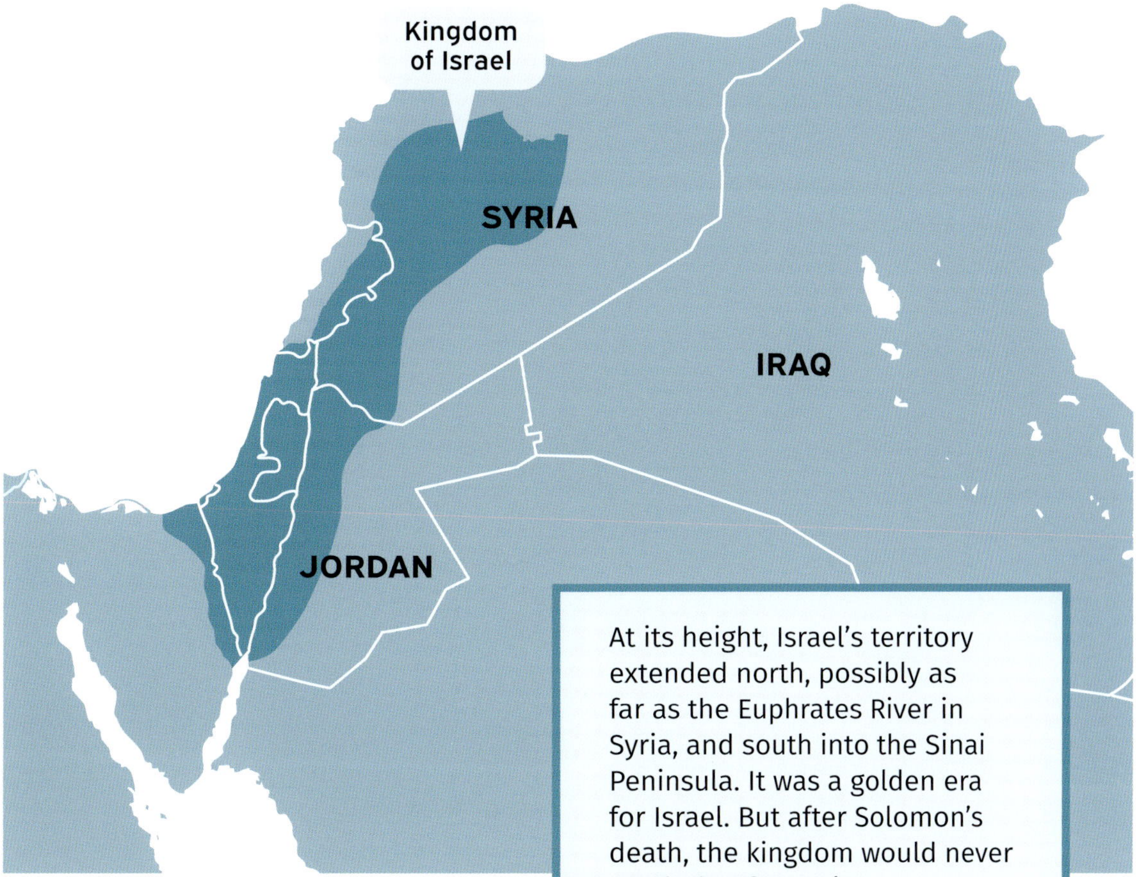

Kingdom of Israel

SYRIA

IRAQ

JORDAN

At its height, Israel's territory extended north, possibly as far as the Euphrates River in Syria, and south into the Sinai Peninsula. It was a golden era for Israel. But after Solomon's death, the kingdom would never reach that far again.

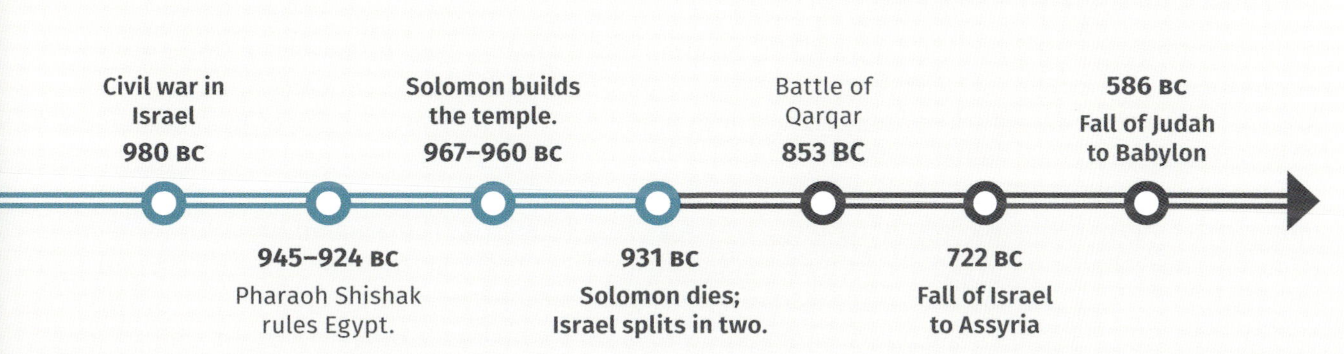

Samuel and the Philistines

Samuel was born in response to his mother Hannah's fervent prayers. Hannah dedicated her son to service at God's sanctuary at Shiloh (1 Sam. 1:1–28). Soon it became clear that God spoke more intimately with the boy Samuel than with the high priest Eli. When Samuel grew up, he exhorted God's people to repent from their sin of idolatry, and he led them to victory against the Philistines (1 Sam. 7:1–17). In Samuel's later years, the people demanded a king to rule over them, and God directed Samuel to anoint Saul. But Saul failed to be a king who was obedient to the King of Kings.

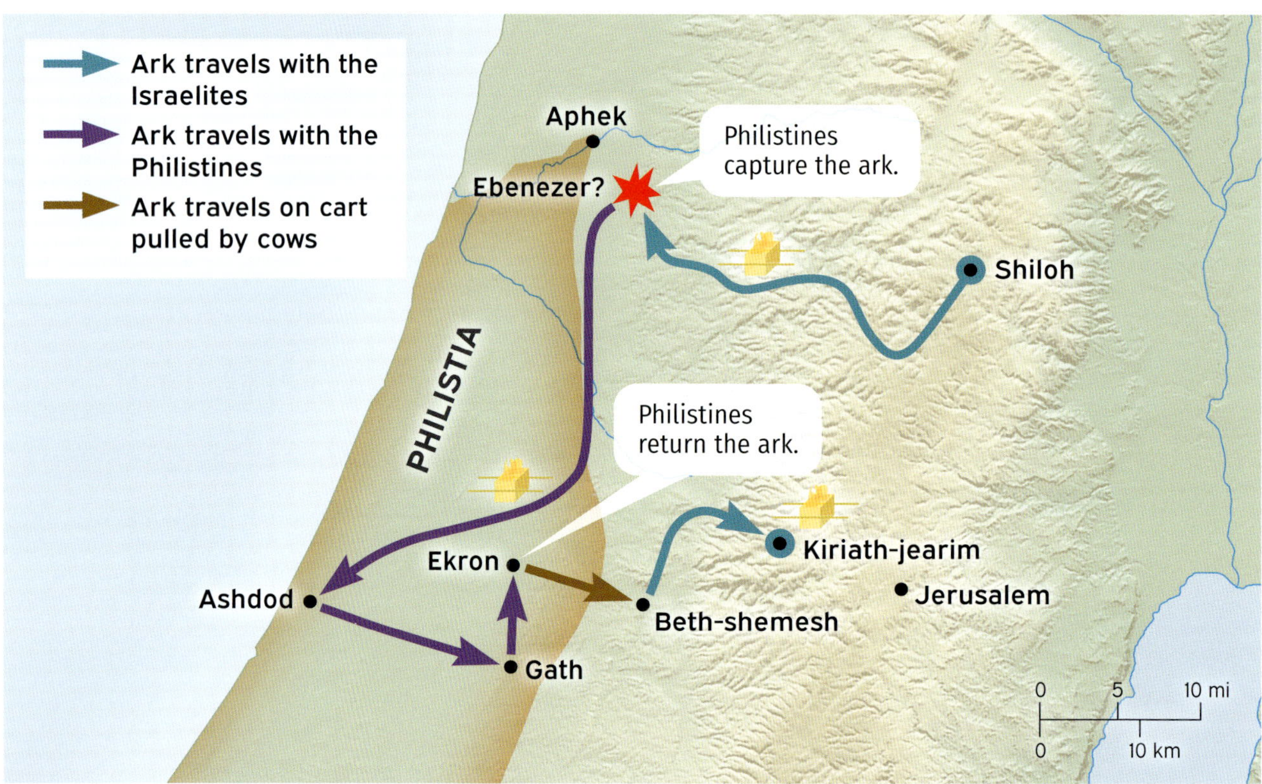

The Ark among the Philistines (1 Sam. 3–6)

While Samuel was still a boy, God gave him a prophecy: The high priest Eli and his wicked sons would face divine judgment. This prophecy came to pass in Israel's battle with the Philistines. After a devastating defeat, the Israelites regrouped and decided to bring the ark of the covenant into battle against their Philistine foes. Supposing it had special powers to protect them, they carried the ark from Shiloh to the battlefield. Again, the Israelites were defeated, but this time the Philistines captured the ark. When the news was reported to Eli that the ark had been lost and two of his sons had died in the conflict, Eli fell backward from his seat and died. The ark was no talisman, but it represented the Lord's holy presence. In captivity, pagan idols fell before the ark, and in each city where the Philistines relocated it, God sent a plague. Exasperated, the Philistines wanted nothing more to do with the ark, so they sent it back into Israelite territory.

Philistine Migration into Canaan

The Philistines were "Sea Peoples" (as the Egyptians called them) who had arrived in southwest Canaan from Crete and the Aegean islands, possibly as early as 1200 BC.

They established five main cities: Ashdod, Ashkelon, Ekron, Gaza, and Gath. Far from being unsophisticated, the Philistines were fierce warriors who were politically capable and technologically advanced. Their use of iron made them a powerful presence in Canaan (1 Sam. 13:19–22).

They were constant adversaries of the Israelites in the era of judges and the early monarchy. Israel's first king, Saul, died in battle against them. David fought and defeated the Philistine threat during his reign.

Egyptian relief depicting Philistine captives

Saul the Reluctant King

Saul, who stood a head taller than everyone else, was at first a reluctant king who lacked military confidence. Nevertheless, Saul had some early successes in battle, but over time he made rash and foolish choices and failed to obey God commands. So God sent the prophet Samuel to the small town of Bethlehem to anoint a new king for Israel.

Saul's Victory at Jabesh-Gilead (1 Sam. 11)

Jabesh in Gilead, east of the Jordan River, was vulnerable to attack, as evidenced by the siege by King Nahash of Ammon. When the people of Jabesh-gilead sent runners to Saul asking for help, Saul responded by traveling from Gibeah, mobilizing Israel at Bezek, and attacking within seven days. Saul's swift blow gained the support of the eastern tribes and reduced the Ammonite threat on the frontier—a tremendous boost for the new king's prestige. Years later, the men of Jabesh-gilead repaid their deep debt to Saul when the king died on Mount Gilboa, rescuing his body from humiliation (1 Sam. 31:8–13; 1 Chron. 10:8–12).

David the Shepherd

David was born in Bethlehem as Jesse's youngest son, and his lineage traced back to Judah, son of Jacob. As a youth, David was a shepherd watching his family's flocks (1 Sam. 16:11; 17:15). Young David's life took an unexpected turn when the prophet Samuel arrived and anointed him as the next king of Israel! But it would take years until Israel recognized whom God had chosen. David's first act of valor that propelled him onto the national scene was his famous defeat of the Philistine warrior Goliath. David then became a faithful servant to King Saul. David's kingship did not come about by a coup or assassination; it was by God's hand.

Bethlehem was a small agricultural town in the hill country of northern Judah. Situated about 5 miles (8 km) south of Jerusalem, it was the setting of the story of Ruth, the hometown of King David, and the birthplace of Jesus Christ.

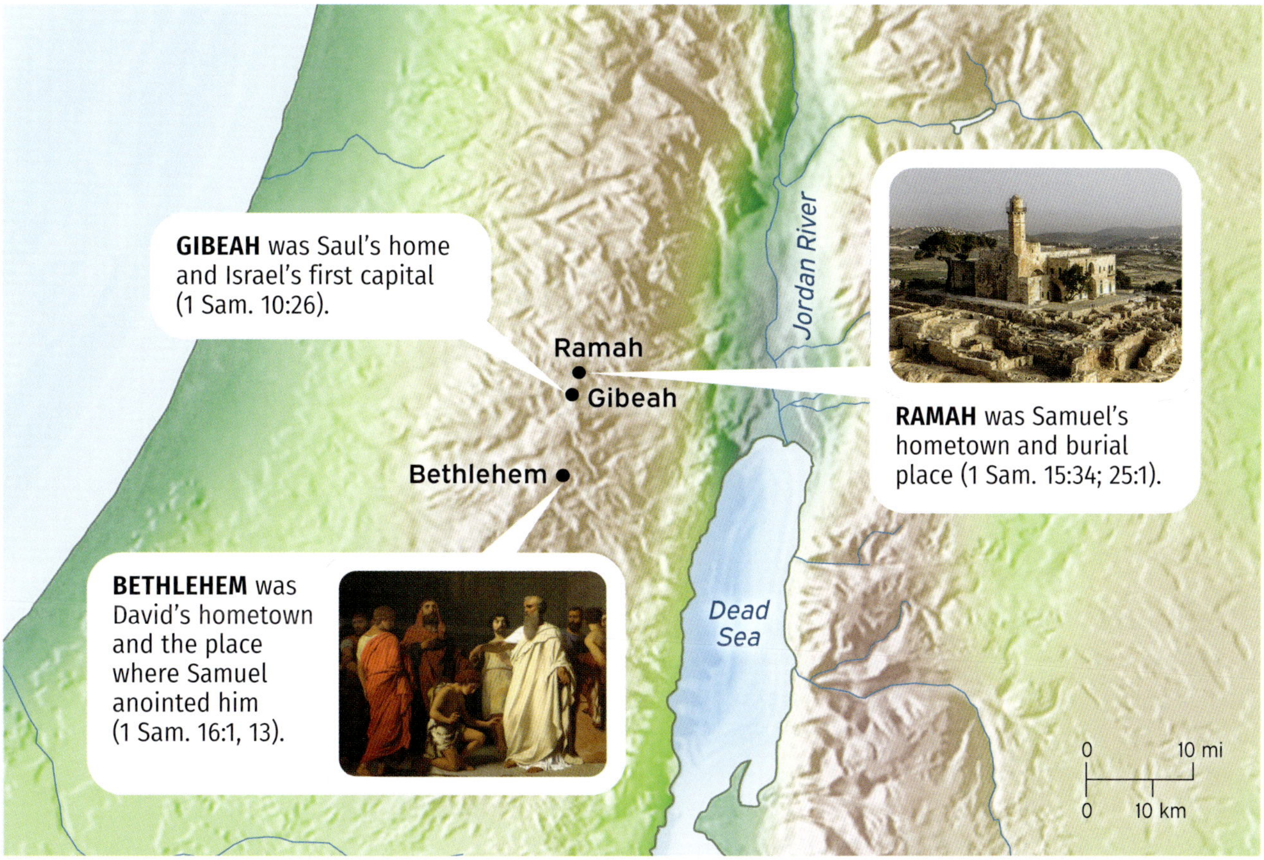

GIBEAH was Saul's home and Israel's first capital (1 Sam. 10:26).

RAMAH was Samuel's hometown and burial place (1 Sam. 15:34; 25:1).

BETHLEHEM was David's hometown and the place where Samuel anointed him (1 Sam. 16:1, 13).

Ramah
Gibeah
Bethlehem
Jordan River
Dead Sea
0 10 mi
0 10 km

The Valley of Elah, the place where David faced Goliath, is shown here from the site of Azekah, on the west side of the valley. The Philistines controlled Azekah until Israel gained control of it in the Battle of Elah. Decades later, King Rehoboam fortified Azekah against attack from the west (2 Chron. 11:5–12).

to Ekron
Beth-shemesh
VALLEY OF ELAH
Israel's camp
Gath
Azekah
Socoh
PHILISTIA
JUDAH
Philistine camp
Adullam
0 3 mi
0 5 km
Shechem
Jordan River
Gezer
Gibeah
Ekron
Jerusalem
Gath
Azekah
Socoh
Bethlehem
Dead Sea
PHILISTIA
JUDAH
0 10 mi
0 10 km

David versus Goliath (1 Sam. 17)

In ancient times, rival forces would sometimes agree to let selected individuals from each side decide a conflict. The Philistine champion was the nine-foot-tall Goliath from the city of Gath. David, armed with only a shepherd's staff, a sling, and five smooth stones, faced Goliath in the Valley of Elah. With one shot, David toppled the giant. The Philistine army fled toward their homeland, and the Israelites chased them westward along the valley floor, killing them "as far as Gath and the gates of Ekron" (1 Sam. 17:52).

David the Fugitive

After defeating Goliath, David joined Saul's army, leading to more victories. He married Saul's daughter Michal and befriended Saul's son Jonathan. The king grew deeply suspicious of David and plotted against him, causing David to flee for his life. David spent nearly a decade as a fugitive, hiding out in caves and even living with the Philistines to escape Saul's pursuit. But during this time, David's entourage grew, as relatives and others disaffected with Saul's reign joined him.

Death of King Saul

The end of Saul's life was far from glorious for Israel's first king. He had become a despot, trying to kill David and to cling to power at any cost. The king was severely wounded in battle against the Philistines, so he chose to fall on his own sword. David mourned the death of Saul and of his friend Jonathan (Saul's son) who was killed in the battle. The king's death, as well as that of the close heirs to the throne, created an opportunity for David to fulfill his anointing and become Israel's next king.

The Battle at Mount Gilboa

Camped with his army in Jezreel as the Philistines approached from Aphek, King Saul sought counsel from the deceased Samuel through a medium at nearby Endor (1 Sam. 28:1–25). The spirit of Samuel gave him nothing but bad news: Saul and his sons would die tomorrow! The prophecy came to pass when the Philistines attacked, and Saul and his sons, including Jonathan, were killed in battle on the slopes of Mount Gilboa where his army had fled to. The Philistines hung their bodies on the wall of Beth-shan, but the warriors of Jabesh-gilead later retrieved them for proper burial (1 Sam. 31:1–13).

Mount Gilboa is a weathered limestone ridge reaching 1,700 feet (500 m) above sea level. The mountain towers over the fertile Jezreel Valley.

David the King

After Saul's death, David was well-positioned at age thirty to begin ruling Judah in the south from the city of Hebron (2 Sam. 2:11). Seven years later, with the northern tribes leaderless, David was crowned king over the north, uniting all of Israel (2 Sam. 5:1–5). King David's successes continued: He captured Jerusalem (Jebus) from the Jebusites and made it his capital city; he brought the ark of the covenant into Jerusalem; his military victories expanded Israel's borders in all directions.

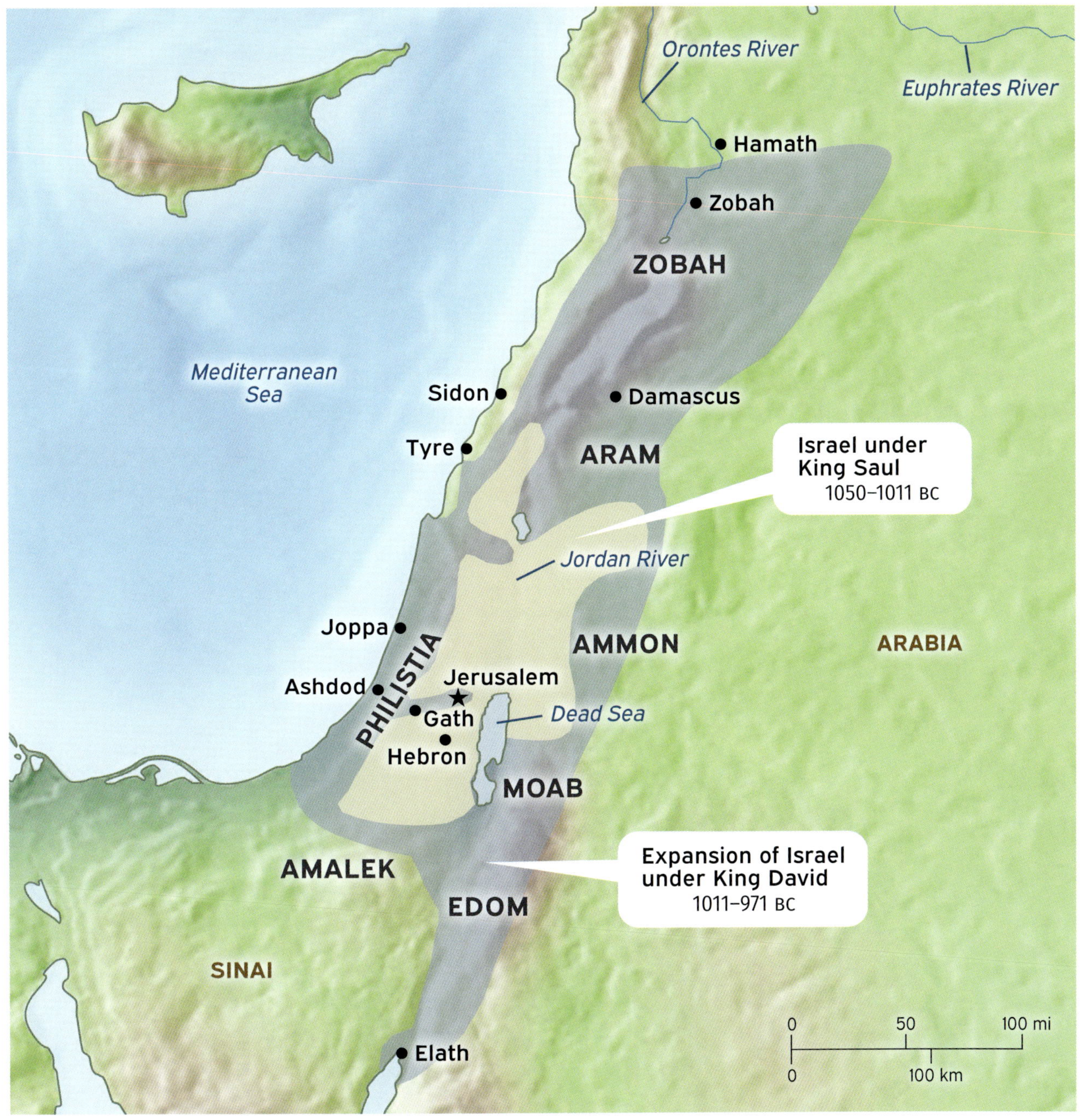

Old City Hebron in the West Bank

Hebron, a city about 19 miles (30 km) southwest of Jerusalem, was where David was made king of Judah (2 Sam. 2:1–4). Hebron had strong ties to the patriarchs of ages past: Abraham had lived in Hebron (Gen. 13:14–18) and purchased a cave as a family burial plot (Gen. 23:1–20).

David's Military

The numbers shown here are the armed warriors from the tribes of Israel who joined David in Hebron, supporting David's rise to the throne of Israel (1 Chron. 12:23–40).

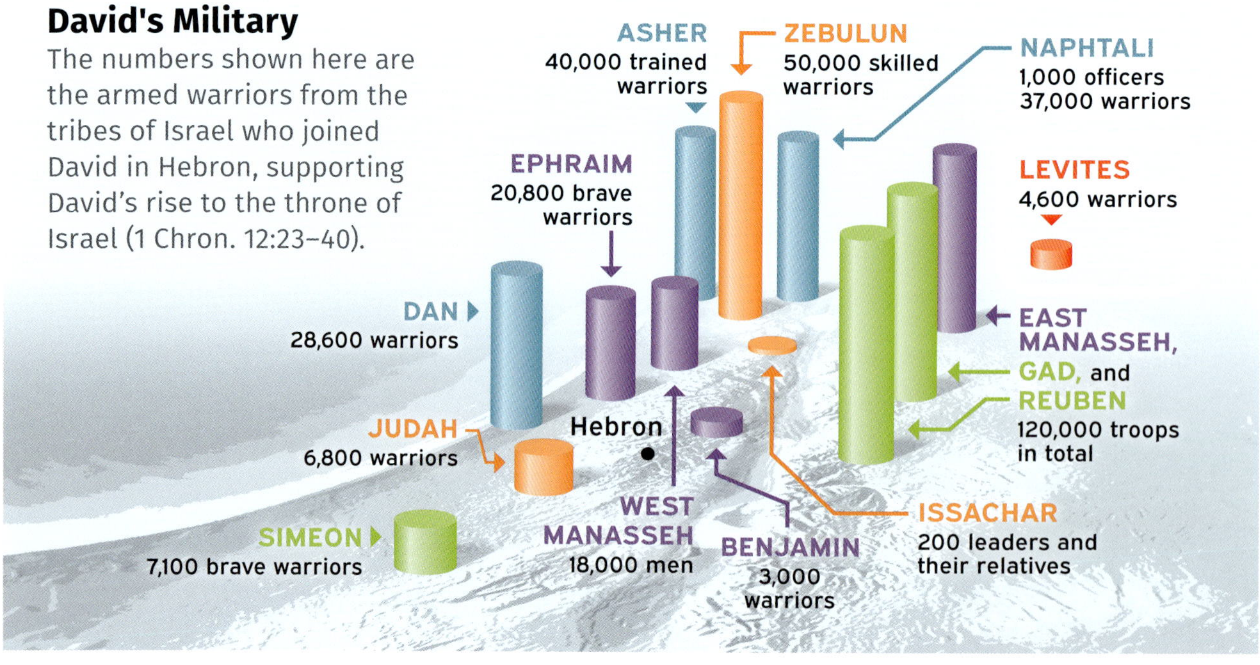

ASHER
40,000 trained warriors

ZEBULUN
50,000 skilled warriors

NAPHTALI
1,000 officers
37,000 warriors

EPHRAIM
20,800 brave warriors

LEVITES
4,600 warriors

DAN
28,600 warriors

EAST MANASSEH, GAD, and REUBEN
120,000 troops in total

JUDAH
6,800 warriors

Hebron

WEST MANASSEH
18,000 men

BENJAMIN
3,000 warriors

ISSACHAR
200 leaders and their relatives

SIMEON
7,100 brave warriors

A Kingdom in Turmoil

At a time when a king should have been on the battlefield with his army, David was lounging on his palace roof. Seeing a beautiful woman, he wanted her, and like a Near Eastern despot, he took her. Bathsheba was a married woman, and her husband, Uriah, was an elite warrior in David's army, so the king quietly arranged for Uriah's death. Rebuked by God through the prophet Nathan, David repented of his sins, but his kingdom was never the same. From this point on in the narrative of 2 Samuel, David's family devolves into violence and revenge, and his son Absalom launches a coup.

Jerusalem in the Time of David

Jerusalem in the time of David was a small fortress city, well-situated in the Judean hills. After reigning over Judah for seven years in Hebron, David captured Jerusalem from its Jebusite inhabitants and made it the capital of his kingdom.

The threshing floor on the top of **MOUNT ZION** was owned by a Jebusite named Araunah. David purchased the site, dedicating it as the place where the temple would later be built (1 Chron. 21:1–22:1; 2 Chron. 3:1–2).

CENTRAL VALLEY

Mount Zion/ Mount Moriah

KIDRON VALLEY

When David had to leave Jerusalem during Absalom's rebellion, he and his men traveled east across the **KIDRON VALLEY** toward the Jordan River (2 Sam. 15:13–23).

King David's Legacy

David's kingdom survived his son's insurrection, but its later years were marked by rebellion, famine, plague, and war again with the Philistines. Before his death, the king appointed Solomon (Bathsheba's son) as heir to the throne (1 Kings 1:1–53). Though David's faults were many, he remains one of the most monumental figures in biblical history. God made a covenant with David: "Your house and your kingdom will continue before me for all time, and your throne will be secure forever" (2 Sam. 7:16). This promise reverberates throughout the New Testament in the person of Jesus the Messiah, the descendant of King David (Matt. 1:1).

Battles of the Old Testament

The Old Testament records more than one hundred battles between the Israelites and their opponents. Thirty-five different nations went to war against Israel, and sometimes Israel lost battles. But God was faithful and preserved his people—even when they went to war against each other.

Battles under	WINS	LOSSES	OTHER*
Joshua	8	3	
David	19	0	
Solomon	3	0	
Judah's Kings	8	14	1
Israel's Kings	10	6	2
Other	12	4	12
Total: 102	60	27	15

** Civil Wars, Treaties, Mixed, Unspecified*

Israel's major opponents	Number of battles
Philistines	18
Arameans	14
Canaanites	10
Ammonites	9
Moabites	6
Assyrians	5
Amalekites	5
Amorites	5
Edomites	5
Jebusites	4
Other opponents	33
Coalitions	
Civil wars	12

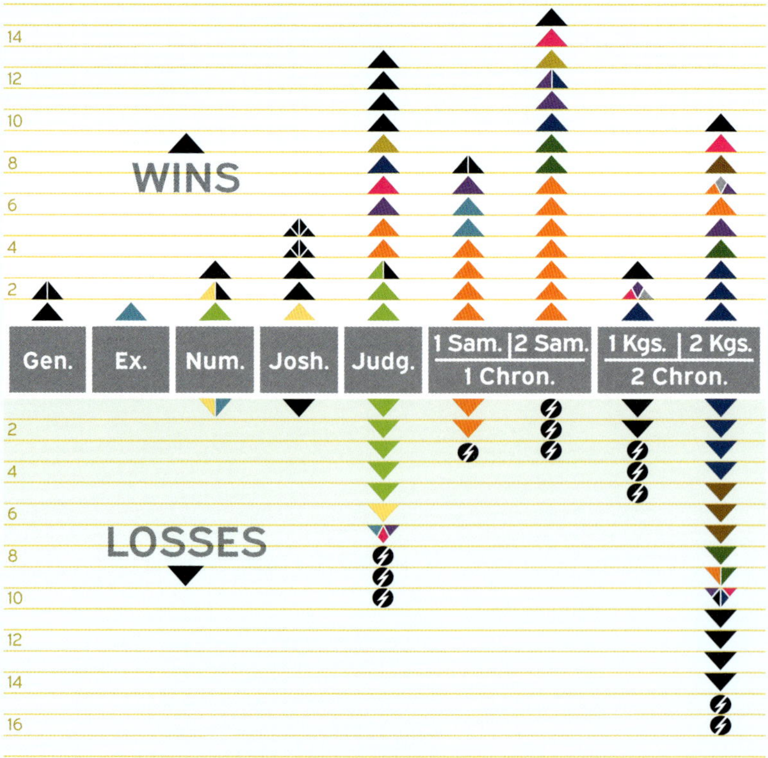

WINS
LOSSES
Gen.
Ex.
Num.
Josh.
Judg.
1 Sam. | 2 Sam.
1 Chron.
1 Kgs. | 2 Kgs.
2 Chron.
2 4 6 8 10 12 14 16

Solomon's Kingdom

Solomon was the third king of Israel and the second son of David and Bathsheba. The new king chose wisdom over riches, fame, or a long life—and in the end, God gave him all these (1 Kings 3:4–15). Solomon governed his kingdom with wisdom, reigning over a golden age for Israel. He built a magnificent temple in Jerusalem and increased his nation's wealth and security.

The king made numerous foreign alliances by marrying the daughters of powerful rulers. In Solomon's old age, these wives turned his heart away from the Lord and toward their pagan gods (1 Kings 11:1–6). Solomon had begun with promising confidence in God but ended his life as an idol-worshiper whose kingdom would be irreparably fractured after his death.

Eilat, near ancient Ezion-geber

Solomon's Fame

Solomon built a fleet of trading ships at Ezion-geber, which brought gold from Ophir and many exotic goods from faraway lands. He also conducted international business, buying horses and chariots from Egypt and Cilicia and reselling them to the Arameans and Hittites. Solomon gained such fame throughout the region that even the queen of Sheba came to visit him to witness his kingdom for herself.

Solomon's Wealth

GOLD

25 tons of gold annually from tributes
16 tons of gold from Ophir
9,000 pounds of gold from Sheba

LABOR

3,600 foremen
30,000 Israelite men
70,000 common laborers
80,000 quarry laborers

MILITARY

1,400 chariots
4,000 stalls for chariot horses
12,000 horses

TERRITORY

45,000 square miles
(120,000 sq km)

WOMEN

700 wives
300 concubines

DAILY FOOD REQUIREMENTS

300 bushels of meal
150 bushels of choice flour
100 sheep or goats
20 pasture-fed cattle
10 oxen
Plus deer, gazelles, roe deer, and choice poultry

Remains of Solomon's multi-chambered gate at Gezer

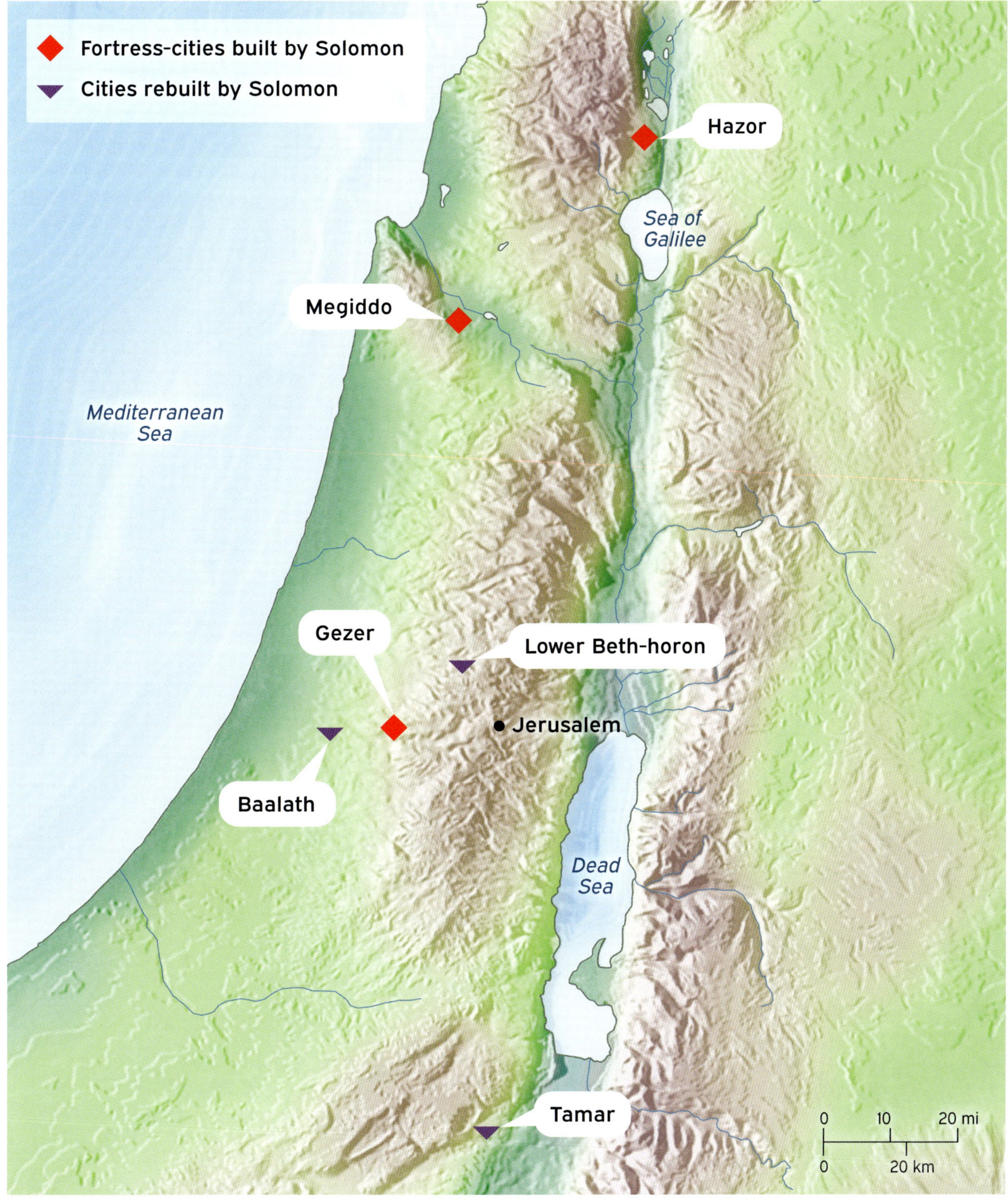

Solomon's Cities

With his vast wealth, King Solomon developed Israel's infrastructure and undertook many building projects. He not only rebuilt existing cities but created new fortress-cities to strengthen his kingdom (1 Kings 9:15).

Where Was the Temple Built?

Solomon built the temple of the Lord on the site of the threshing floor of Araunah, which David had purchased. This was also considered the location of Mount Moriah, where Abraham had nearly sacrificed Isaac.

The temple stood in the northeastern corner of Jerusalem in a new section that Solomon had fortified so that a large flat area could accommodate the temple as well as the king's living quarters.

Today, the gold Dome of the Rock, an Islamic shrine first built in the seventh century AD, tops the Temple Mount in Jerusalem.

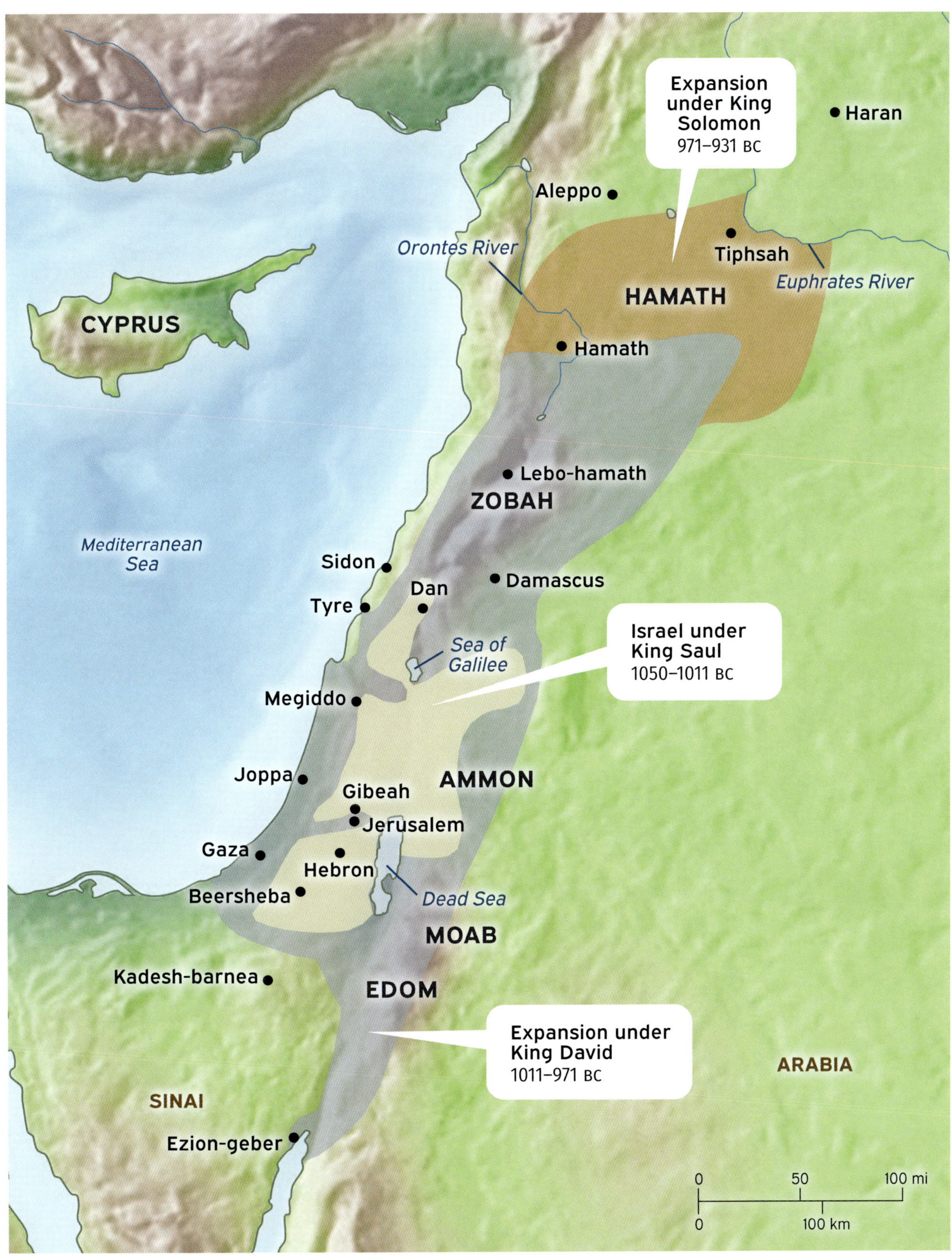

Expansion under King Solomon
971–931 BC
Haran
Aleppo
Tiphsah
Orontes River
Euphrates River
HAMATH
CYPRUS
Hamath
Lebo-hamath
ZOBAH
Mediterranean Sea
Sidon
Damascus
Dan
Tyre
Sea of Galilee
Israel under King Saul
1050–1011 BC
Megiddo
Joppa
AMMON
Gibeah
Jerusalem
Gaza
Hebron
Beersheba
Dead Sea
MOAB
Kadesh-barnea
EDOM
Expansion under King David
1011–971 BC
ARABIA
SINAI
Ezion-geber
0 50 100 mi
0 100 km

THE BOOKS OF WISDOM & POETRY

Poetic writings can be found throughout the Old Testament, but a collection of five books of poetry and wisdom stand out. In these books, human beings express their joyful and troubled prayers to God in songs (Psalms); give practical advice for wise living (Proverbs); struggle with the meaning and apparent unfairness of life (Job, Ecclesiastes); and celebrate God's creation in marriage and love (Song of Songs). These five books have a strong experiential tone, and though they are presented more from a human perspective than other parts of Scripture, God's voice still speaks clearly and authoritatively.

The five books consist almost entirely of poetic writings, with a few sections of Ecclesiastes and Job written in prose. In Psalms, the poetry is expressed lyrically through song. In Job, however, the poetry comes in the form of dialogue. The books can also be considered wisdom literature, with the books of Proverbs, Job, and Ecclesiastes especially focused on attaining wisdom and on understanding God's ways in the world.

The contents of these books were spoken, sung, written, edited, and compiled over a long time span of Old Testament history. The setting for the story of Job may have been as early as the time of Abraham in the 2000s BC, and portions of Proverbs were compiled as late as the 700s BC during the reign of Hezekiah.

JOB, PSALMS, PROVERBS, ECCLESIASTES, AND SONG OF SONGS

The book of Job examines suffering and refutes those who say suffering is always earned or that God is unjust. Psalms is a collection of the songs of Israel, which express faith and hope in God's mercy and protection. Proverbs provides a compass to navigate life with wisdom. Ecclesiastes peers through the apparently meaningless vapor of life to find purpose. Song of Songs celebrates romance, sexual intimacy, and love in marriage.

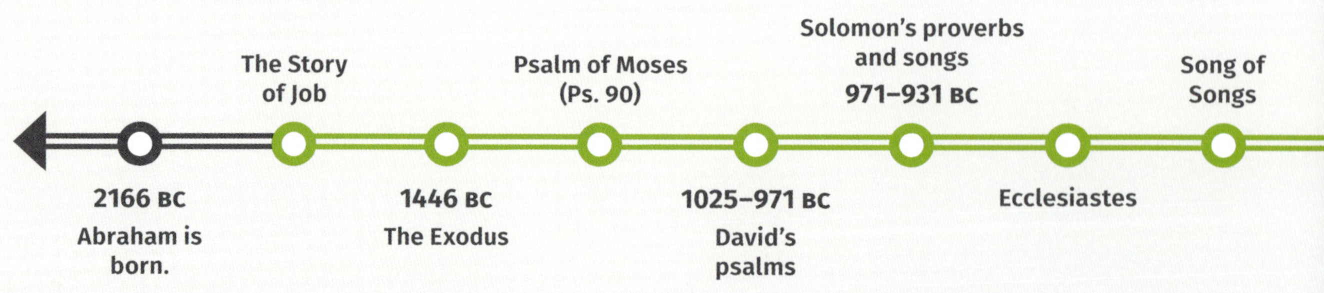

SYRIA
IRAQ
Jerusalem
JORDAN
Uz?

The poetry and wisdom books focus on Israel and Jerusalem (Zion), with one notable exception: Job, which is set in Uz, a land outside of Israel. Zion is the Hebrew name for the mountain in Jerusalem on which Solomon built the temple. It is used as a synonym for Jerusalem, but it also evokes a greater meaning as the locale or kingdom of God that transcends any geographical region.

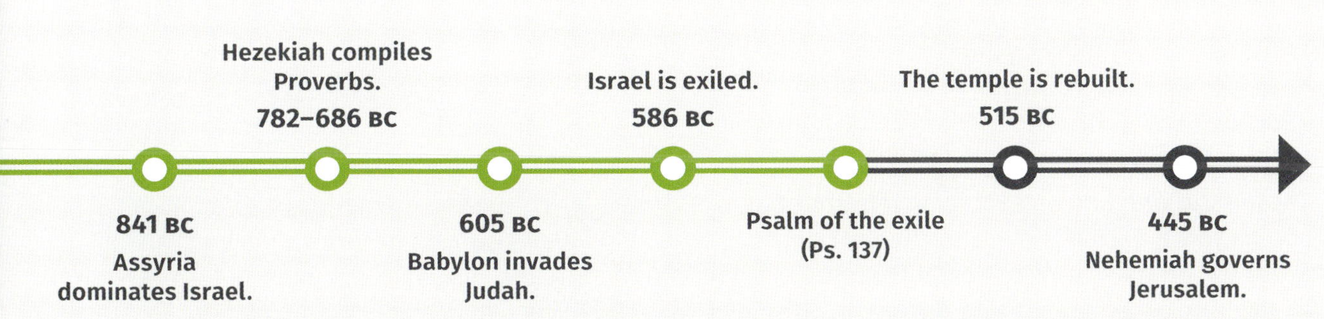

The Wisdom Books

The books of Job, Proverbs, and Ecclesiastes are especially focused on imparting wisdom to their readers and exploring the human struggle to gain understanding. Wisdom is not the same as intelligence or knowledge. Knowledge is a mastery of facts and ideas, and intelligence is the ability to gain that mastery. By contrast, wisdom is the ability to see the right time and the best way to say or do something.

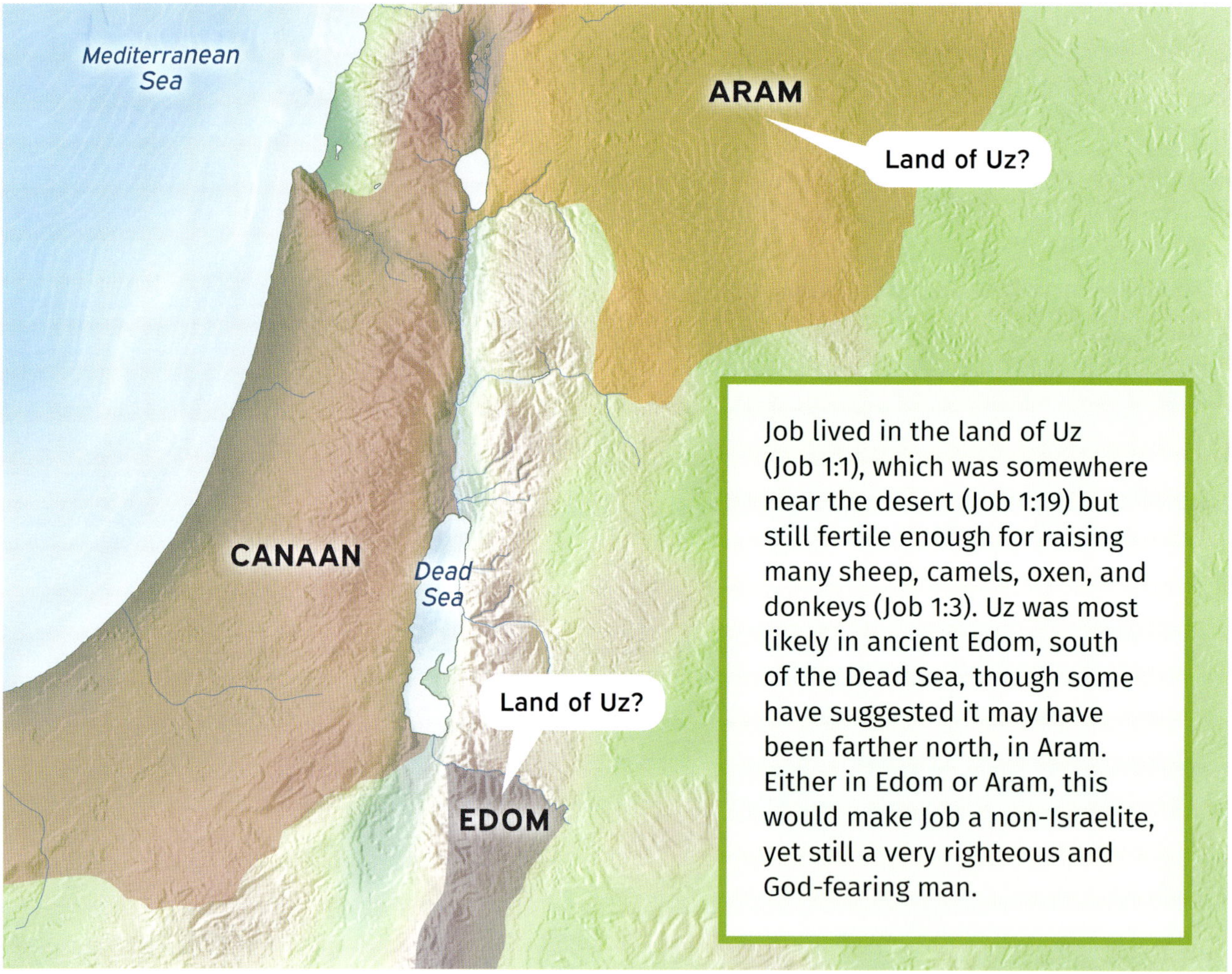

Mediterranean Sea

ARAM

Land of Uz?

CANAAN

Dead Sea

Land of Uz?

EDOM

Job lived in the land of Uz (Job 1:1), which was somewhere near the desert (Job 1:19) but still fertile enough for raising many sheep, camels, oxen, and donkeys (Job 1:3). Uz was most likely in ancient Edom, south of the Dead Sea, though some have suggested it may have been farther north, in Aram. Either in Edom or Aram, this would make Job a non-Israelite, yet still a very righteous and God-fearing man.

When Did Job Live?

Though no one knows exactly when the book of Job was written, the setting for the narrative seems to be during the era of the patriarchs in the 2000s BC, centuries before the law of Moses. Clues in the text point to the patriarchal era: the money Job and his relatives used is termed *kesitah* in Hebrew, as it was during Jacob's day (Gen. 33:19; Job 42:11); the length of Job's life (140 years; Job 42:16) is similar to the unusually long lifespans of Abraham, Isaac, and Jacob.

Village of Dana, Jordan, southeast of the Dead Sea in the region of the ancient Edomites

Wise King Solomon

King Solomon's wisdom was said to exceed that of "all the wise men of the East and the wise men of Egypt" (1 Kings 4:30). His "wise and understanding heart" was a special gift from God (1 Kings 3:12). We are told in 1 Kings 4:32 that Solomon "composed some 3,000 proverbs and wrote 1,005 songs."

Ecclesiastes was written by Solomon, "the Teacher" (Eccl. 1:1).

Proverbs is a collection of wise sayings from various sages, but especially from Solomon (Prov. 1:1; 25:1).

Song of Songs—or Song of Solomon as it is also called—may have been composed in part by Solomon (Song 1:1) or, more likely, either written *for* Solomon or written much later and attributed to the era of Solomon.

Themes in Proverbs

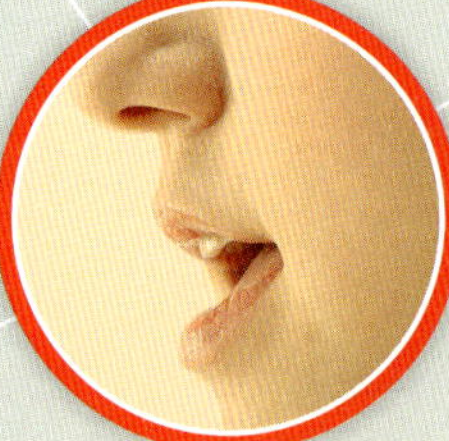

Speaking
10:11; 15:4, 23; 16:23-24; 18:4, 21; 26:23

Arguing
3:30; 10:12; 13:10; 15:18; 16:28; 17:14, 19; 18:19; 20:3; 21:19; 22:10; 25:8; 26:4-5, 17, 20-21; 29:22; 30:33

Lying
6:16-19; 10:31; 12:19-22; 13:5; 14:25; 17:7, 20; 19:9; 21:6, 28; 25:18; 26:18-19, 24, 28; 28:13; 30:5-8

Honesty
2:7; 11:1, 3, 20; 12:19, 22; 14:25; 16:13; 19:1; 20:7, 10; 24:26, 28; 28:6, 13, 23

Flattery
7:4-5, 21; 26:28; 28:23; 29:5

Gossip
6:16, 19; 10:12; 11:9, 12-13; 16:27-28; 17:4, 9; 18:8; 20:19; 25:9-10, 23; 26:20-22

Mocking
3:34; 9:7-8, 12; 13:1; 14:6; 15:12; 17:5; 19:25; 21:24; 22:10; 24:9; 29:8; 30:17

Wisdom
1:7; 2:6; 3:13-20; 4:5-13; 5:1-2; 8:1-9:6; 9:10-12; 11:2; 14:33; 15:33; 16:16; 17:24; 18:4; 19:8; 24:3, 7, 14; 28:26; 30:24-28

Understanding
2:2-7; 3:5; 14:6, 29, 33; 15:32; 16:21; 17:10, 27; 18:2; 19:8; 20:5; 21:30; 28:16

Knowledge
1:4-7; 2:3-6, 10-12; 8:9-12; 9:10; 10:14; 11:9; 12:23; 14:6-7, 18; 15:2, 14; 18:15; 19:2, 27; 22:12; 23:12; 24:3-5; 28:2

Counsel
1:20-33; 5:1-2; 6:20-23; 7:1-2; 10:31; 11:14; 12:5, 26; 13:13; 15:7, 22; 19:20; 20:5, 18; 23:9; 27:9

Correction
1:8, 20-33; 3:11-12; 4:1; 9:7-8; 10:17; 12:1; 13:1, 18; 15:5, 12, 32; 17:12; 25:12; 27:17; 28:23

Good Judgment
1:4; 3:21-26; 4:1-7; 5:1-2; 9:1-6, 10; 14:8, 15; 21:5; 22:3; 23:23; 27:12

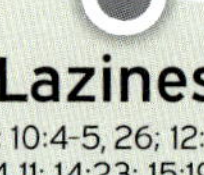

Foolishness
1:7, 22, 32; 8:5; 9:13-18; 10:8, 18, 23; 11:29; 12:15-16, 23; 13:16, 19-20; 14:7-9, 16-18, 29; 15:5, 14; 17:10, 16, 24, 28; 18:2, 13; 19:3; 20:3; 21:20; 22:15; 26:1-12; 28:26; 29:11; 30:32

Haste
18:13; 19:2; 21:5; 25:8; 28:20, 22; 29:20

Laziness
6:6-11; 10:4-5, 26; 12:11, 24, 27; 13:4, 11; 14:23; 15:19; 18:9; 19:15, 24; 20:4, 13; 21:5, 25; 24:30-34; 26:13-16; 28:19

Wickedness
3:31-33; 4:14-19; 5:22-23; 6:12-15; 10:6-7, 24-30; 11:10-11; 12:5-7, 10; 17:23; 21:7, 29; 26:23-26; 28:4; 29:7, 12

Bad Company
4:14-19; 13:20; 14:7; 16:19; 20:19; 22:5, 24-25; 23:6-8, 20-21; 24:1-2, 21-22

Anger
12:16; 14:17, 29; 15:1, 18; 19:11, 19; 21:14; 22:24-25; 29:8, 22; 30:33

Temptation
1:10; 4:23-27; 10:9; 11:5-6; 14:12, 16, 22; 15:3; 16:6, 17; 19:21; 21:15; 28:26; 29:6

Envy
3:31; 14:30; 23:17; 24:1-2, 19-20

Cheating
11:1; 16:8; 20:23; 22:28; 23:10; 28:8

Stealing
6:30-31; 22:22; 28:24; 29:24; 30:7-9

Revenge
6:34; 20:22; 24:28-29; 25:21-22

Hating
6:16-19; 8:13; 9:8; 10:12, 18; 13:5, 24; 14:17; 15:17; 26:24, 26, 28; 28:16; 29:10

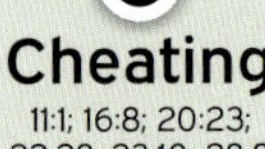

Pride
8:13; 11:2; 13:10; 16:18-19; 18:12; 21:4, 24; 22:4; 26:12; 29:23; 30:32

Humility
3:34; 11:2; 12:15; 13:10; 15:5, 33; 16:19; 18:12; 22:4; 29:23

Trust in the Lord
3:5-6; 11:28; 16:20; 20:24; 21:22, 31; 22:17-19; 28:25-26; 29:25; 30:4-5; 31:11

Fear of the Lord
1:7; 2:1-5; 3:7-8; 8:13; 9:10; 10:27; 14:2, 26-27; 15:16, 33; 16:6; 19:23; 22:4; 23:17-18; 24:21; 28:14; 29:25; 31:30

Strength
3:7-8; 10:29; 11:7; 17:22; 18:10-11; 20:29; 21:22; 24:3, 5, 10; 30:25; 31:17, 25

Harmony/ Peace
1:33; 10:10; 11:12; 12:20; 14:30; 16:7; 17:1; 29:17

Happiness
3:18; 8:32-36; 10:28; 12:25; 15:13, 15, 30; 16:20; 17:22; 23:25; 24:17; 28:20; 29:18

Justice
2:8-9; 8:20; 12:5; 13:23; 16:10-12; 17:15, 23, 26; 18:5; 19:28; 21:3, 7, 15; 22:8, 22; 24:11; 25:5; 28:5; 29:4, 26-27; 31:8-9

Faithfulness
3:3; 11:13; 14:22; 16:6; 17:17; 19:22; 20:6, 28; 23:26-28; 25:13, 19; 28:20

Self-control
14:29; 16:32; 19:11; 23:1-3; 25:28

Friendship
3:32; 11:30; 12:26; 14:20; 16:28; 17:9, 17; 18:19, 24; 19:4, 6-7; 20:6; 22:11, 24; 24:26; 27:6, 9-10, 17; 28:7; 29:5

Kindness
3:3; 11:17; 16:24; 26:25; 28:8; 31:26

Sexuality
5:3-23; 6:20-35; 7:4-27; 22:14; 23:26-28; 30:20-23; 31:3

Love
3:11-12; 7:4; 8:17, 21; 9:8; 10:12; 13:24; 14:22; 15:9, 17; 16:6; 17:9, 17; 18:19, 24; 19:8; 20:28; 21:17, 21; 27:5-6, 9-10; 29:3

Righteousness
3:33; 4:18; 11:11, 30-31; 13:21; 14:2; 15:8, 19, 29; 16:13; 21:12, 21; 29:6, 10, 27

Mercy
11:16-17; 18:23; 19:17; 21:10; 28:13

Marriage
5:18; 12:4; 18:22; 19:13-14; 31:10-11

Parents
1:8-9; 4:1-4; 10:1; 15:20; 17:21, 25; 19:26; 20:20; 30:11-12, 17

Obedience
1:8-9; 3:1-2; 4:1-13, 20-22; 5:1-2; 6:20-23; 7:1-3; 10:17; 19:16; 23:22; 28:4, 7; 29:18

Children
1:8-9; 3:1-2; 4:1-4; 10:1; 13:22; 15:20; 17:21, 25; 19:18, 26; 20:7; 22:6, 15; 23:13-14; 29:15, 17

Goodness
2:20; 3:27; 11:3, 6, 17, 27, 30; 12:2; 13:22; 14:14, 19, 22; 15:3; 17:13, 26; 20:8; 28:10, 21; 31:10-12

Generosity
3:9-10, 27-28; 11:24-25; 21:26; 22:9; 23:6; 25:14, 21-22; 28:27

Poverty
10:15; 13:8; 15:16; 16:8; 28:27; 29:7, 14

Loans/Debt
6:1-5; 11:15; 17:18; 20:16; 22:7, 26-27; 27:13

Wealth/ Prosperity
3:9-10; 10:2-4, 15, 22; 11:4, 25, 28; 13:7-8, 11, 22; 14:20, 24; 15:6, 16-17; 16:20; 18:11; 19:4; 20:21; 21:5-6; 22:4, 7, 16; 23:4-5; 28:11, 19-20, 22, 25; 30:8-9

Money
1:19; 3:14; 10:16; 11:28; 20:15; 22:1

Working
6:6-11; 10:4-6; 12:11, 24, 27; 13:4; 14:4, 23; 21:5; 22:29; 27:23-27; 28:19; 31:10-31

Greed
1:18-19; 15:16, 27; 21:26; 22:1; 25:16; 27:20; 28:6, 8, 22, 25; 29:4

Bribes
15:27; 17:8, 23; 18:16; 21:14; 28:21; 29:4

The Psalms

The 150 psalms provide windows into the souls of the ancient saints who wrote them. The theological reflections in this collection of prayers and songs are not simplistic. The psalmists model depth of character, wisdom, authenticity, and very human struggles. Through the psalms, God teaches about who he is as the sovereign and loving Creator, the great things he has done in this world, and what he expects from his people. The psalms were written, sung, recited, and collected throughout Israel's history. Many were composed by or for David, and some are connected to Solomon (Pss. 72; 127) and one was even by Moses (Ps. 90).

The book of Psalms mentions many different places, ranging thousands of miles, possibly from Spain (Tarshish?) to Africa (Sheba?), and perhaps even as far as India (Ophir?).

Most Quoted Books

The number of times these Old Testament books are quoted in the New Testament:

Most Quoted Verses

The Old Testament verses that are quoted most often in the New Testament:

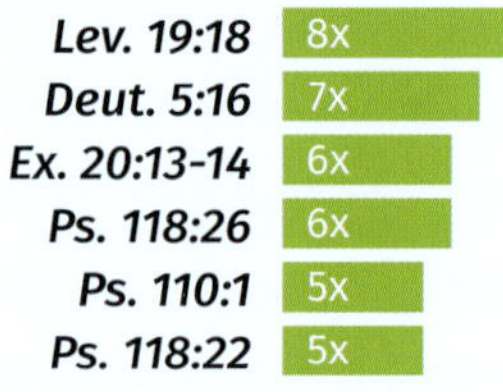

> **"Bless the one who comes in the name of the LORD. We bless you from the house of the LORD."**
>
> PSALM 118:26

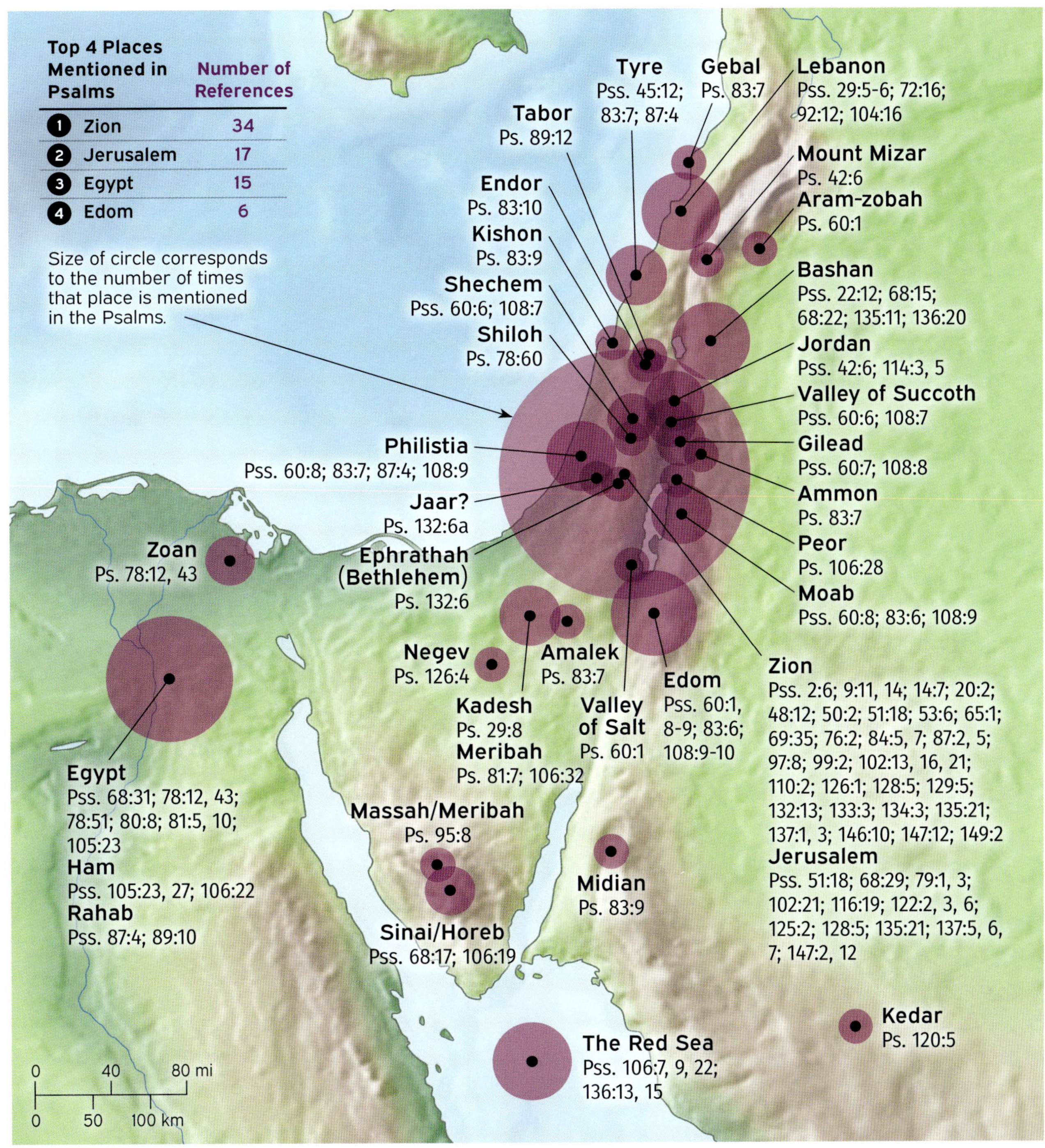

Places in the Psalms

In Psalms, the names of places are not just terms or geographical notes. They have rich meaning and emotional impact. For example, the name "Zion" to the Israelites expressed their most beloved home, the center of their hopes and aspirations. In contrast, the name "Assyria" evoked horror and "Babylon" brought dread because of what those powerful nations had done to Israel in the past and might do in the future. In this way, the book of Psalms gives us insight into the world that God's people inhabited in their hearts and minds.

Themes in Psalms

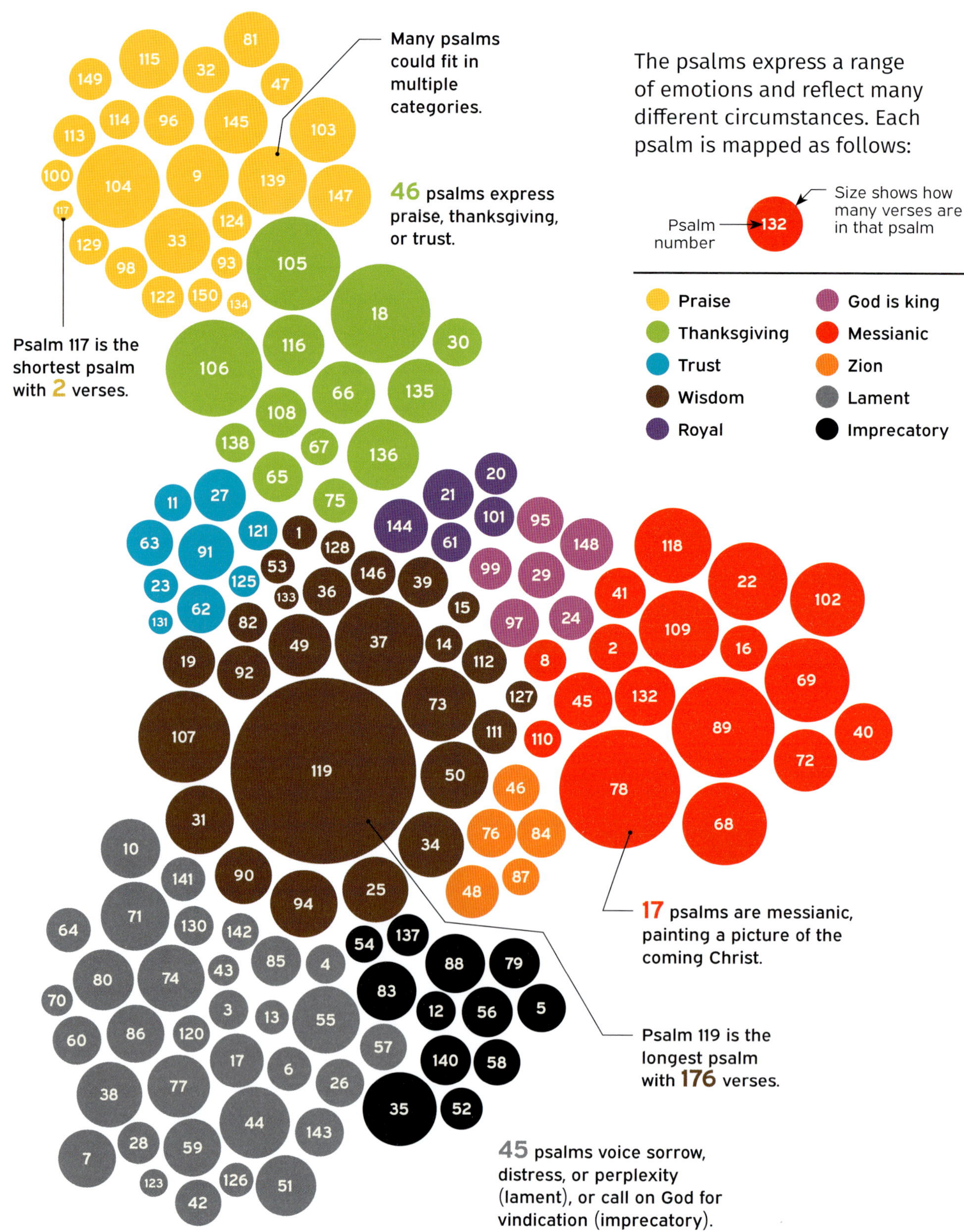

Song of Songs

As a song dedicated to the celebration of human love and passion, Song of Songs is unique in the Bible. It is composed of short speeches, primarily by an unnamed young groom and bride. The book never mentions God, but it bears witness that the Creator has graciously provided his human creatures with good gifts of intimacy and sexuality.

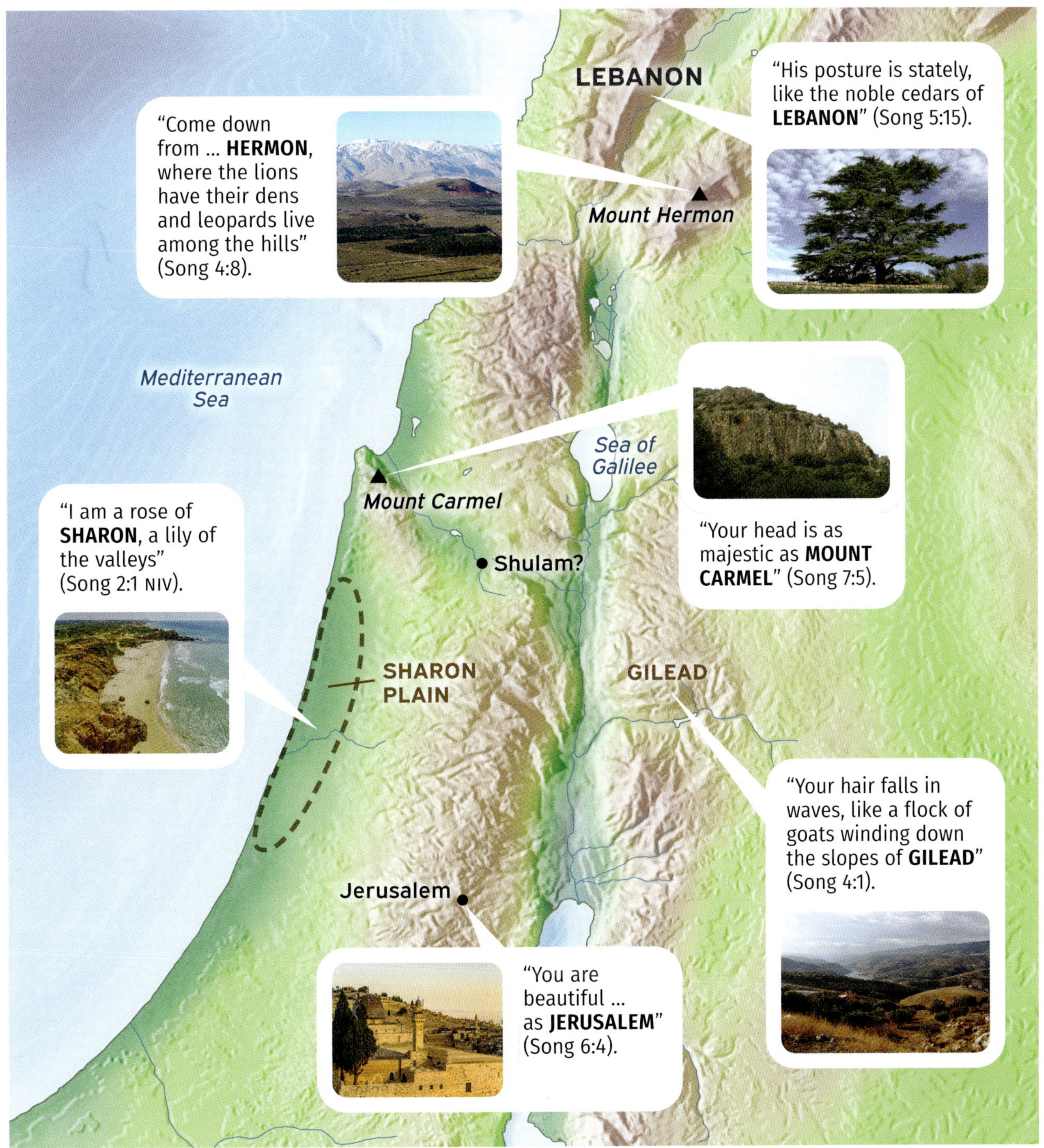

Lachish relief

THE KINGS & PROPHETS

God's judgment came quickly after King Solomon died. The northern tribes rebelled against Solomon's son and heir, Rehoboam. They chose a new king, Jeroboam, and established the Northern Kingdom of Israel, while the tribe of Judah in the south remained loyal to the Solomonic line. Both kingdoms rapidly fell into political instability, power struggles, and the worship of false gods. In the biblical books of Kings and Chronicles, the rulers of Israel and Judah are evaluated not on their military might or economic success but on whether they kept the covenant of God or foolishly "did what was evil in the LORD's sight" (2 Kings 8:18).

Throughout this divided kingdom era, God spoke through the prophets, calling his people to repentance and warning of judgment. Most kings did not heed the words of the prophets, but some listened, such as Hezekiah and Josiah who led spiritual reforms.

The kingdoms of Israel and Judah ran parallel with each other for two centuries, until the Assyrian Empire conquered Israel in 722 BC. The kingdom of Judah continued nearly a century and a half longer, until the Babylonian Empire destroyed Jerusalem in 586 BC. God's people were sent into exile—but they had a divine promise of hope: "The remnant left in Israel, the survivors in the house of Jacob, will no longer depend on allies who seek to destroy them. But they will faithfully trust the LORD, the Holy One of Israel. A remnant will return; yes, the remnant of Jacob will return to the Mighty God" (Isa. 10:20–21).

KINGS, CHRONICLES, AND THE PROPHETS

The books of 1 and 2 Kings and 2 Chronicles record the reigns of the kings of Israel and Judah. The major and minor prophetic books form the last section of the Old Testament, but they are not arranged chronologically. Prophets who ministered during the divided kingdom era include Amos, Jonah, Hosea, Isaiah, Micah, Nahum, Zephaniah, and Habakkuk, among others.

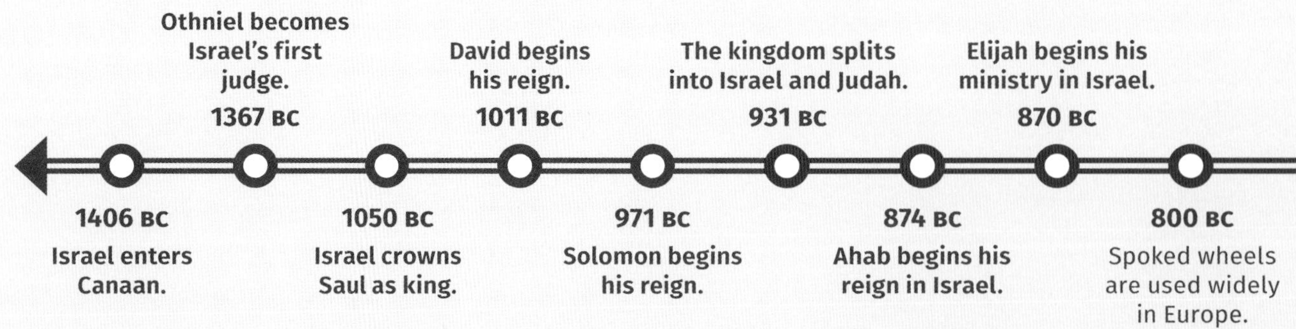

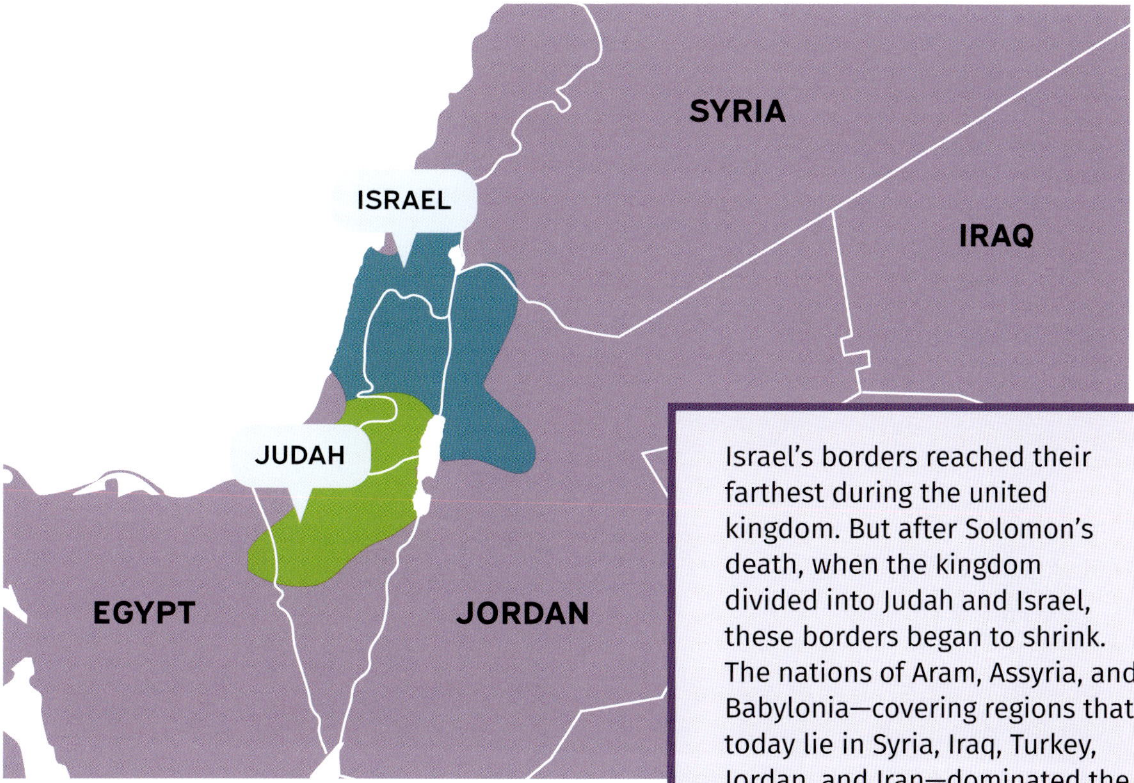

Israel's borders reached their farthest during the united kingdom. But after Solomon's death, when the kingdom divided into Judah and Israel, these borders began to shrink. The nations of Aram, Assyria, and Babylonia—covering regions that today lie in Syria, Iraq, Turkey, Jordan, and Iran—dominated the ancient Near East.

792 BC
Uzziah begins his reign in Judah

Homer's Iliad and Odyssey written down.

776 BC
The first known Olympic Games are held in Greece.

760 BC
Hosea prophesies in Israel.

755 BC
Jonah prophesies in Nineveh.

753 BC
Rome is founded on the Tiber River.

728 BC
Hezekiah begins his reign in Judah.

722 BC
Assyria conquers Israel.

Sargon II becomes king of Assyria.

695 BC
Sennacherib builds a thirty-mile water canal for Nineveh.

586 BC
Babylon destroys Jerusalem and the temple.

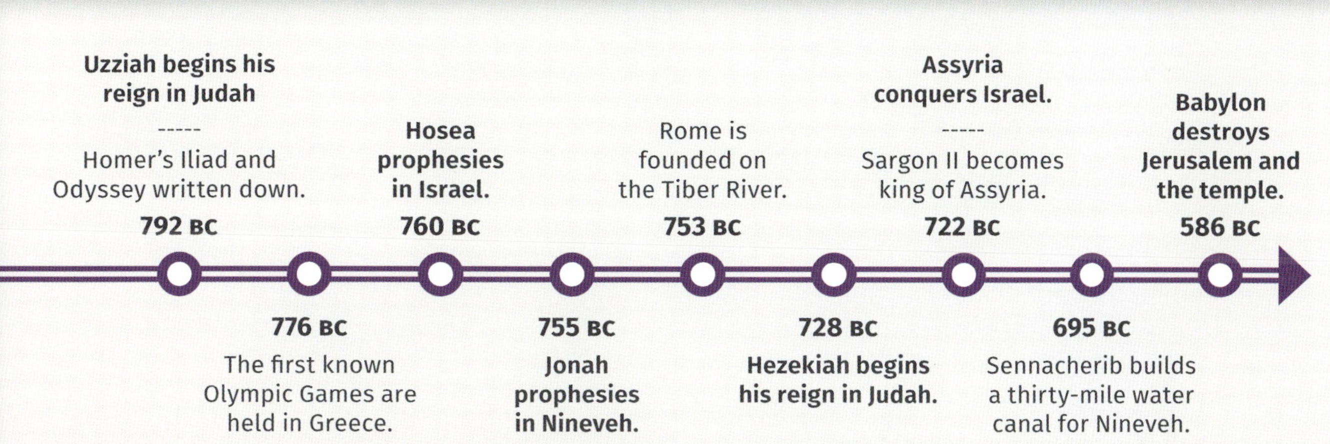

Two Foolish Kings

After Solomon's death, the rapid downfall of the kingdom began with two foolish kings. In the south was Rehoboam, Solomon's son. In the north was Jeroboam, Solomon's former labor manager. Rehoboam listened to his young advisors who told him to be even harsher to the people of Israel than his father had been (1 Kings 12:8–15). The ten northern tribes responded in revolt, and they crowned Jeroboam their new king. Rehoboam and the people of Judah "imitated the detestable practices of the pagan nations" (1 Kings 14:24). Meanwhile, Jeroboam—fearful that his people would be drawn back to Judah because the temple of the Lord was in Jerusalem, in Rehoboam's territory—set up golden calves in Bethel and Dan for the people to worship there. Because this provoked God's anger, God sent an ominous message to Jeroboam: "Since you have turned your back on me, I will bring disaster on your dynasty" (1 Kings 14:9).

> **"On the advice of his counselors, the king made two gold calves. He said to the people, 'It is too much trouble for you to worship in Jerusalem. Look, Israel, these are the gods who brought you out of Egypt!'"**
>
> 1 KINGS 12:28

Shown here is Tel Dan, one of the places where King Jeroboam placed a golden calf so that the people could worship it. A metal frame demonstrates how large the altar for sacrifices may have been.

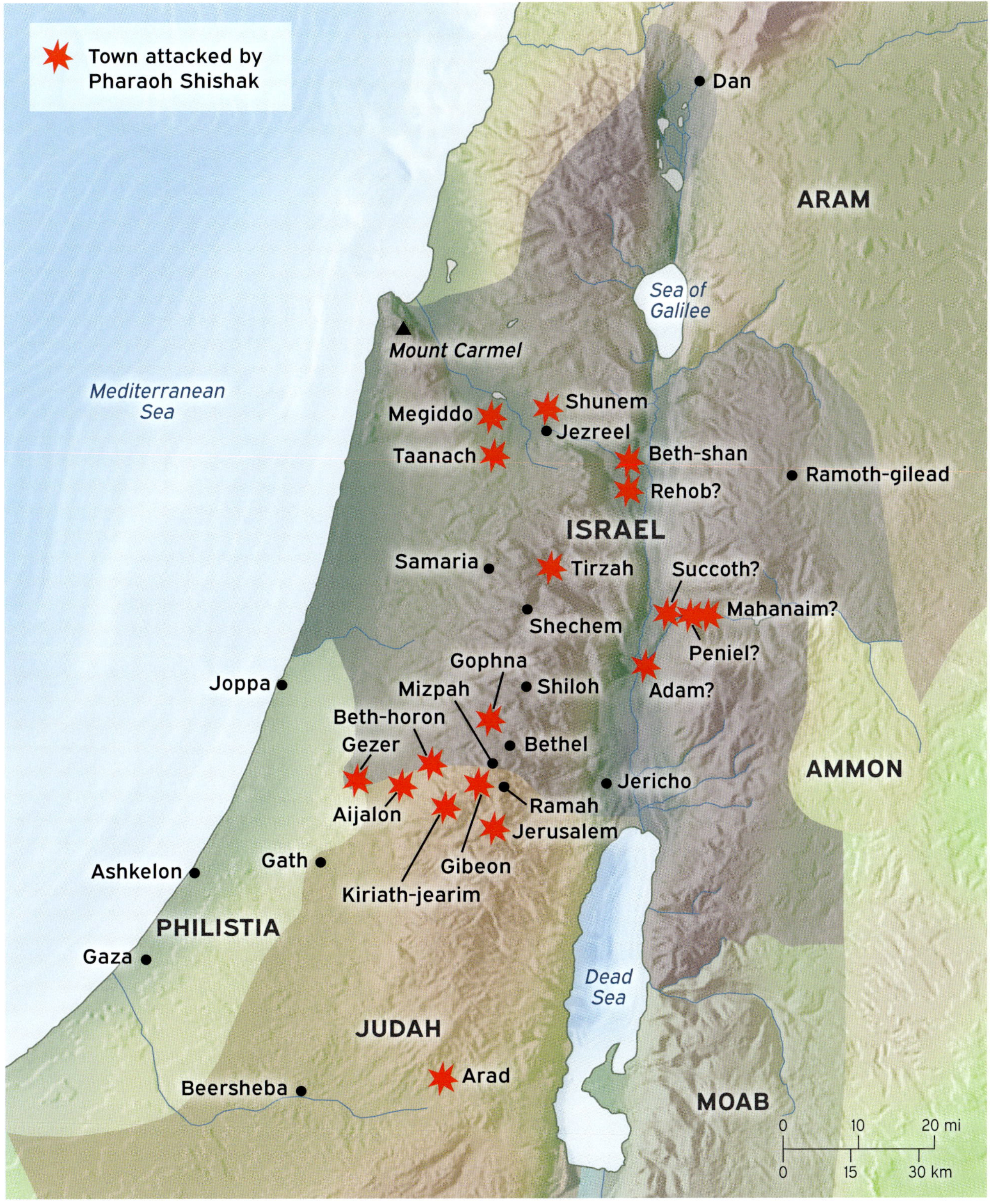

Around 926 BC, five years after the division of Israel, Pharaoh Shishak of Egypt saw a weakened and fractured kingdom. He ransacked Jerusalem and cities throughout Judah and Israel (1 Kings 14:25; 2 Chron. 12:1–12). Battles shown on this map are sites listed in the Pharaoh's own annals.

Northern Kingdom of Israel

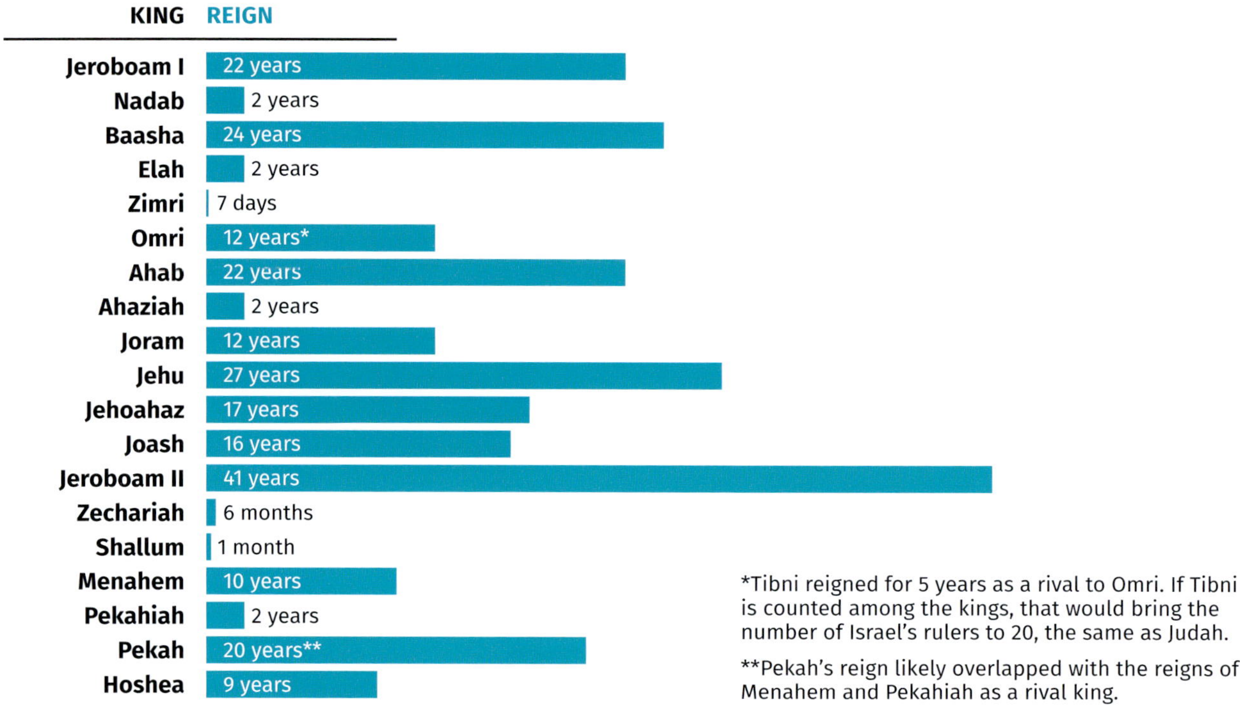

*Tibni reigned for 5 years as a rival to Omri. If Tibni is counted among the kings, that would bring the number of Israel's rulers to 20, the same as Judah.

**Pekah's reign likely overlapped with the reigns of Menahem and Pekahiah as a rival king.

Southern Kingdom of Judah

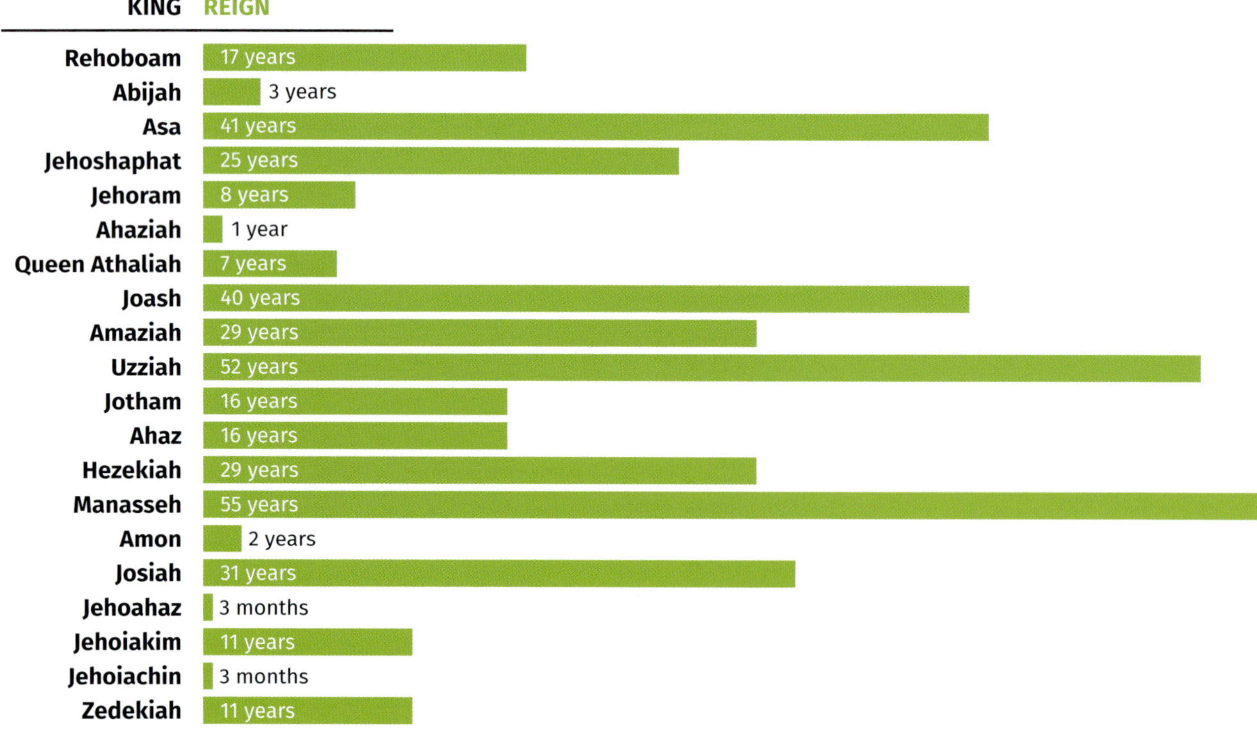

King Ahab and Queen Jezebel

One of the most wicked duos in the Old Testament was King Ahab and Queen Jezebel of the Northern Kingdom of Israel. They worshiped the Canaanite god Baal and built an altar to him in their capital city of Samaria. Militarily, Ahab had some success. He achieved victories over the Arameans (1 Kings 20:1–43) and led a coalition of kings against Assyrian king Shalmaneser III, defeating him at the Battle of Qarqar (853 BC). At home, however, Ahab and Jezebel exploited their own people (1 Kings 21:1–29), and Jezebel tried to exterminate God's prophets, particularly Elijah (1 Kings 18:4; 19:2). Both Ahab and Jezebel met gruesome ends: Ahab was killed in battle and his blood on his chariot was "washed beside the pool of Samaria, and dogs came and licked his blood" (1 Kings 22:37–38); Jezebel was thrown from a window in Jehu's violent coup, her body trampled by horses and eaten by dogs (2 Kings 9:30–37).

> **"[King Ahab] did what was evil in the LORD's sight, even more than any of the kings before him."**
>
> 1 KINGS 16:30

War Between Israel and Aram (1 Kings 20–22)

King Ben-hadad of Aram and his allies tried to besiege Samaria, but King Ahab of Israel met them in battle and defeated them. A year later, Ben-hadad tried again at Aphek, believing that the Israelites' gods would be powerless on the plains, but Ahab defeated them again. Despite warnings from the prophet Micaiah, Ahab and King Jehoshaphat of Judah attacked the Arameans to take back the town of Ramoth-gilead. Ahab was killed by an Aramean arrow and his army lost the battle.

Elijah

Elijah, whose name means "My God is Yahweh," was single-minded in his devotion to the one true God. At the end of his long life and ministry, Elijah was caught up into heaven in a whirlwind with a chariot of fire.

Elisha

Elisha was Elijah's assistant and successor. Like Elijah's prophetic ministry, Elisha's was characterized by amazing miracles and risky encounters with powerful rulers.

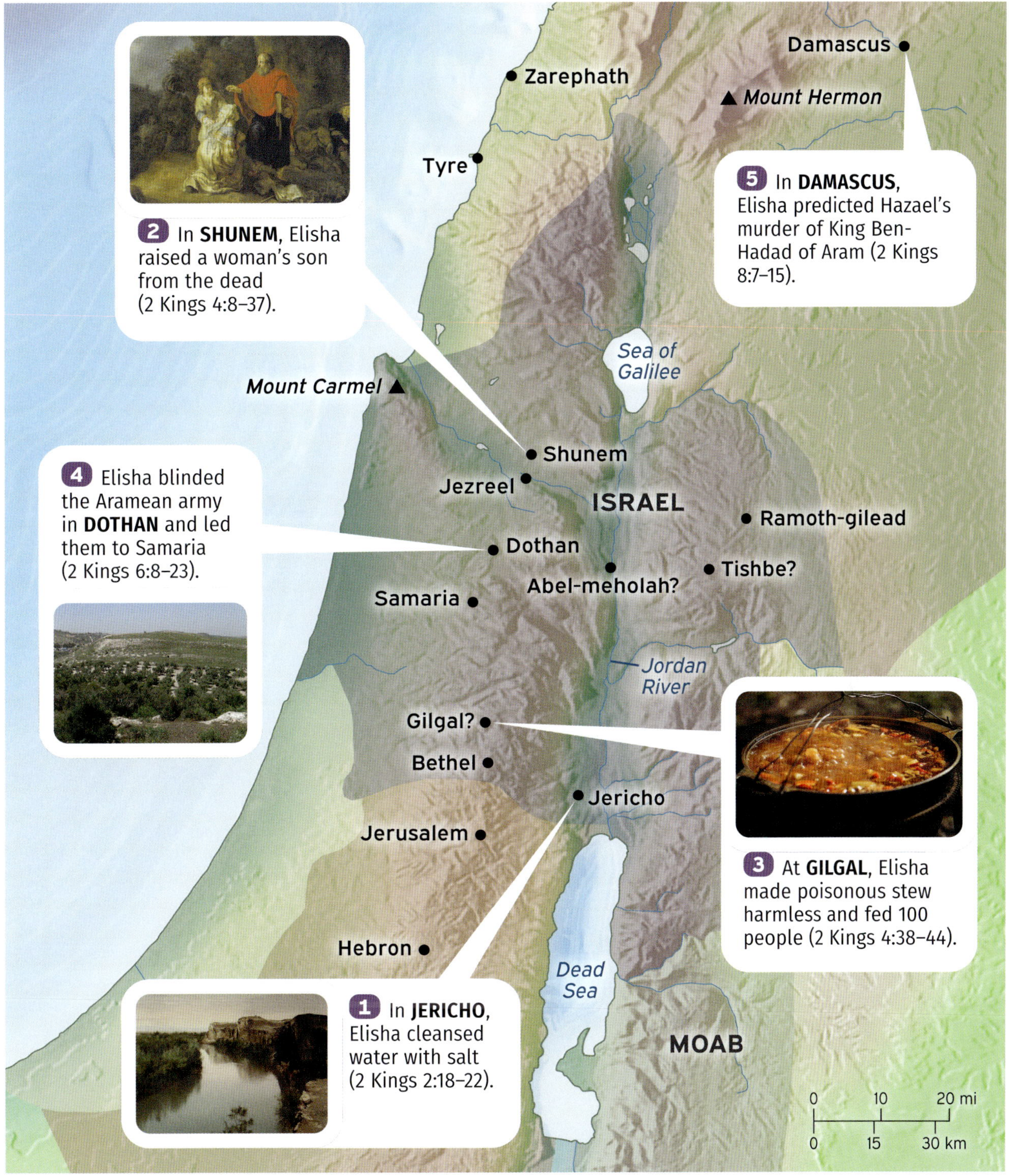

7 Nebuchadnezzar II of Babylon destroyed the Assyrian and Egyptian armies at the Battle of **CARCHEMISH** in 605 BC, ending Assyrian dominance (Jer. 46:1–12).

Haran

Carchemish

Aleppo

Qarqar

1 A coalition of kings (including King Ahab of Israel) fought the advancing Assyrian army at the Battle of **QARQAR** in 853 BC.

Damascus

2 King Jehu of **ISRAEL** paid tribute to Assyrian King Shalmanesser III in 841 BC.

Mediterranean Sea

ISRAEL

Samaria

Jerusalem

JUDAH

5 Assyria besieged **JERUSALEM** in 701 BC, but King Hezekiah sought the Lord and the Assyrian army failed.

4 Assyria conquered **SAMARIA**, ending the Northern Kingdom of Israel in 722 BC.

EGYPT

The Rise and Fall of Assyria

Assyria was a symbol of terror and tyranny in the ancient Near East for more than three centuries. At its height, it reached from the Persian Gulf to Egypt. In the biblical account, we learn about Assyria's power and ruthlessness in its treatment of the people of Israel and Judah. But its fortune rose and fell with the strength of its leaders. Eventually, the dominant Assyrian Empire, which had conquered Israel and attacked Judah, fell to a more powerful ascendant empire: Babylonia.

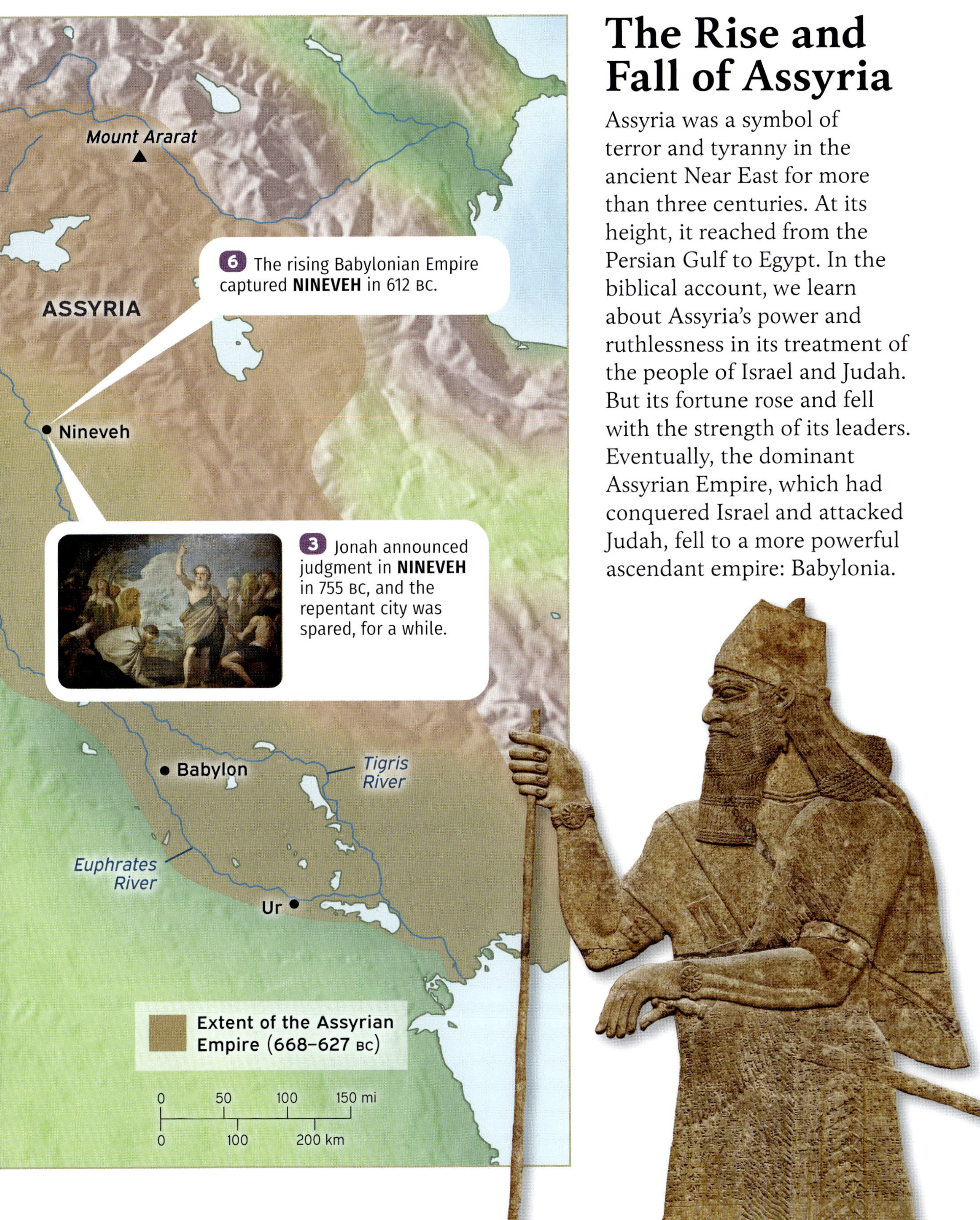

TARSHISH may have been the port city of Tartessos in Spain, Tarsus of Asia Minor (in Turkey today), or simply a general term for any place accessible by sea.

Tarsus

Haran

ASSYRIAN EMPIRE

Mediterranean Sea

To Tarshish?

Damascus

ISRAEL

Gath-hepher

Samaria

Joppa

Jerusalem

JUDAH

EGYPT

Jonah's hometown was **GATH-HEPHER**, which in Hebrew means "winepress of the well" (2 Kings 14:25).

Jonah boarded a ship at the port of **JOPPA**, today a suburb of Tel-Aviv (Jon. 1:3).

0 50 100 150 mi

0 100 200 km

Jonah's Journey

Jonah prophesied to the Northern Kingdom of Israel during the prosperous but spiritually dark reign of Jeroboam II in the eighth century BC (2 Kings 14:25).

When God called Jonah to prophesy judgment in Nineveh, Assyrian power was at a low point, but the Assyrians had already proven to be brutal enemies. So when the prophetic call came, Jonah fled in the opposite direction. He took a ship toward Tarshish, an unidentified location probably somewhere at the far end of the Mediterranean Sea.

After three days in the belly of "a great fish" (Jon. 1:17), the reluctant prophet accepted God's call and traveled to Nineveh to preach to the enemies of Israel. Though spared God's wrath after Jonah's warning, Nineveh eventually fell to Babylon in 612 BC, almost a century and a half after Jonah.

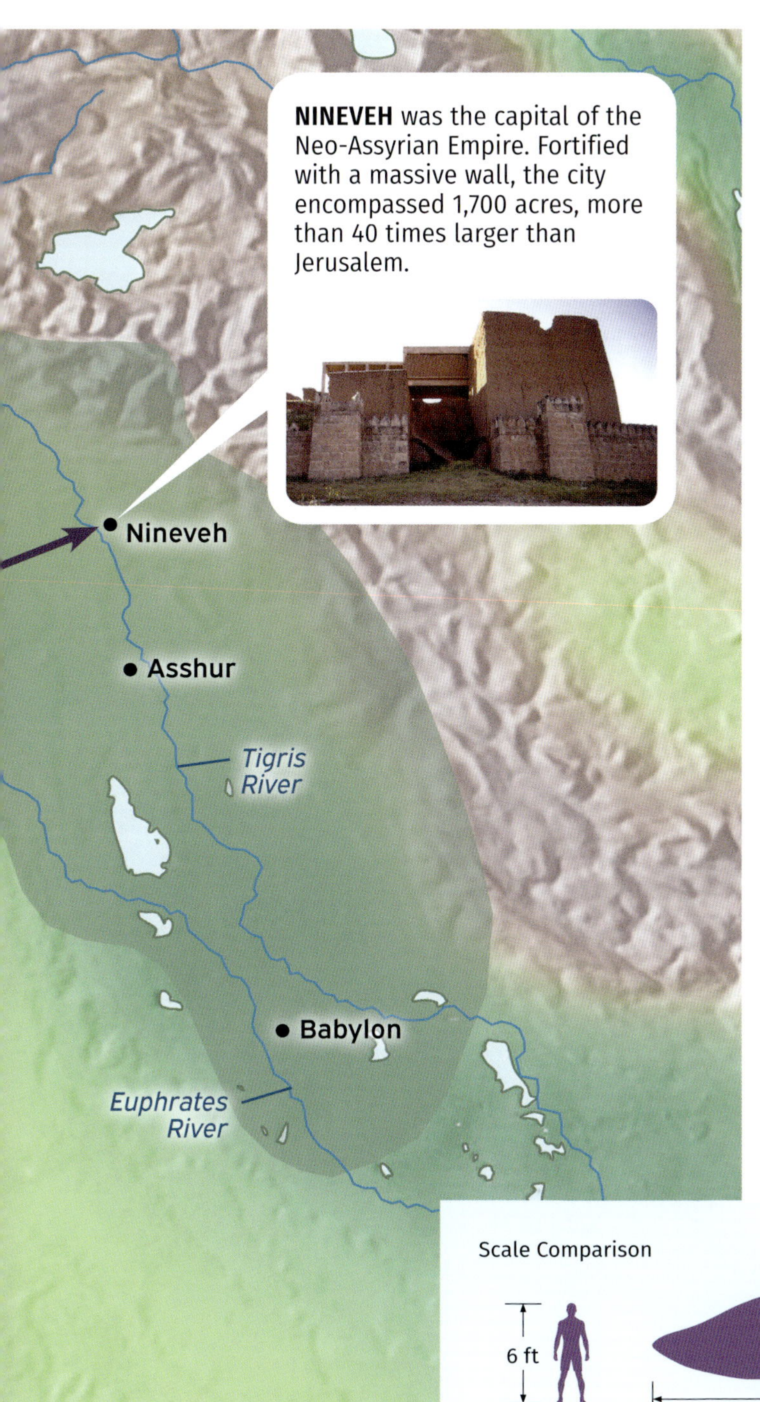

Scale Comparison

6 ft

avg 40 ft

It is not known what kind of "great fish" swallowed Jonah, but the whale shark has been suggested. Averaging 40 feet (12 m) long, the adult whale shark is an enormous but docile filter feeder. It does not bite, but feeds swimming with its mouth open, straining out the water and swallowing what it scoops up.

Books of the Prophets

The prophetic books in the Old Testament are often divided into two parts: Major Prophets and Minor Prophets. "Major" and "Minor" indicate the length of the prophets' books, not the importance of their messages.

The prophets' messages cluster around the two great judgments that Israel experienced: the destruction of the northern kingdom of Israel by Assyria (722 BC), and the destruction of the Southern Kingdom of Judah by Babylonia (586 BC). The prophets warned the people of impending judgment because they had abandoned God and violated the covenant. Some spoke from within the time of judgment and looked to the future, to the time when God would restore his people and once again show them his favor.

Major Prophets
Minor Prophets
Words per Book
Years of Ministry

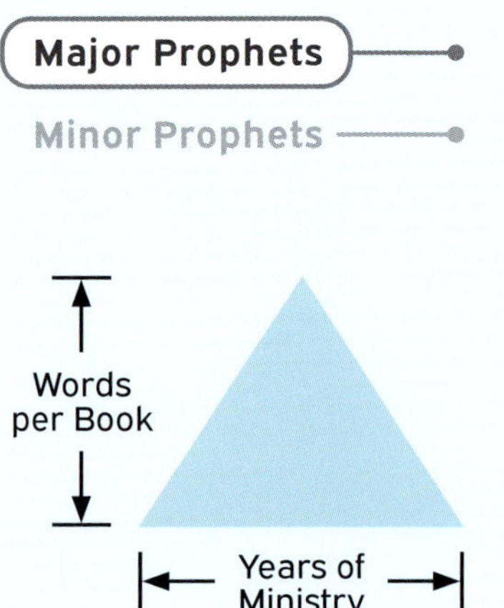

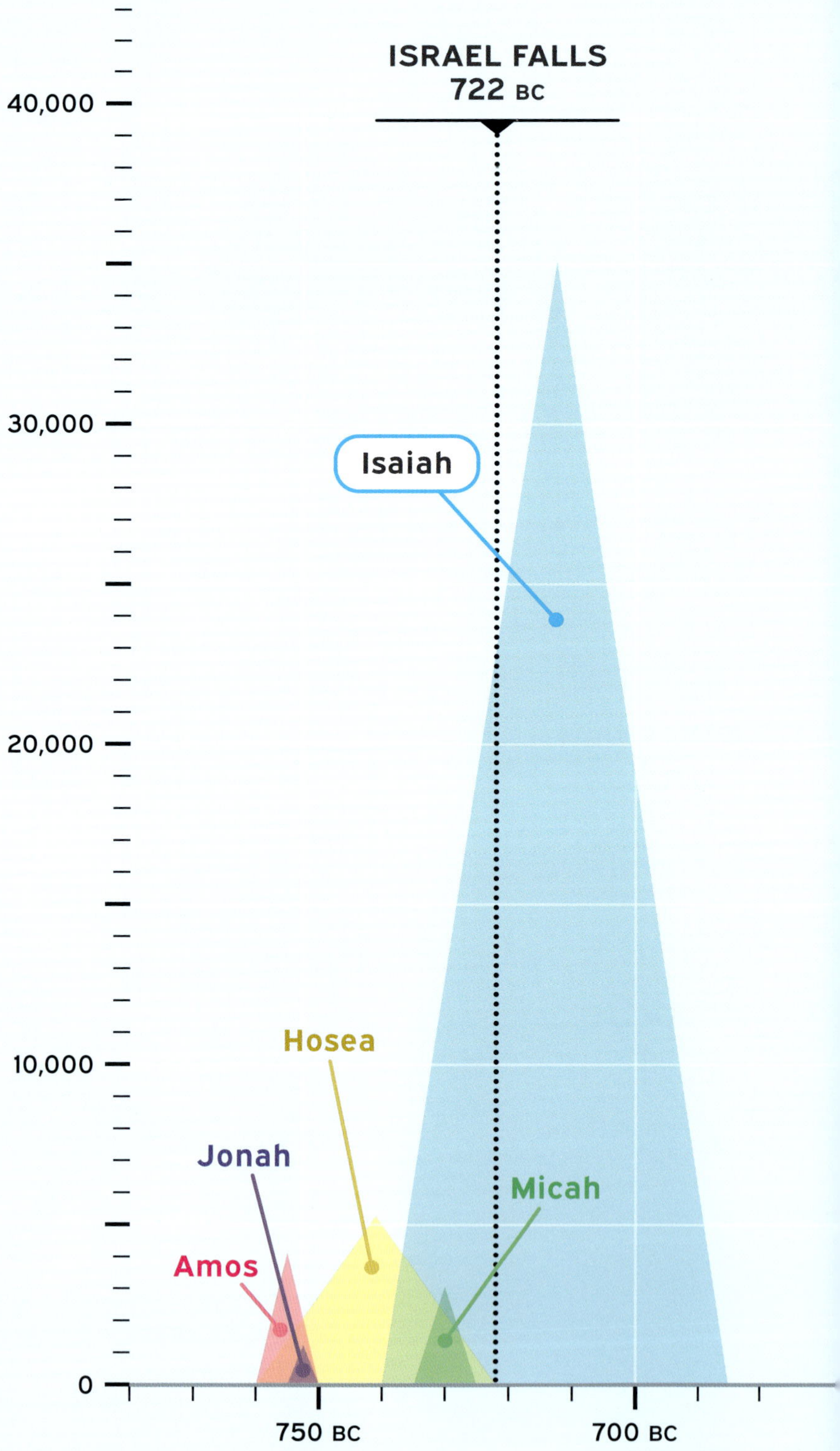

ISRAEL FALLS
722 BC
40,000
30,000
20,000
10,000
0
Isaiah
Hosea
Jonah
Micah
Amos
750 BC
700 BC

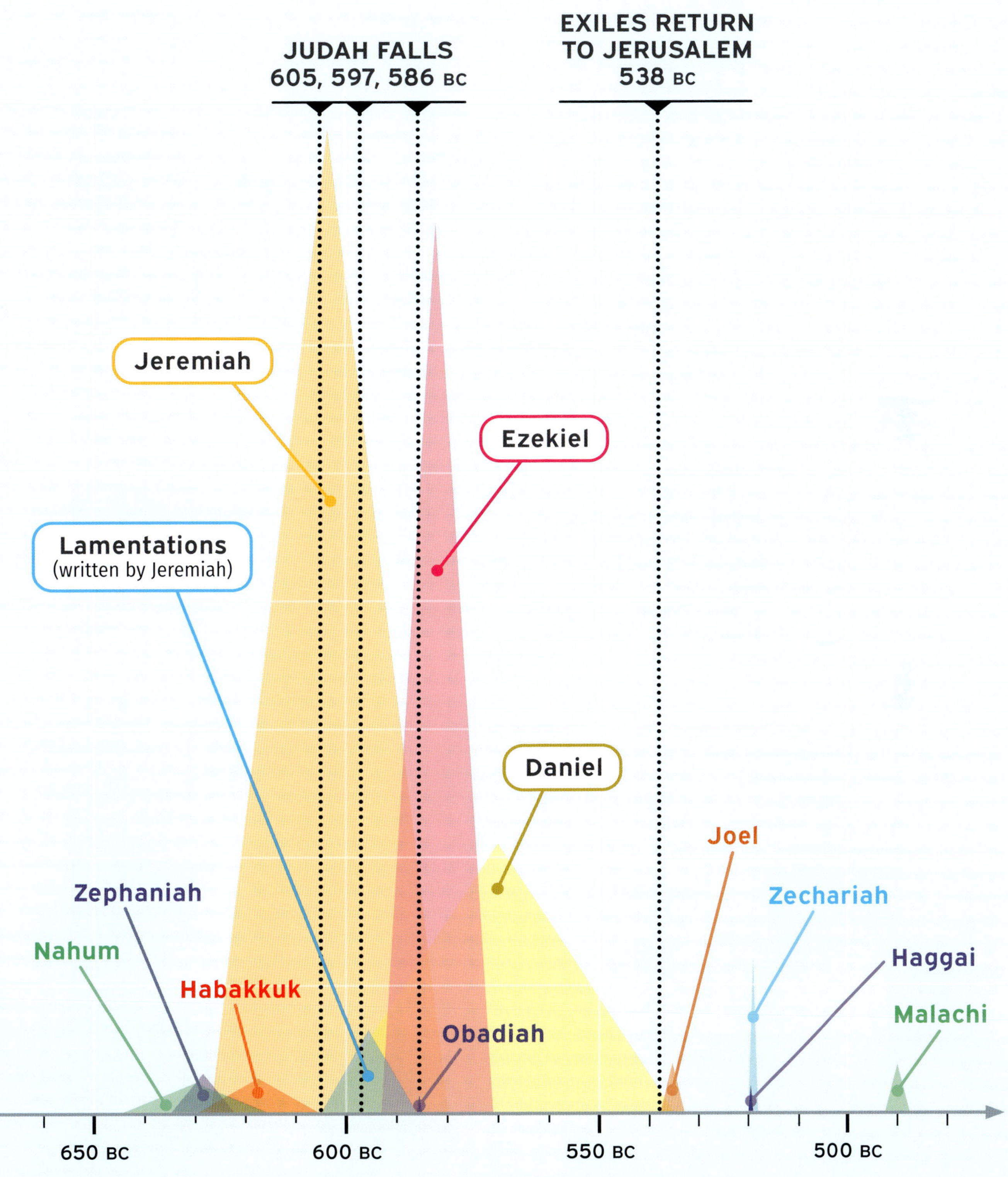
JUDAH FALLS
605, 597, 586 BC
EXILES RETURN
TO JERUSALEM
538 BC
Jeremiah
Ezekiel
Lamentations
(written by Jeremiah)
Daniel
Joel
Zephaniah
Zechariah
Nahum
Haggai
Habakkuk
Malachi
Obadiah
650 BC
600 BC
550 BC
500 BC

The Prophets

The early prophets who ministered during the united kingdom and the beginning of the divided kingdom—like Nathan, Elijah, and Elisha—did not collect their messages into books. But the prophecies of those in the mid to late divided kingdom and during the exile were written and assembled as anthologies named after the prophets. These are the prophetic books of Isaiah through Malachi in the Old Testament. While many of their prophecies concern matters immediately facing people at the time, they also tell about the future and speak of a Messiah who, in the words of Zechariah, would be a king coming to you "righteous and victorious, yet he is humble, riding on a donkey—riding on a donkey's colt" (Zech. 9:9; Matt. 21:46).

The Fall of Israel

In 744 BC, Tiglath-pileser III usurped the Assyrian throne and consolidated control of Assyria's territories. He established his empire as the dominate military and economic power. His successors Shalmaneser V, then Sargon II, advanced Assyria deeper into the heart of Israel. The reigns of the final kings of the northern kingdom of Israel were marked by idolatry, violence, assassinations, and obeisance to Assyria. King Menahem of Israel paid a large tribute of silver to appease Assyria. King Pekah, instead of looking to God, established alliances with neighboring rulers to fend off the encroaching Assyrians, something condemned by the prophet Isaiah. Finally, when King Hoshea failed to pay the tribute, Shalmaneser V destroyed Israel's capital, Samaria, in 722 BC, thus ending the Northern Kingdom (2 Kings 17:3–41).

King Hezekiah

Hezekiah was one of Judah's best kings. His father, King Ahaz, betrayed the Lord, but Hezekiah promoted true worship of God. Reversing the damage done by his father, Hezekiah took down the pagan worship sites, repaired the doors of God's temple, had the Levites sanctify themselves, and invited people throughout Judah to celebrate Passover in Jerusalem. Though Hezekiah made mistakes during his twenty-nine-year reign—such as showing Babylonian rulers the temple treasures (2 Kings 20:12–19)—he listened to the words of the prophet Isaiah and sought the Lord in prayer. During Hezekiah's rule, the Assyrian Empire failed to conquer Judah.

> **"Hezekiah trusted in the LORD, the God of Israel. There was no one like him among all the kings of Judah, either before or after his time. He remained faithful to the LORD in everything, and he carefully obeyed all the commands the LORD had given Moses."**
>
> 2 KINGS 18:5–6

Assyrian Invasion (2 Kings 18:13–19:37)

Hezekiah reigned in Judah when the Assyrians defeated the Northern Kingdom of Israel and deported its inhabitants. In 705 BC, Sennacherib came to power in Assyria, triggering a widespread rebellion and bitter wars. Hezekiah stopped paying tribute to appease Assyria, and in 701 BC Sennacherib invaded Judah, intent on conquering Jerusalem. Hezekiah's prayers to the Lord were heard, and God's powerful hand struck down the Assyrian army as they besieged Jerusalem, forcing them to abandon their plans and return to Nineveh.

Jerusalem (767–643 BC)

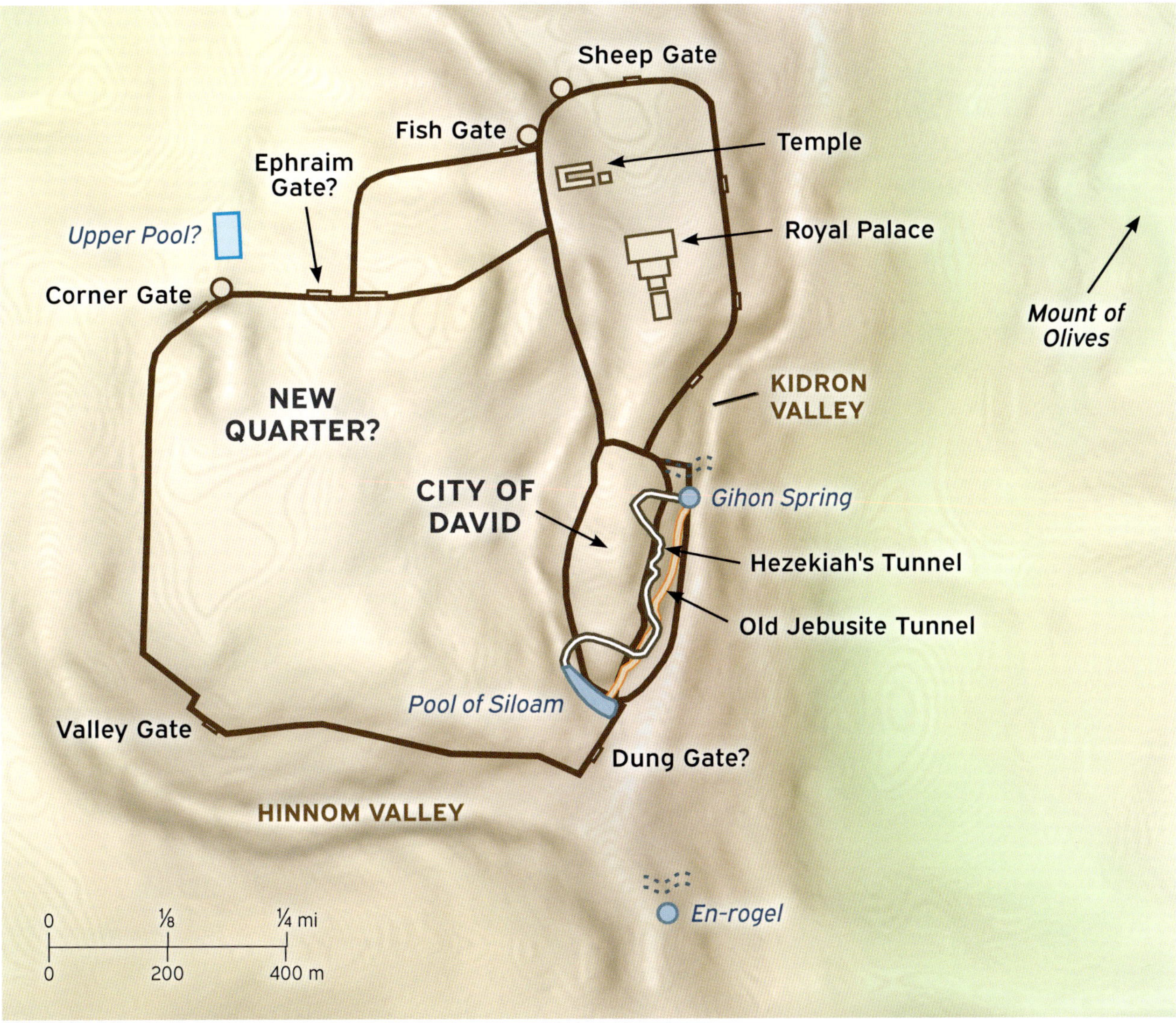

Sheep Gate
Fish Gate
Temple
Ephraim Gate?
Royal Palace
Upper Pool?
Corner Gate
Mount of Olives
KIDRON VALLEY
NEW QUARTER?
CITY OF DAVID
Gihon Spring
Hezekiah's Tunnel
Old Jebusite Tunnel
Pool of Siloam
Valley Gate
Dung Gate?
HINNOM VALLEY
En-rogel
0 ⅛ ¼ mi
0 200 400 m

Preparing for an Attack

Various kings of Judah repaired and augmented the walls of Jerusalem to prepare the city for defending itself against Assyrian attacks. These kings included Uzziah, Jotham, Hezekiah, and Manasseh (2 Chron. 26:9; 27:3; 32:1–5; 33:14). Hezekiah knew that refusing to pay Assyria the annual tribute would probably result in a siege of Jerusalem, so he prepared by building a pool and digging a tunnel ("Hezekiah's Tunnel") to bring water into the city from outside the city walls (2 Kings 20:20; 2 Chron. 32:30). The tunnel was 1,777 feet (541.4 m) long, and it carried water from the Gihon Spring to the pool of Siloam.

Hezekiah's Tunnel

The Wise Prophet Isaiah

Isaiah was a Judean prophet during the reigns of four kings: Uzziah, Jotham, Ahaz, and Hezekiah. He lived in Jerusalem, was well educated, was married to a prophetess, and had two sons (Isa. 7:3; 8:3). As Judah's political and religious counselor, he had access to kings, and he was apparently also a court historian (2 Chron. 26:22; 32:32). Isaiah opposed social and political evil at all levels. He rebuked kings for their willful indifference and denounced the wealthy for ignoring their responsibilities to others. His prophecies, recorded in the book that bears his name, tell of a coming Messiah: the peaceful Prince of God's kingdom (Isa. 11:1–11) who would also be an obedient, suffering Servant (Isa. 53:3–12).

The book of Isaiah records a series of warnings for Israel, Judah, and the surrounding nations, demonstrating that all people are accountable to the Lord for their actions.

Josiah, the Last Good King

Josiah was crowned king at only eight years old and reigned for thirty years. Unlike many of his predecessors who led Judah into idolatry and wickedness, Josiah "turned to the LORD with all his heart and soul and strength" (2 Kings 23:25). At age twenty, he began eradicating pagan places of worship, thus fulfilling a prophecy made centuries earlier (1 Kings 13:1–3; 2 Kings 23:15–18). When Josiah repaired God's temple in Jerusalem, the Book of the Law was found and read to him (2 Kings 22:8–20). Moved by the book's pronouncements against apostasy, Josiah, supported by the prophets Zephaniah and Jeremiah, celebrated Passover and led a spiritual renewal in Judah (2 Kings 23:1–25). Josiah's reforms, however, did not outlive his reign, as the next (and final) four kings of Judah "did what was evil in the LORD's sight" (2 Kings 23:32).

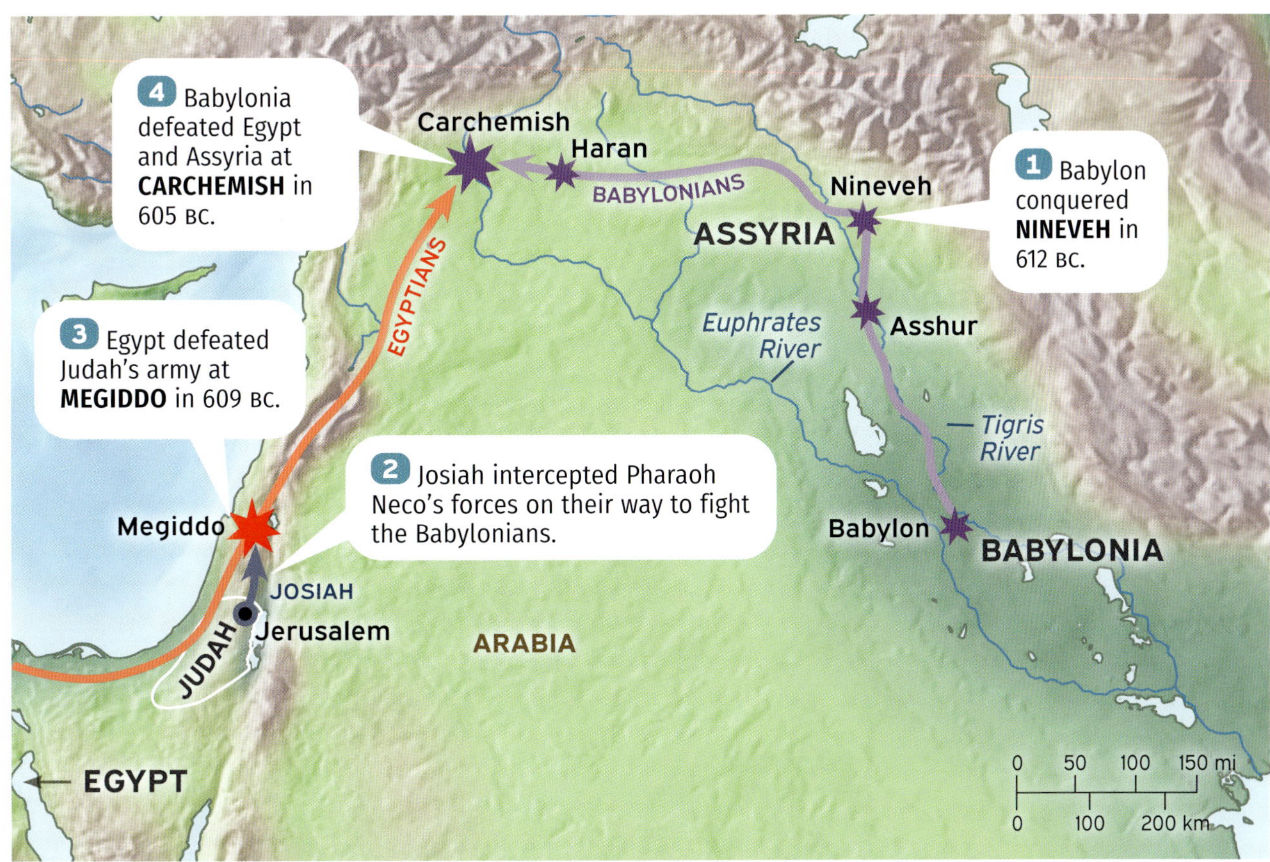

The Battle of Megiddo (2 Chron. 35:20–25)

During Josiah's kingship, Assyrian power diminished, while the Babylonians were on the rise. The Babylonian Empire toppled the Assyrian capital of Nineveh in 612 BC, then pursued the remaining Assyrian army to Carchemish. A few years before the Battle of Carchemish, King Josiah fatefully tried to intercept the Egyptian army on its way to aid the Assyrians. Judah lost the Battle of Megiddo against Egypt, and Josiah was fatally wounded in the conflict. Egypt continued its march to Carchemish, where it was roundly defeated.

The Babylonians

Babylon is one of the world's oldest cities and the center of the ancient Babylonian civilization. In the biblical narrative, Nimrod founded Babylon a few generations after the great flood (Gen. 10:8–10) and Babylon was likely the site of the Tower of Babel (Gen. 11:1–9).

In the seventh century BC, the Chaldean prince Nabopolassar seized the throne of Babylon (625–605 BC) and put an end to Assyrian dominance. Under his son, Nebuchadnezzar II (reigned 605–562 BC), the revived Babylonian Empire spread its influence and power across the region. It was Nebuchadnezzar II who conquered Judah and destroyed the temple in Jerusalem, sending God's people into exile, a judgment foretold by God's prophets.

Hattusha
Tarsus
Carchemish
Aleppo
Hamath
Tadmor
Riblah
Mediterranean Sea
Sidon
Damascus
ARAM
ISRAEL
Samaria
Jerusalem
JUDAH
EGYPT

Nebuchadnezzar II invaded **JERUSALEM** three times, finally destroying and plundering the temple in 586 BC.

The Babylonians deported many survivors, including prophets Daniel and Ezekiel, to **BABYLONIA**.

BABYLON was the capital of the Babylonian Empire (612–539 BC) and home to the legendary Hanging Gardens, one of the Seven Wonders of the Ancient World.

Persepolis, Iran

THE EXILE

During the reign of Josiah, the last good king of Judah, the Babylonian Empire was busy defeating the once-powerful Assyrians. After Josiah's death and the fall of Assyria, the Babylonians turned their attention to Judah. For nearly twenty years under King Nebuchadnezzar II of Babylon, they raided Judah, eventually breaking through the walls of Jerusalem and setting fire to the temple. Many of the people in Jerusalem were taken as captives to Babylon. Jerusalem was left as a heap of burned-out buildings and broken-down walls. The temple was ransacked and stripped of its beauty. Survivors either lived among the ruins or migrated to neighboring nations. The people must have wondered where their God was in all this mess.

The prophets Jeremiah, Daniel, and Ezekiel lived through this terrible period, prophesying in Judah and in exile. They warned of doom before Jerusalem fell, but they also prophesied about a future restoration.

That restoration did arrive (at least in part), but only after decades of exile. The Babylonian Empire fell to the Persians in 539 BC, resulting in a new ruler, King Cyrus II, who issued a proclamation allowing exiled Jews to return to their homeland. This, Scripture tells us, was the work of God: "The LORD fulfilled the prophecy he had given through Jeremiah. He stirred the heart of Cyrus to put this proclamation in writing" (Ezra 1:1). Under leaders like Ezra and Nehemiah, the people returned by the thousands to rebuild Jerusalem.

EZRA, NEHEMIAH, ESTHER, AND THE PROPHETS

The books of Ezra and Nehemiah tell about the rebuilding of Jerusalem and the temple. Prophets like Jeremiah (who wrote Lamentations), Ezekiel, Daniel, Obadiah, Joel, Haggai, Zechariah, and Malachi ministered to the struggling remnant in exile and in Judah. The book of Esther is a story about God's protection of the Jews exiled in foreign lands.

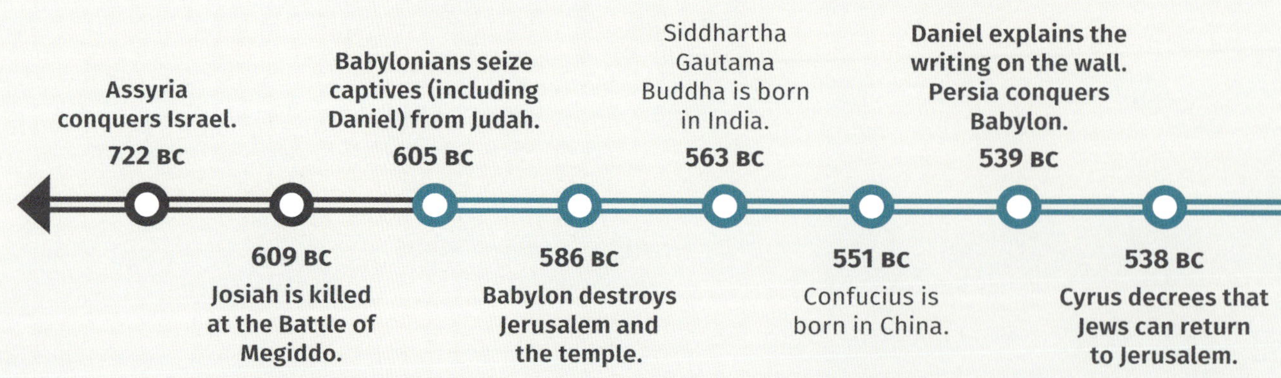

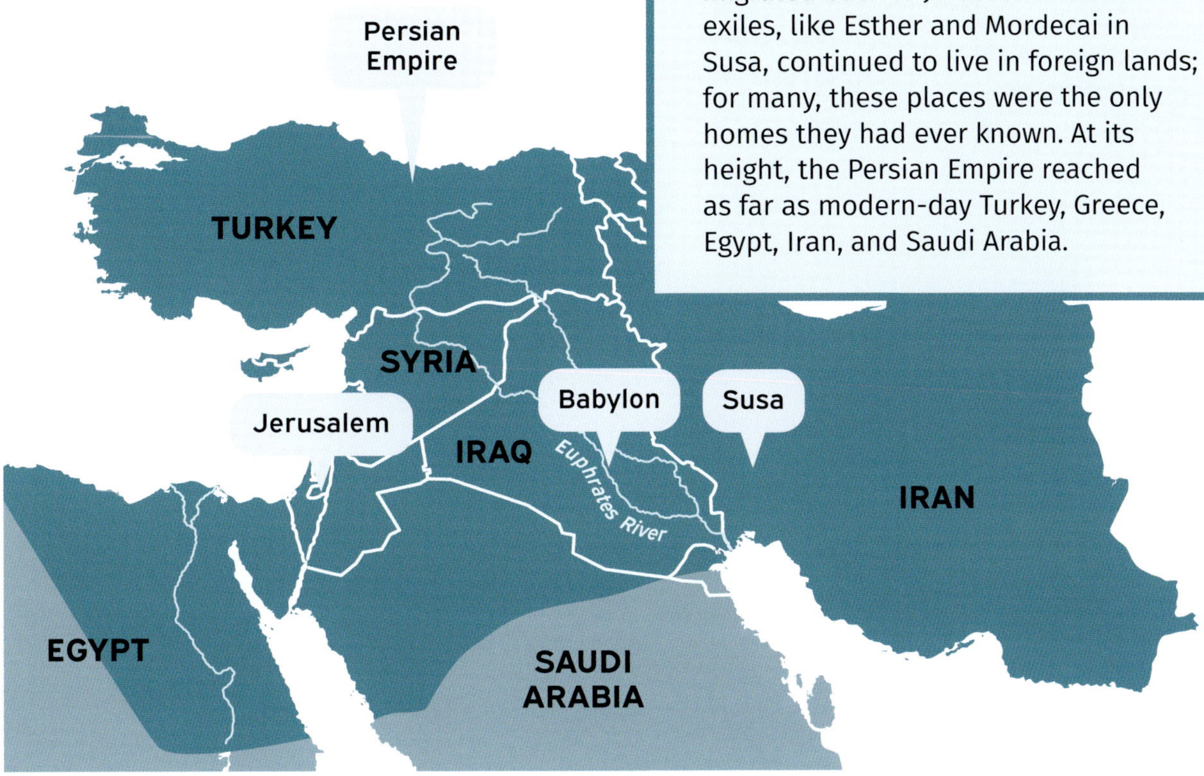

Persian Empire
TURKEY
SYRIA
Jerusalem
IRAQ
Babylon
Susa
Euphrates River
IRAN
EGYPT
SAUDI ARABIA

After Babylon fell to Persia, many Jews migrated back to Jerusalem. Other exiles, like Esther and Mordecai in Susa, continued to live in foreign lands; for many, these places were the only homes they had ever known. At its height, the Persian Empire reached as far as modern-day Turkey, Greece, Egypt, Iran, and Saudi Arabia.

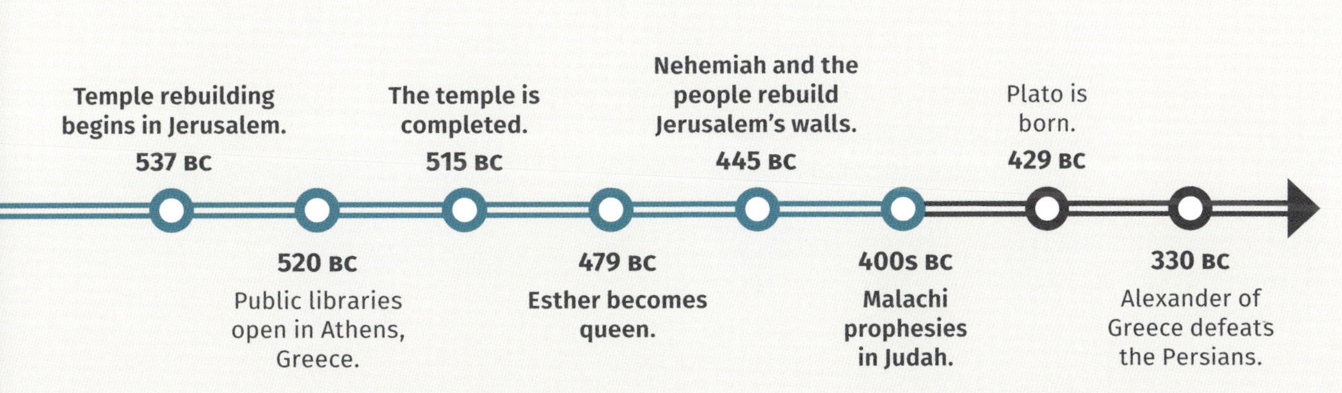

Jeremiah, the Weeping Prophet

Jeremiah, a prophet who lived through the destruction of Jerusalem, is sometimes called "the weeping prophet" because he shared his deep personal anguish as he delivered God's messages. Jeremiah warned the people of Judah to repent. But they did not listen. Judgment came when the Babylonians sacked Jerusalem and killed or exiled Judah's leaders. The book of Lamentations, which contains poems lamenting Jerusalem's fall, is believed to have been written by Jeremiah (2 Chron. 35:25). The prophet foretold that the exile would be temporary and that God would one day establish a new covenant with his people (Jer. 25:1–14; 31:31–34; see also Luke 22:20). He remained with the remnant left in Judah, but in the end, he was taken by them to Egypt.

The Assassination of Gedaliah (Jer. 40:7–41:18)

After the fall of Jerusalem, Babylon set up a puppet governor, Gedaliah, over the Jews left in Judah. Gedaliah came from a high ranking family in Judah, and Gedaliah's father once saved Jeremiah's life (Jer. 26:24).

Gedaliah's governorship did not last long. Judean guerrilla bands led by Ishmael assassinated Gedaliah in Mizpah and took captives. Ishmael and the captives were headed toward Gibeon, when Johanan, another military leader, intercepted them and rescued the prisoners. Ishmael escaped eastward to Ammon. Fearing retribution by Babylon for the assassination, many Judeans fled to Egypt.

Back to Egypt (Jer. 42:1–43:13)

Despite stern warnings from the Lord through the prophet Jeremiah that they should remain in Judah, the people sought refuge in Egypt—much like their ancestors, Abraham and Jacob, had done centuries earlier. The Judean refugees settled in Egypt near Migdol, Tahpanhes, and Memphis, as well as in southern (Upper) Egypt (Jer. 44:1).

> **"The Lord, who scattered his people,**
> **will gather them and watch over them**
> **as a shepherd does his flock.**
> **For the Lord has redeemed Israel**
> **from those too strong for them."**
>
> JEREMIAH 31:10–11

Jeremiah was born near Jerusalem in Anathoth (Jer. 1:1), a town that belonged to the Levites (Josh. 21:3, 18). Just before Judah fell, Jeremiah bought a field in Anathoth as a sign that Israel would one day be restored to its land (Jer. 32:6–9). Years later, 128 men of Anathoth returned from exile and resettled the town (Ezra 2:1–2, 23). Biblical Anathoth is believed to be in the area of Anata today.

Ezekiel, the Watchman in Exile

Ezekiel was a thirty-year-old priest living in exile near Babylon when he was called by God to be a prophet, "a watchman" of Israel (Ezek. 1:1; 3:17). Ezekiel probably had been deported from Jerusalem in 597 BC, about a decade before the Babylonians razed Jerusalem and burned the temple. Ezekiel's ministry was characterized by incredible visions and strange demonstrations meant to draw people's attention to the coming catastrophe. At first, his messages were rejected, but later, his prophecies were vindicated as they began to come true when Jerusalem was toppled. After Jerusalem fell, Ezekiel's messages became more hopeful. He saw a vision of a glorious future temple situated in a new promised land (Ezek. 40–48).

Ezekiel's New Promised Land (Ezek. 45:1–8; 47:13–48:29)

In the book of Ezekiel, the prophet sees a future with strong links to the past, for the land of Israel is still a promised land and the temple still the place where God dwells. The geography in Ezekiel's vision does not resemble the earlier allotment of territories to the tribes in Joshua's day (Josh. 13:1–21:45). Instead, each tribe has an equal portion of land, arranged with the temple at the center of Israel. This seems to indicate that old tribal jealousies and hatreds will be gone, for each tribe will be on exactly the same footing. Likewise, the future temple does not appear to be a blueprint for construction but instead represents an ideal. These are theological statements expressed through land and a building. It will be a new world in which God returns to his temple and his land to dwell with his people (Ezek. 10:3–4, 18; 11:22–23; see also Rev. 21:1–3).

Daniel, the Prophet of Empires

Daniel was a young man of Judah's royal family when the Babylonian army first attacked Jerusalem. He was deported to Babylon to serve the growing empire (605 BC). Though forced into service to the king who was destroying his homeland, Daniel stood strong as an example of faith, wisdom, and endurance while living in a pagan environment. He was also a prophet who interpreted dreams and was given visions about the future. His ministry spanned multiple kings, from Nebuchadnezzar of Babylon to Cyrus of Persia. While many of Daniel's prophecies are difficult to understand in detail, their overall message is clear: Evil forces are now in power, but God is in control and will save his people.

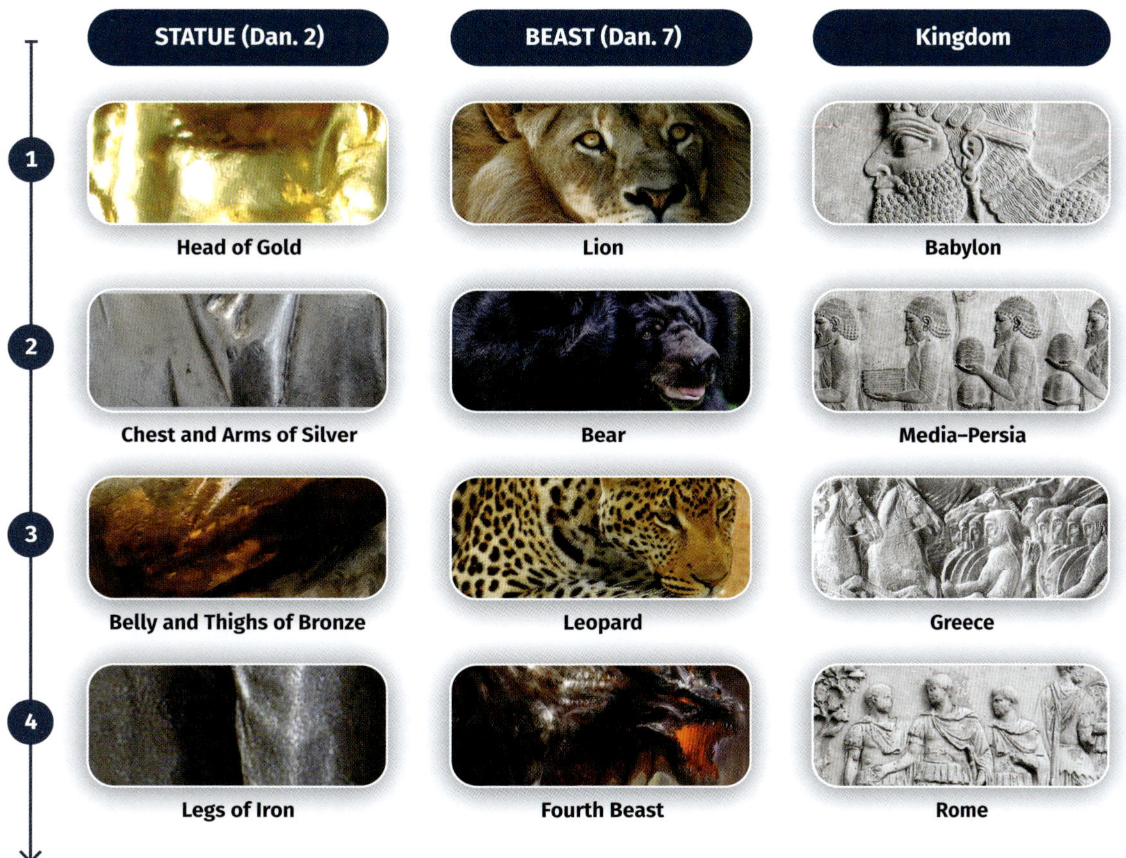

Four World Kingdoms

In chapter 2, Nebuchadnezzar has a disturbing dream about a statue made of four metals. In chapter 7, Daniel sees four huge beasts emerging from the sea. The parts of the statue and the beasts from the sea represent four powerful empires. But it is an eternal kingdom—the "rock … not [made] by human hands" (Dan. 2:34)—that destroys the statue of empires, and it is the one "like a son of man coming with the clouds of heaven" who has a "kingdom [that] will never be destroyed" (Dan. 7:13–14; see also Matt. 24:30). (The four world empires have traditionally been identified as shown above.)

4 After the fall of Jerusalem in 586 BC, many Judeans fled to **EGYPT.** Jeremiah was taken with them (Jer. 43:1–7).

3 Jeremiah lived in **JERUSALEM** through the three Babylonian invasions (605–586 BC) (2 Chron. 36:6–21).

1 Daniel was taken during Nebuchadnezzar's first invasion of Jerusalem in 605 BC to serve in the palace at **BABYLON**.

2 Ezekiel lived near the **KEBAR RIVER**, likely in Nippur, a Jewish settlement of exiles, where he received his call to be a prophet in 593 BC (Ezek. 1:1).

A Remnant Restored

The fall of Judah was horrific, but it was not the final word for God's people. The Lord had promised to bring his people back to their land. The mighty Babylonian Empire collapsed, falling to the Persians in 539 BC. Quickly, things changed. The Persian king, Cyrus II, permitted the Jews to return and rebuild the temple in Jerusalem (2 Chron. 36:22–23; Ezra 1:1–5). The books of Ezra and Nehemiah chronicle this return, spanning close to a century. God sent prophets like Haggai and Zechariah to encourage the people to complete the rebuilding of the temple when construction stalled. The priest Ezra brought spiritual renewal while the governor Nehemiah brought civic restoration.

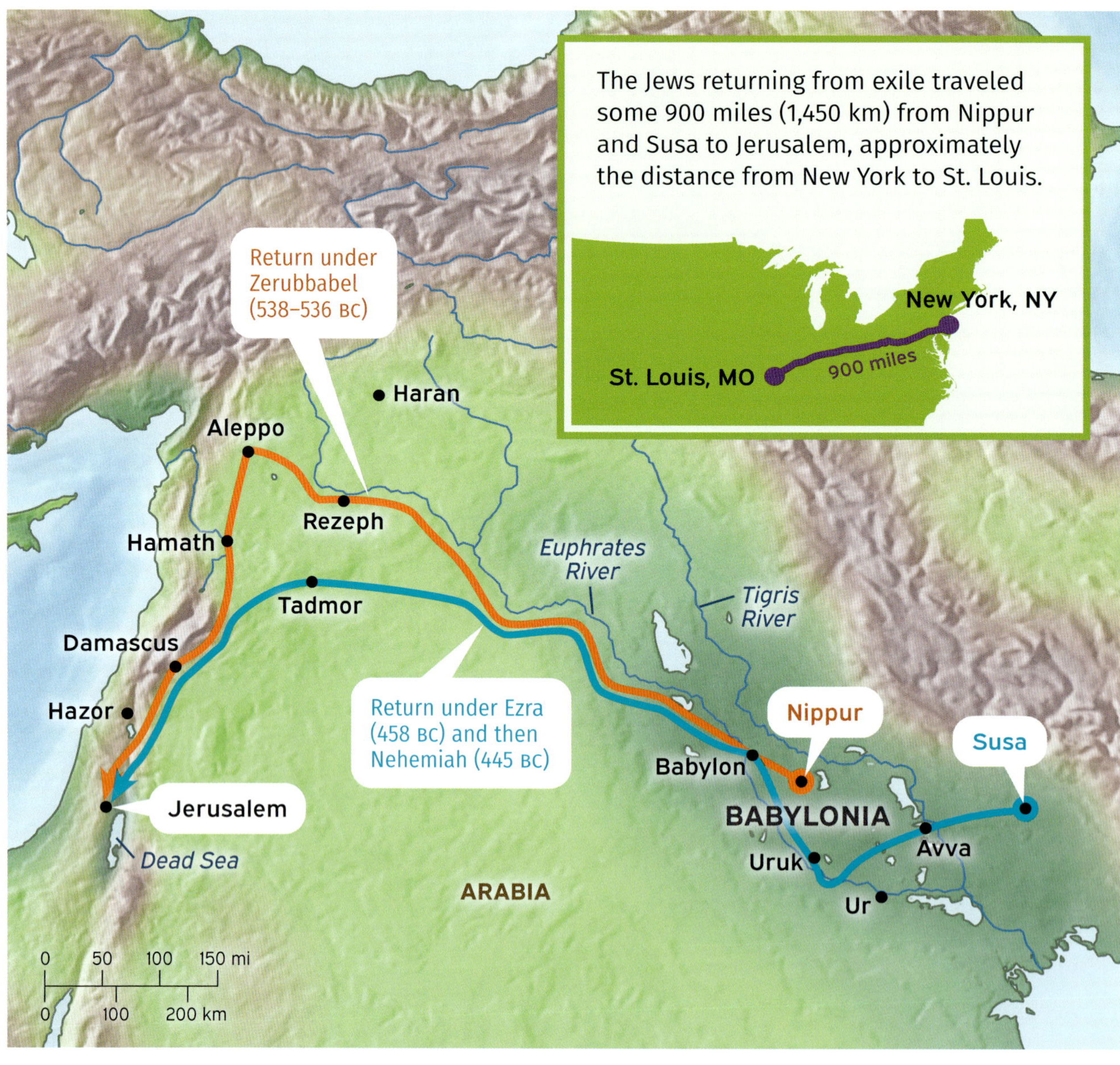

Ezra and Nehemiah

As a scribe and priest, Ezra was a disciplined student of God's laws. He taught, preached, and interpreted Scripture (Ezra 7:1–10). He was an important official who assisted the king with Jewish affairs in the Persian Empire. Upon arriving in Jerusalem, one of his first reforms was to call the people (especially the priests) to live separately from the peoples around them, and that even meant divorcing themselves from their pagan wives and children (Ezra 10:1–4).

Nehemiah was cupbearer to the Persian king, making him a trusted adviser. When Nehemiah heard reports about Jerusalem's sad state, he was moved with compassion, and with the king's permission he traveled to Jerusalem to rebuild the city's walls (Neh. 1:1–2:9).

Together, Ezra and Nehemiah led the rebuilding of Jerusalem and the reinstitution of worship at the temple, Sabbath observance, and religious festivals (Neh. 8:13–18; 10:1, 32–39; 13:15–22).

Judean Desert near Bethlehem

Rebuilding Jerusalem

The first wave of Jewish exiles who returned to Jerusalem were, at first, enthusiastic about rebuilding the temple of God (Ezra 3:7–13). But construction stalled when they faced opposition (Ezra 4:1–5). Prophets Haggai and Zechariah urged the people to finish the temple they had started, which they did complete in 515 BC, seventy years after the fall of Jerusalem (Ezra 5:1–2; 6:16–22).

Decades later, during the time of Ezra and Nehemiah, though the temple had been rebuilt, the walls of Jerusalem lay in ruins (Neh 2:17). The crumbling walls were a shameful reminder that the people had broken their covenant with God and had lost divine protection. Therefore, rebuilt walls would be a sign that God was bringing the

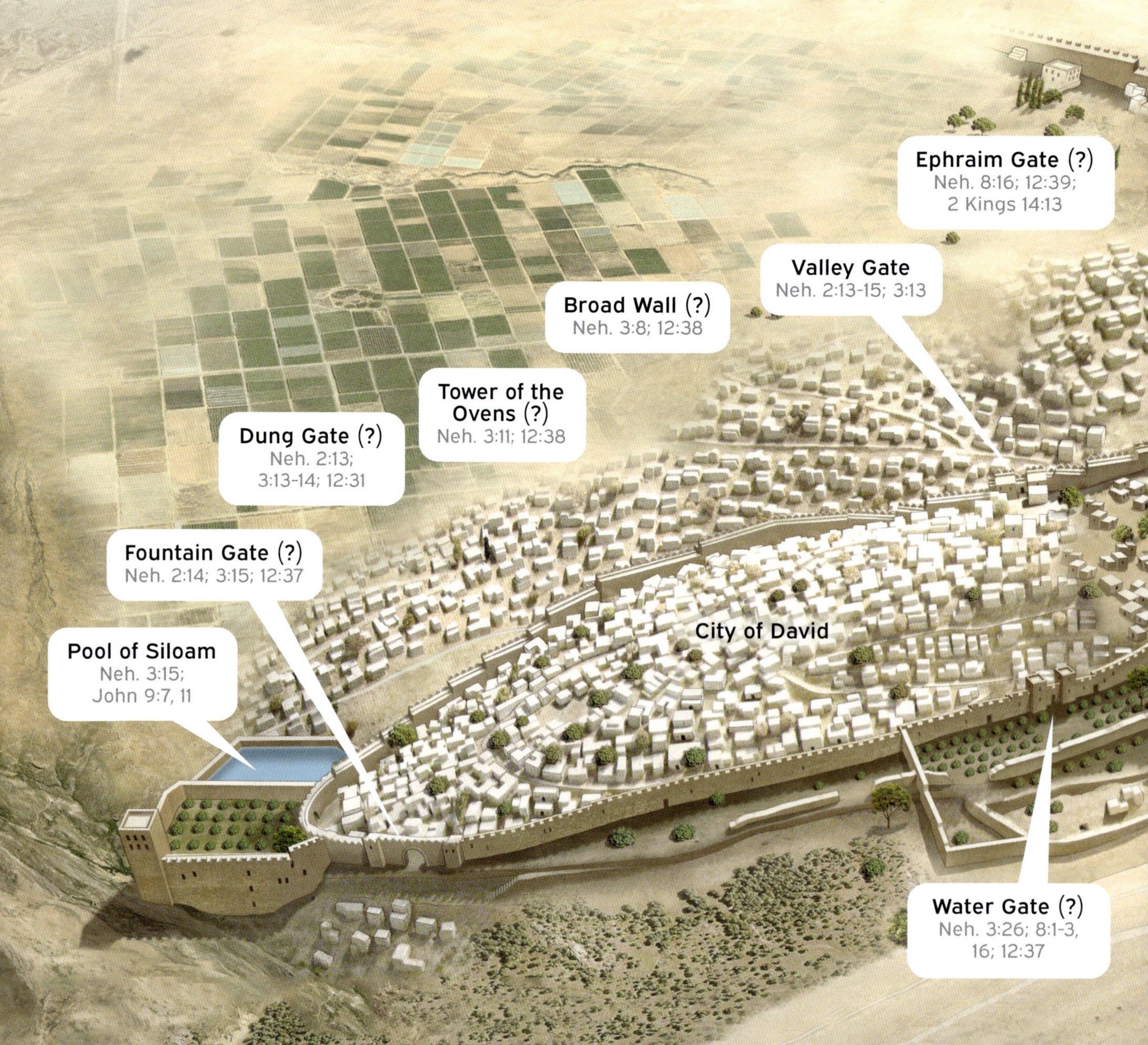

promised restoration to his covenant people. Israel's enemies knew that if the walls were rebuilt, the Jews would gain political power, security, and self-determination, so Nehemiah was met with fierce opposition. But under his leadership, the people rebuilt the city's walls in only fifty-two days! The speed and success of the reconstruction was a witness to everyone that—with God's help—his people can accomplish amazing things (Neh. 2:18; 4:14–15, 20; 6:15–16).

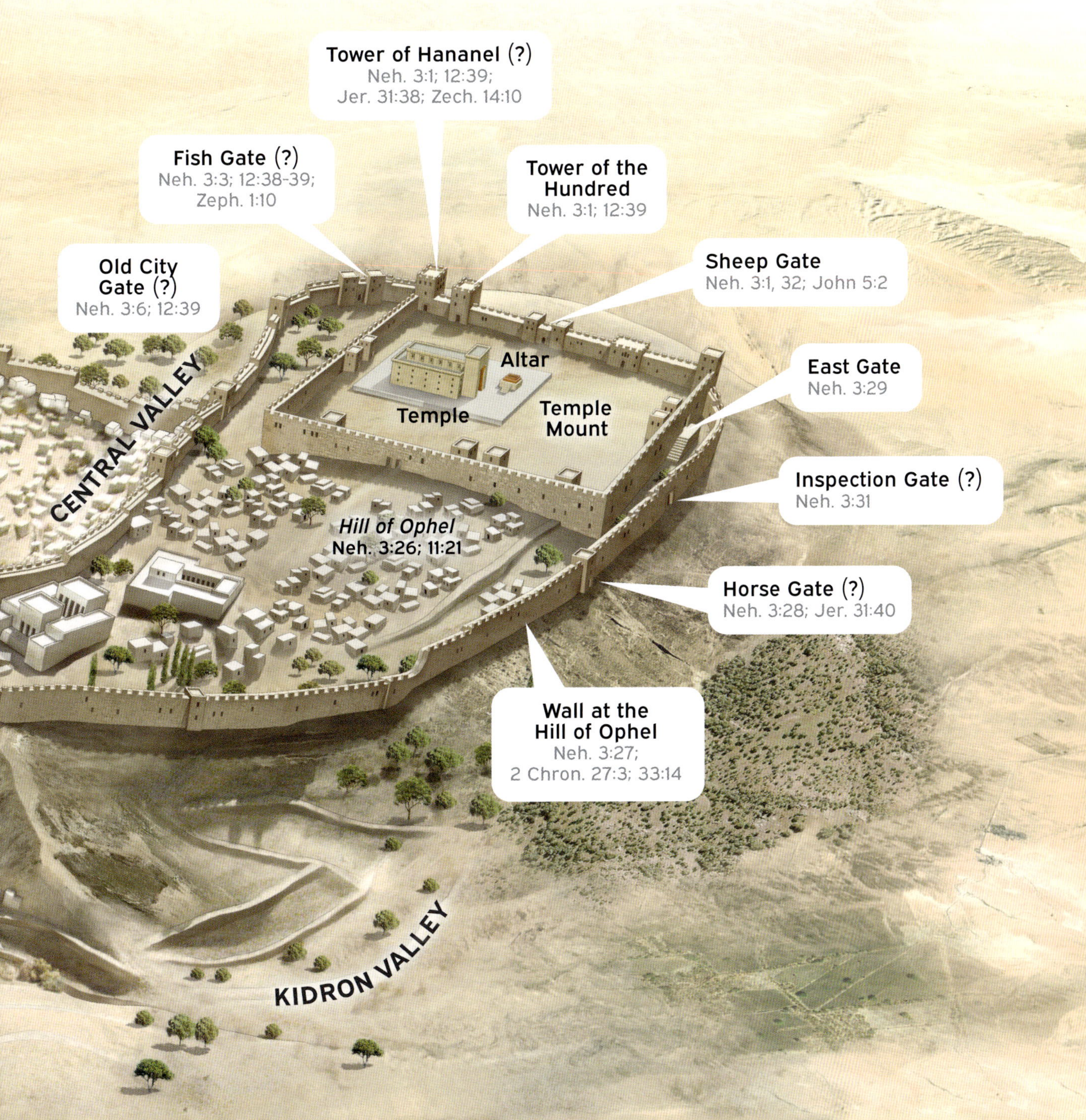

Persia

Cyrus II, king of Persia (559–530 BC), founded the vast Persian Empire. When his father was king, Persia was a small nation subject to the nearby kingdom of Media. But Cyrus conquered the Medes and combined the two nations into one (sometimes called the Medo-Persian Empire). The city of Babylon, after suffering years of neglect by Babylonian rulers, fell easily to Cyrus, without even a fight. Cyrus brought Babylonia into the Persian Empire, earning him the nickname Cyrus the Great.

Because Cyrus allowed Jews in exile to return to their homeland and rebuild their temple and society, he is viewed favorably in the Old Testament. Isaiah named him as Judah's future deliverer and even called him the Lord's anointed (Isa. 44:28–45:13).

The Persian Empire

THRACE
LYDIA
ARMENIA
MEDIA
MARGUS
BACTRIA
PARTHIA
DRANGIANA
PERSIA
BEYOND THE RIVER
EGYPT
Mediterranean Sea
Arabian Sea

Persian Royal Road
Ancyra
Mazaka
LYDIA
Sardis
Issus
Mediterranean Sea
BEYOND THE RIVE
Byblos
Tyre
Jerusalem
Memphis
EGYPT

3 Exiled Jews returned to **JERUSALEM** (538 BC) and rebuilt the temple (515 BC).

Extent of the Persian Empire (559–530 BC)

0 100 200 mi
0 100 200 300 km

1 Cyrus II of Persia captured **ECBATANA** and defeated the Medes in 549 BC, joining Media and Persia.
5 In **SUSA**, Esther became queen to Xerxes I of Persia (486–465 BC) and saved her people.
7 Nehemiah traveled from **SUSA** to Jerusalem to rebuild the city walls (445 BC).
ARMENIA
MEDIA
Nineveh
Arbela
Ecbatana
Tigris River
Euphrates River
Susa
Babylon
Pasargadae
Persepolis
PERSIA
6 Ezra led exiles from **BABYLON** to Jerusalem (458 BC).
2 **BABYLON** fell to Cyrus II and the Persians in 539 BC.
4 King Darius I of Persia (521–486 BC) made **PERSEPOLIS** his capital.

Queen Esther

Esther was queen of Persia during the reign of Xerxes I (Ahasuerus, 486–465 BC). She was a young woman of the Diaspora ("scattering"), descended from Jews who had been scattered among the nations at the time of the exile. Her family had not returned to Judea, as others had. Orphaned and raised by her cousin Mordecai, she kept her Jewish identity a secret when she became queen. But when the Jews in Persia were threatened with massacre by an enemy, Esther revealed who she really was and used her influence to save her people. Esther and Mordecai rose to power in Persia and established the festival of Purim to commemorate the Jews' victory over their enemies.

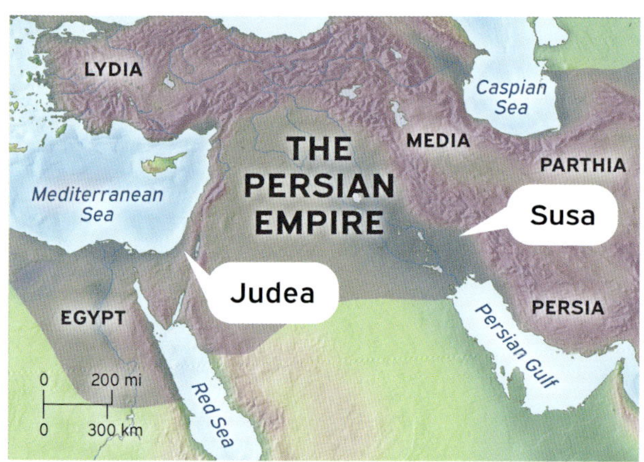

> **"Who knows if perhaps you were made queen for just such a time as this?"**
>
> ESTHER 4:14

Ruins of Susa near Shush, Iran

Alexander and the Greeks

In 546 BC, the Greek colonies in Asia Minor fell under the rule of Persia. Over the next six decades, Persia and Greece saw constant battles until the Greeks finally wrested control of their lands from the Persians. But later, it was a young Macedonian by the name of Alexander who set out from Greece to conquer the vast Persian Empire, which he did with lightning speed. Though Alexander died about as quickly as he conquered, he spread Greek culture and influence throughout the ancient world. The resulting conflict between Greek and Jewish cultures and religions would last for centuries, well into the Greco-Roman period, the time of Jesus.

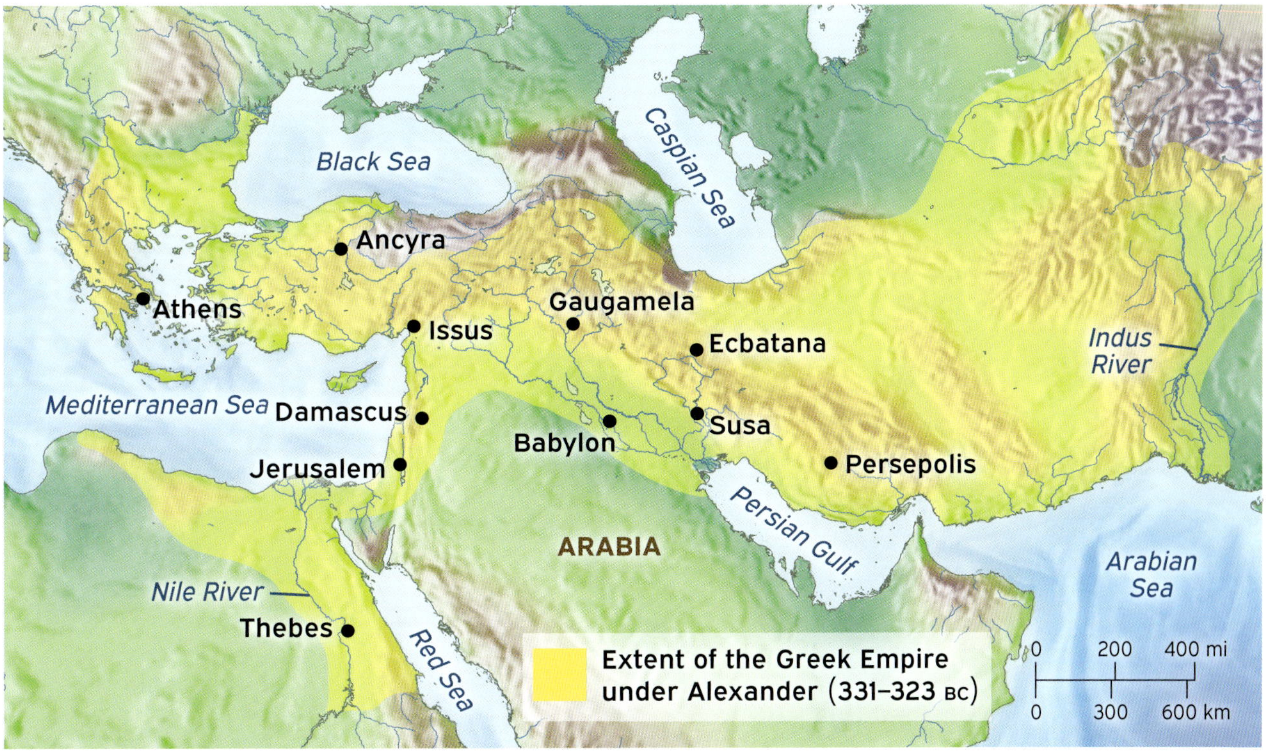

Black Sea
Caspian Sea
Ancyra
Athens
Gaugamela
Issus
Ecbatana
Indus River
Mediterranean Sea
Damascus
Susa
Babylon
Jerusalem
Persepolis
Persian Gulf
ARABIA
Arabian Sea
Nile River
Thebes
Red Sea
Extent of the Greek Empire under Alexander (331–323 BC)
0 200 400 mi
0 300 600 km

Between the Old Testament and the New Testament

In the centuries between the end of the Old Testament and the start of the New Testament, the people of God in Judea were subject to unstable and unpredictable foreign rulers. The Seleucids and Ptolemies ruled large parts of the Greek Empire, often fighting over control of Judea. For a while, the Jews regained independence after the Maccabean Revolt (164 BC), but eventually the new rising empire of Rome conquered Judea (63 BC), leaving the Jewish people once again oppressed, waiting and hoping for a Messiah to arrive.

THE CHRIST

Like the Old Testament, the New Testament starts with a "beginning" (Gen. 1:1; John 1:1). A new, spiritual creation is initiated with the arrival of the incarnate God, Jesus the Messiah—that is, the *Christ* ("Anointed One"). Because of his love for his creation, God intervened in human history to give to the world "his one and only Son, so that everyone who believes in him will not perish but have eternal life" (John 3:16).

Jesus was born in Bethlehem of Judea sometime around 4 BC. His ministry of teaching, healing, and doing miracles lasted for about three years (AD 27–30). Most of his ministry occurred in Galilee where Jews and "so many gentiles live" (Matt. 4:15), but some of his most significant events took place in the heavily Jewish region of Judea.

In Jerusalem, Jesus was brought up on false charges and crucified like a criminal. But he was not only a victim of injustice; he willingly gave his life at God's appointed time (John 7:30; 12:23). He went to the cross in full control. He knew that he would die as a substitutionary sacrifice for humanity (Mark 10:45). Shortly thereafter, his resurrection from the grave proved that he was the glorified Messiah.

The risen Christ appeared many times over a forty-day period, both in Jerusalem and in Galilee. Before he ascended into heaven, he commissioned his followers to carry on the mission by spreading the good news of salvation from Jerusalem to the ends of the world (Matt. 28:19–20).

THE GOSPELS

The Gospels—Matthew, Mark, Luke, and John—present the life of Jesus from different perspectives. Matthew emphasizes how Jesus is the Messiah who fulfills prophecy. Mark shows Jesus as the Son of God who gives his life as a ransom for others. Luke focuses on how Jesus is the Savior and Lord of all. John gives witness to Jesus as the truth and the light of the world.

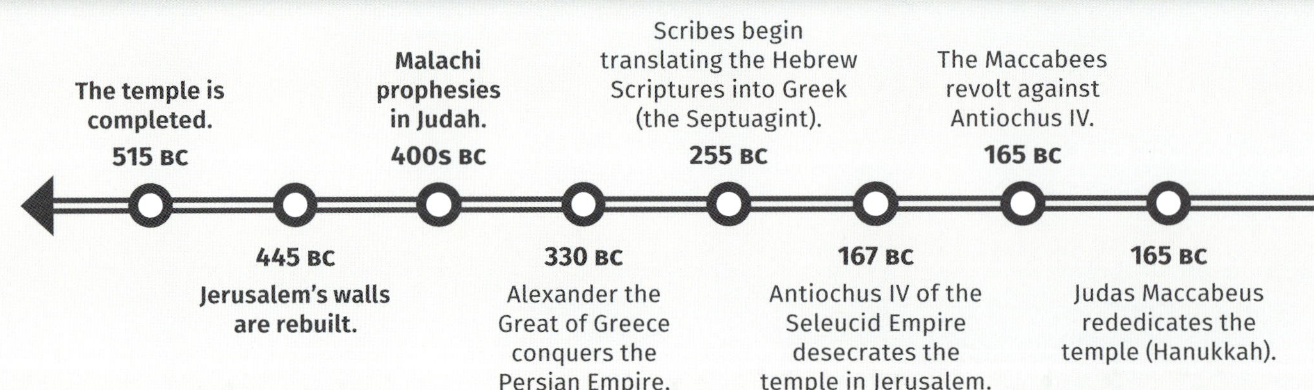

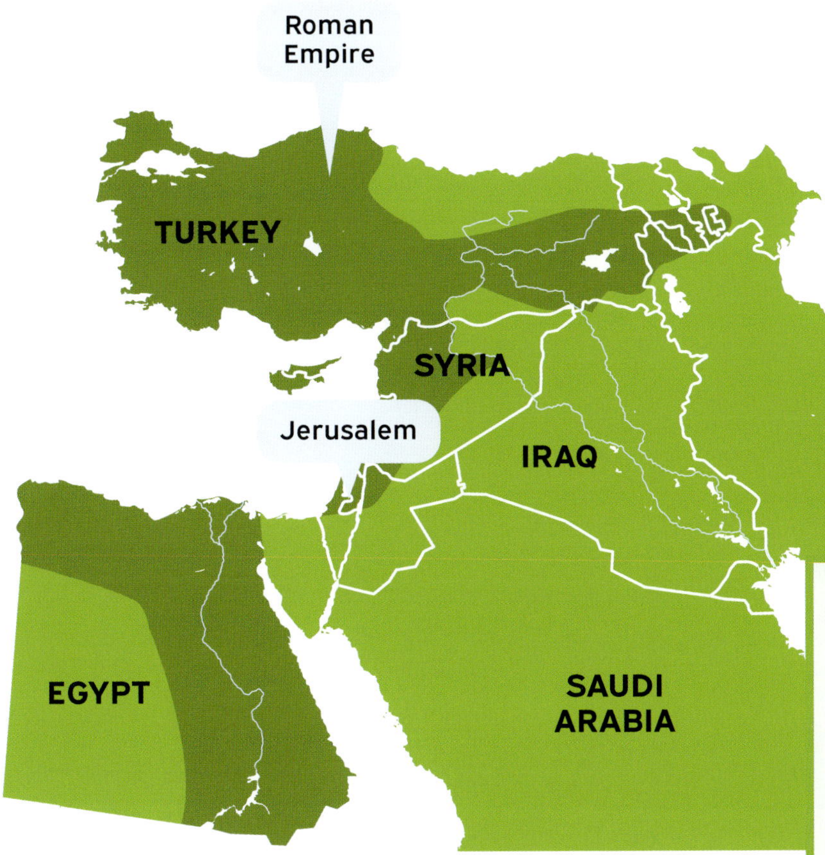

Roman Empire
TURKEY
SYRIA
Jerusalem
IRAQ
IRAN
EGYPT
SAUDI ARABIA

During the time of Jesus, the Roman Empire reached from Spain to Syria and all along the Mediterranean coast. Jerusalem fell under Roman authority in 63 BC and continued to be so for the entire New Testament period.

102 BC The first Chinese ships reach the east coast of India.

55 BC Julius Caesar begins his campaign in Britain.

20 BC Herod the Great begins an expansion of the temple complex in Jerusalem.

4 BC **Jesus is born in Bethlehem.**

AD 27 **Jesus begins his ministry.**

AD 30 **Jesus's death, resurrection, and ascension**

AD 34 **Saul is converted on the road to Damascus.**

AD 37 **Barnabas and Paul go to Jerusalem.**

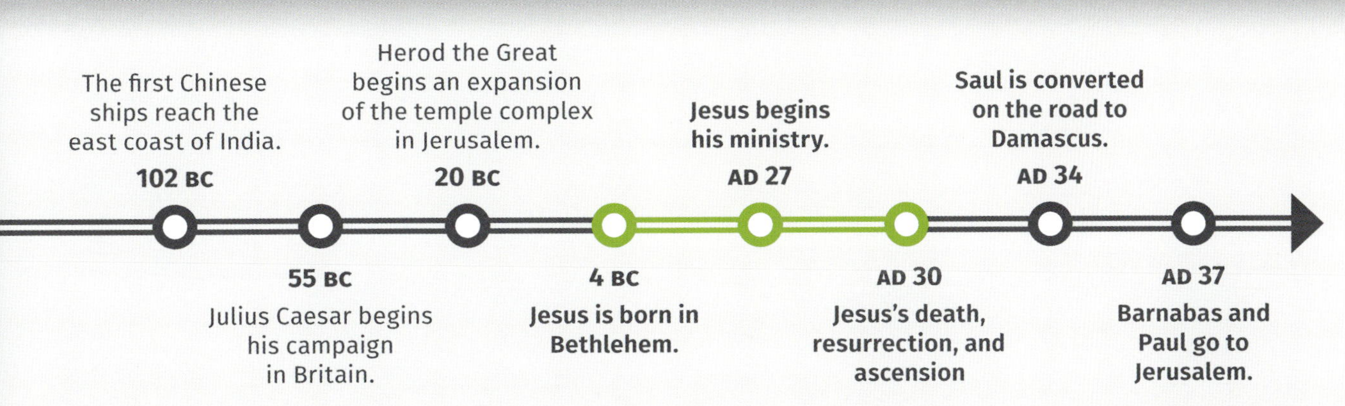

Approximate date for Jesus's birth is between 6 and 4 BC. This timeline follows the 4 BC date.

The Romans

In the second century BC, Jews in Judea won their freedom from their Greek Seleucid rulers in the Maccabean Revolt. But within a century, their independence would again be lost, when Judea came under the authority of the Romans. By the time of Christ in the first century AD, Jewish society and politics were very diverse. Some factions supported the Roman Empire because Rome brought economic prosperity and a measure of stability. Others, however, were violently opposed to the Roman Empire because it spread pagan worship practices and imposed heavy taxes.

Atlantic Ocean

SPAIN

ITALY

Rome

Carthage

4 Julius Caesar crossed the **RUBICON RIVER** in 49 BC and took control of the Roman Republic.

5 Octavian Augustus became the first emperor of **ROME** (27 BC–AD 14).

2 Rome defeated **CARTHAGE** by the end of the Punic Wars (264–146 BC).

Extent of the Roman Empire (AD 60)

1 Rome conquered MACEDONIA in the Battle of Pydna (168 BC).
LMATIA
MACEDONIA
GREECE
Corinth
CRETE
Black Sea
PONTUS
GALATIA
ASIA MINOR
Ephesus
CILICIA
Antioch
SYRIA
CYPRUS
Mediterranean Sea
Cyrene
Alexandria
Jerusalem
EGYPT
3 Roman general Pompey conquered JERUSALEM in 63 BC, ending independent Jewish rule.
0 100 200 300 mi
0 200 400 km

Herod's Greatness and Cruelty

Herod the Great was the Roman-appointed king of Judea (37–4 BC) at the time of Jesus's birth (Matt. 2:1; Luke 1:5). He was a strong military leader, a brilliant politician, and a cruel tyrant. He rose to power by gaining Roman favor, and he retained it by suppressing his opponents. Though Herod was given the title "King of the Jews," the Jewish people never accepted him as legitimate, partly because he was not from the line of David but rather was an Edomite. Once Herod had power, he was paranoid about keeping it. He murdered two of his wives and three of his sons when he suspected them of plotting against him. When Jesus was born in Bethlehem and Herod heard the newborn referred to as a *king*, he ordered the massacre of boys under two years old in the area of Bethlehem (Matt. 2:1–20).

Ruins of Caesarea

Herod was known for his large construction projects, including building up the city of Caesarea into a Roman headquarters. He began an expansion of the Jerusalem temple complex in 20 BC, about fifteen years before Jesus was born. It would be in these temple courts where Jesus would teach his followers and confront the religious rulers of his day (Luke 21:37–38).

Today, there are Jewish, Christian, Armenian, and Muslim Quarters within the Old City district of Jerusalem. A Muslim shrine, the golden Dome of the Rock, tops the Temple Mount.

Jerusalem through the Centuries

Now a sprawling metropolitan city, Jerusalem in Bible times was only a few acres in size. Its most important building, the temple of the Lord, was built, destroyed, rebuilt, and expanded throughout the nation's history.

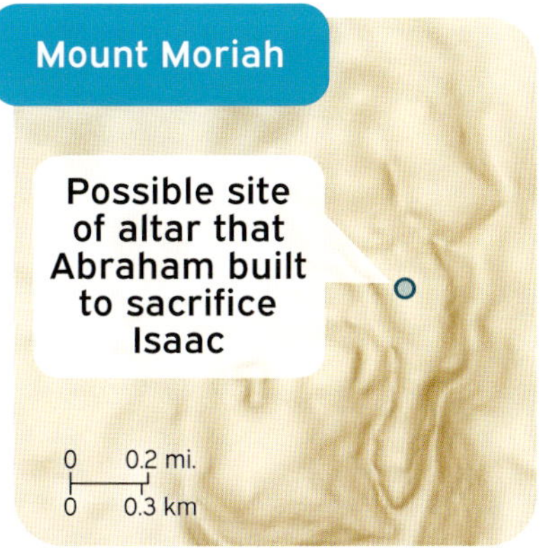

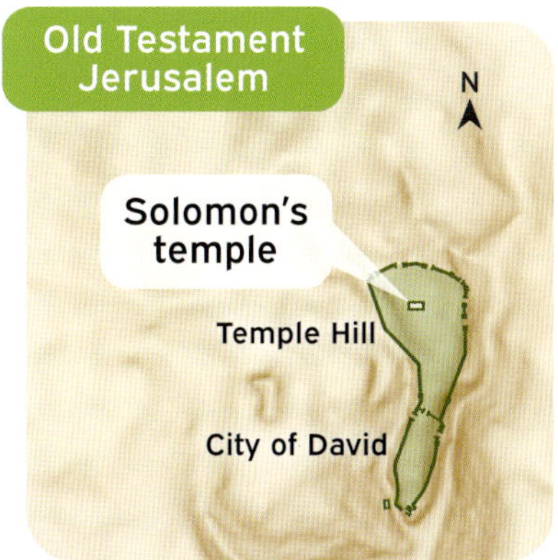

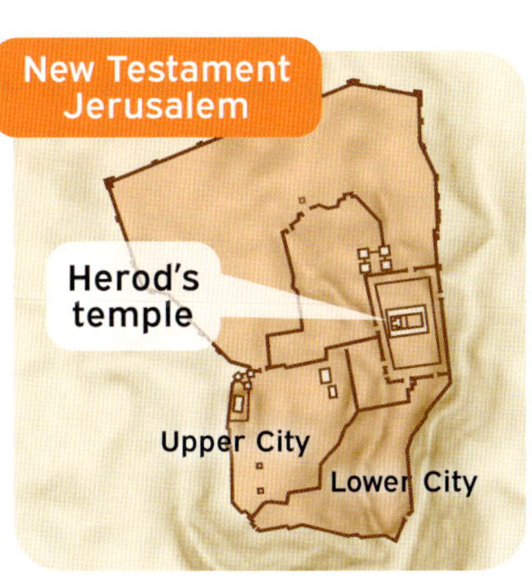

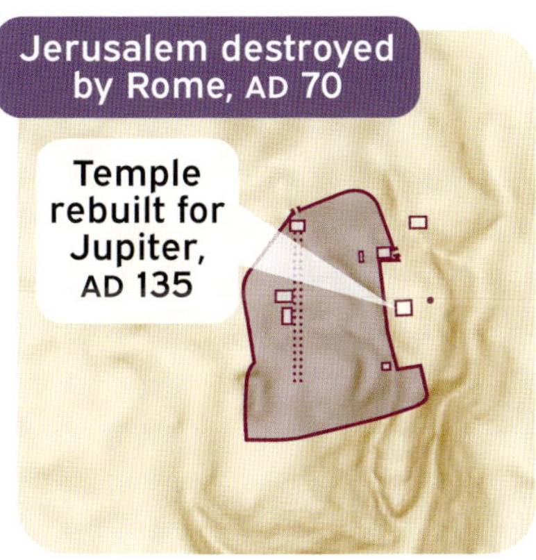

The Birth of Christ

Mary, a young woman in Nazareth of Galilee, was betrothed to Joseph. But before the marriage took place, an angel announced to Mary that she would become pregnant by the power of God's Spirit and give birth to the Son of God, and she should name him Jesus (Luke 1:26–35). Mary responded with extraordinary faith. Because of a Roman census, Mary and Joseph went to Bethlehem. It was in this small town that Jesus was born in a stable because no other lodging was available (Luke 2:1–7). Wrapped in swaddling clothes and laid in a manger, the long-awaited Messiah had a very humble beginning.

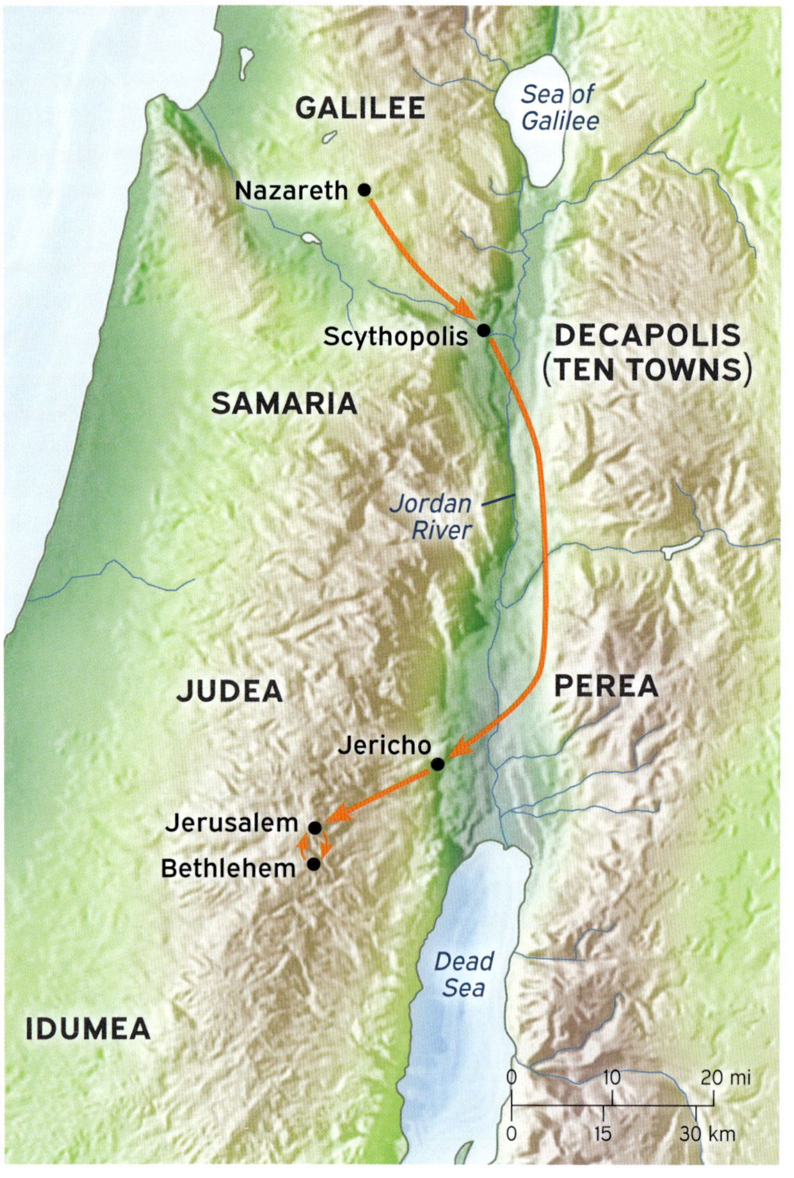

Judean desert near Jericho

Mary and Joseph's Journey to Bethlehem (Luke 2:1–5)

Since Joseph was of the lineage of David, he was required to go to Bethlehem (David's hometown) to register in the census. The route Mary and Joseph probably took bypassed Samaria by crossing into Perea, then back across the Jordan River into Judea. The rocky and hilly journey, which was about 90 miles (145 km) long, may have taken the expectant couple up to two weeks.

Wise Men from the East (Matt. 2:1–12)

Wise men (*magi*) from "eastern lands" arrived in Jerusalem because they witnessed an unusual phenomenon in the sky: a certain star which ultimately led them to Bethlehem. These wise men probably came from a group of gentile priests in Mesopotamia. Many Jews had settled in Babylonian regions, so the men may have been very familiar with the Jewish expectation of a Messiah-King. After finding Jesus and presenting gifts to the newborn king, they returned to their homeland by a different route—presumably one that did not take them through Jerusalem—because they had been warned in a dream not to see King Herod on their way home.

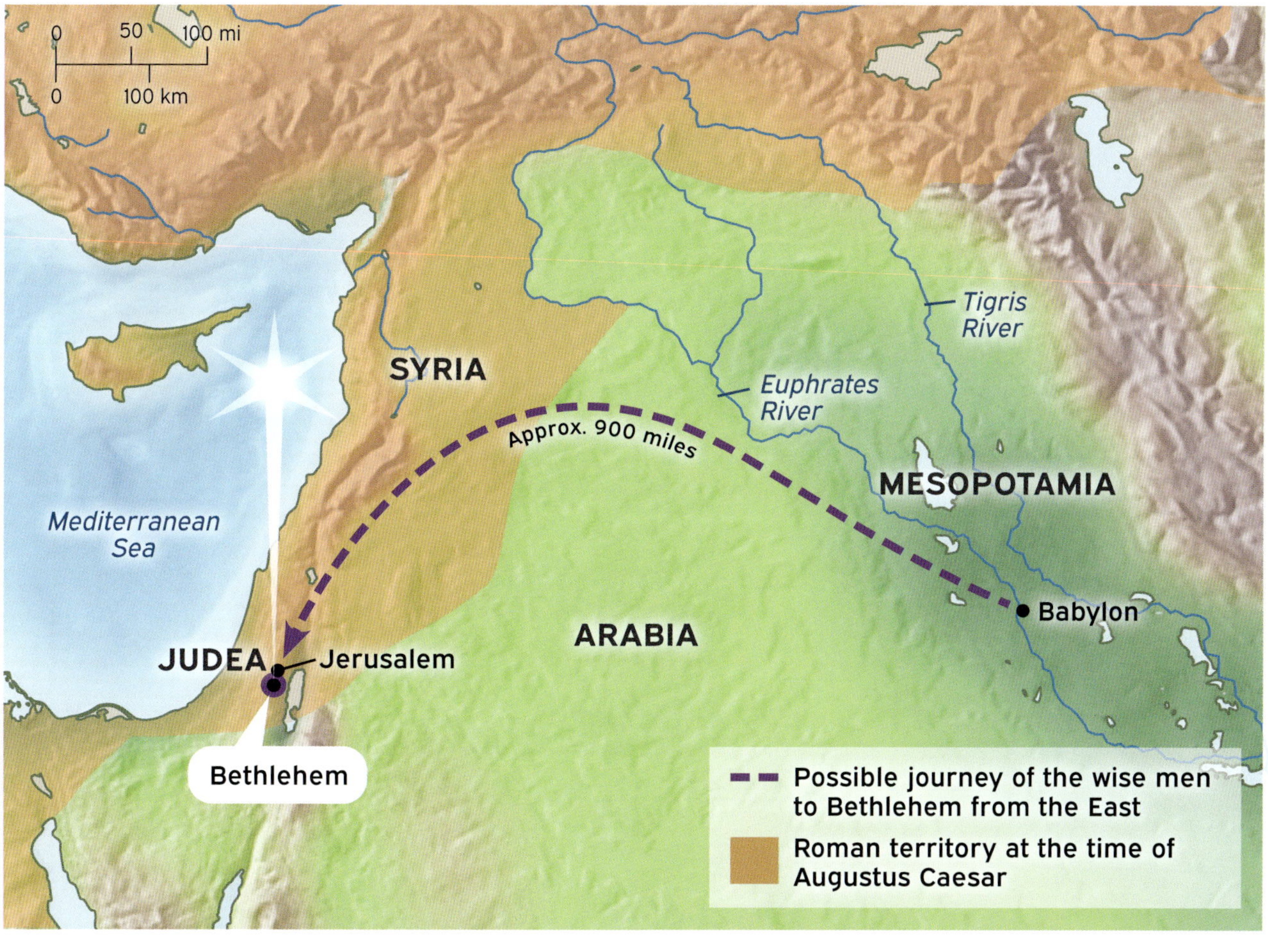

0 50 100 mi
0 100 km
Tigris River
SYRIA
Euphrates River
Approx. 900 miles
MESOPOTAMIA
Mediterranean Sea
Babylon
ARABIA
JUDEA
Jerusalem
Bethlehem
Possible journey of the wise men to Bethlehem from the East
Roman territory at the time of Augustus Caesar

The Escape to Egypt

Prophecies of the Messiah

The Gospels and the book of Acts record many Old Testament prophecies that Jesus fulfilled during his ministry on earth—from his birth in Bethlehem to his sacrificial death on the cross as the sinless "Lamb of God who takes away the sin of the World!" (John 1:29).

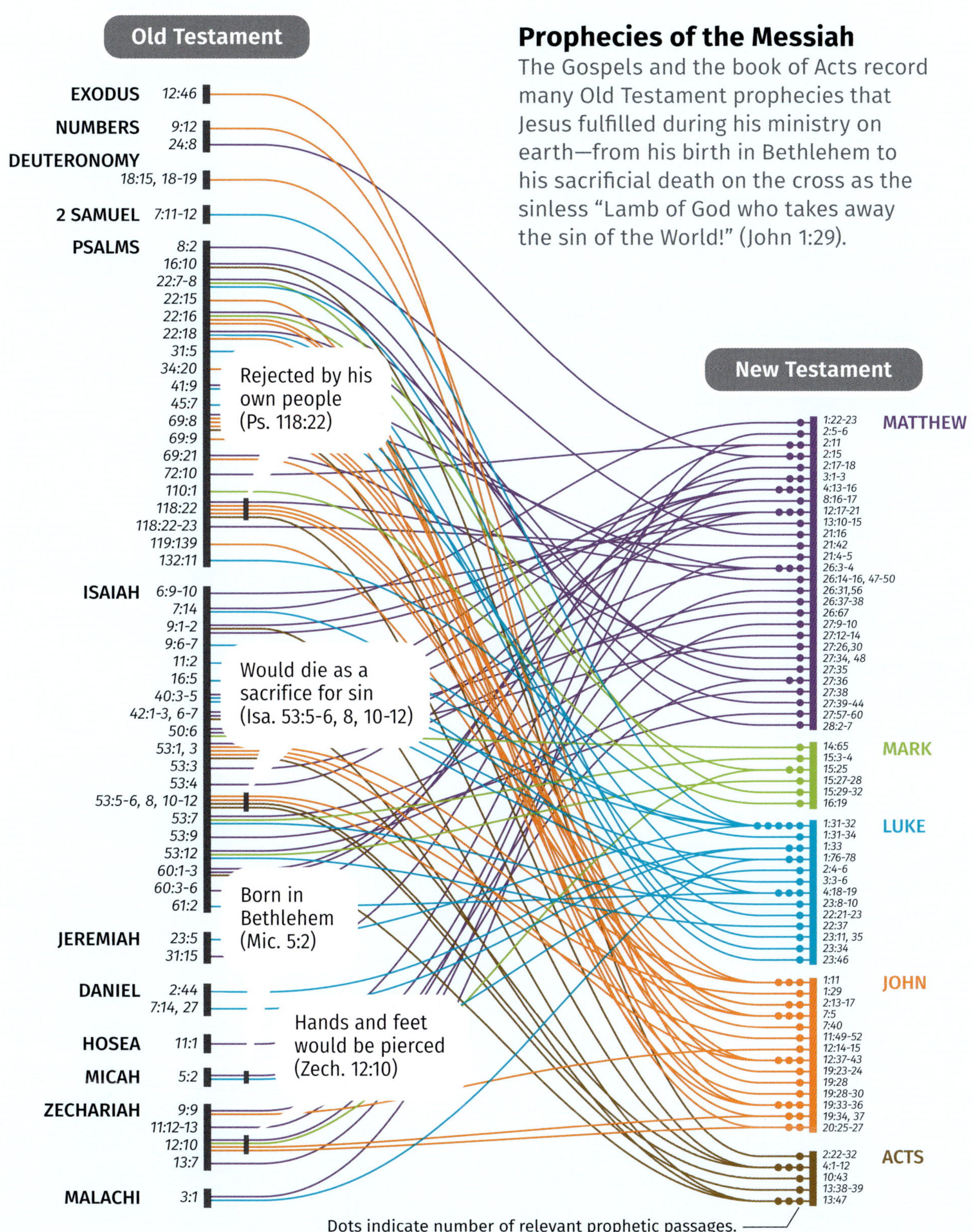

John the Baptist

John was a fiery, Spirit-filled, open-air preacher who called people to repent and be baptized. Dressed in a garment of camel's hair and living on desert foods, John was a relative of Jesus whose life was devoted to preparing the way for the Lord (Mark 1:6; Luke 1:15–17). John baptized Jesus with water, though he felt unworthy to baptize the one who would "baptize ... with the Holy Spirit" (Matt. 3:11). John remained faithful to his calling, even when it cost him his life.

GALILEE

"Galilee of the gentiles" was a racially mixed area in the north and a prominent Jewish population center. Jesus lived most of his life in Galilee. He was raised in Nazareth from a young age and worked in his father's business as a craftsman until he was baptized and began his ministry. His base of operations became Capernaum by the Sea of Galilee. Of his twelve disciples, eleven were Galileans. Jesus also ministered to the gentiles who lived in the areas surrounding Galilee, like when he healed a gentile woman's daughter near Tyre.

SAMARIA

Between Galilee and Judea lay several regions: Perea, a mostly Jewish area; Decapolis ("Ten Towns") with its many Greek-speaking gentiles; and, most notoriously, Samaria. In Old Testament times, Samaria had been home to the Northern Kingdom of Israel. But after the kingdom fell to Assyria, Samaria was repopulated with foreigners from throughout the Assyrian Empire (2 Kings 17:21–41). The Samaritans had a long history of conflict with the Jews of Judea (Ezra 4:1–5; Neh. 4:1–23). By New Testament times, the Samaritans limited their Scriptures only to the Pentateuch (Genesis through Exodus) and centered their worship at their own temple on Mount Gerizim, not Jerusalem. Observant Jews avoided the Samaritans by traveling through Perea instead. But in one memorable occasion, Jesus went through Samaria, resulting in his conversation with the Samaritan woman at the well.

JUDEA

Judea, "the land of the Jews," was a province of the Roman Empire. Jewish society was centered in Judea, particularly in Jerusalem. Though Jesus spent far less time in Judea than in Galilee, Judea is very prominent in the Gospels. Many significant events in the life of Jesus took place in and around Jerusalem, especially the events of his last week—from his triumphal entry to his death, burial, and resurrection. After Christ's ascension, the church got its start in Jerusalem during Pentecost, making Judea an early center of Christianity.

GALILEE (and regions to the north)

A Region of Tyre
Jesus healed a gentile woman's daughter (Matt. 15:21–28).

B Caesarea Philippi
Peter's great declaration of Jesus as the Messiah (Matt. 16:13–20).

C Mount Hermon
- Possible location of the Transfiguration (Matt. 17:1–13). Mount Meron and Mount Tabor are also possible locations.
- Nearby, Jesus healed a demon-possessed boy (Matt. 17:14–21).

D Cana
- Jesus changed water into wine (John 2:1–11).
- Jesus healed a Capernaum official's son (John 4:46–5:4).

E Gennesaret
Possible location of the feeding of multitudes (Matt. 14:13–21; 15:32–39) and many healings (Mark 6:53–56).

F Area of Korazin
- Jesus pronounced judgment on Korazin, Bethsaida, and Capernaum (Matt. 11:20–24).
- Possible area of the Sermon on the Mount (Matt. 5–7).

G Capernaum
- Miraculous catch of fish (Luke 5:1–11).
- An evil spirit cast out (Mark 1:21–28).
- Sermon on the Mount (Matt. 5–7).
- Peter's mother-in-law healed (Matt 8:14–15).
- Officer's servant healed (Matt 8:5–13).
- Paralyzed man healed (Mark 2:1–12).
- Woman with a hemorrhage healed (Mark 5:25–34).
- Jairus's daughter raised to life (Luke 8:40–56).
- Two blind men given sight (Matt 9:27–31).
- Demon-possessed man healed (Matt 9:32–34).
- Twelve disciples sent out to announce the kingdom of heaven (Matt. 10:1–15).
- Man with a deformed hand healed (Matt. 12:9–13).
- A demon-possessed man healed (Matt. 12:22–37).
- Temple tax provided (Matt. 17:24–27).
- Jesus's teachings on the bread of life (John 6:22–59).

H Bethsaida
- Possible location of feeding of multitudes (Matt. 14:13–21; 15:32–39).
- Jesus healed a blind man (Mark 8:22–26).

I Sea of Galilee near Bethsaida
Jesus walked on water (Matt. 14:22–33).

J Sea of Galilee
Jesus calmed the storm (Matt. 8:23–27).

K Gergesa/Gadara
Possible location of casting out demons, which enter pigs (Luke 8:26–39).

L Nazareth
- Jesus's childhood home (Matt. 2:19–23).
- Jesus rejected (Luke 4:16–30).

M Nain
Jesus raised a widow's son (Luke 7:11–17).

N Region of Galilee
- Jesus cleansed a leper (Mark 1:40–45).
- Jesus's resurrection appearances to his disciples (Matt. 28:16–20).

Caesarea •

Mount Hermon
C
A
Tyre
B
Caesarea Philippi
TYRE
UPPER GALILEE
F
Lake Hula
G
E
Mount Meron
H
Ptolemais (Acco)
LOWER GALILEE
Korazin
Bethsaida
N
Capernaum
Gennesaret
Sea of Galilee
I
Cana
Magdala
Gergesa
D
Tiberias
J
Kishon River
Sepphoris
K
Nazareth
Mount Tabor
L
Gadara
Nain
M
DECAPOLIS (TEN TOWNS)
SAMARIA
Jordan River
Salim
Miracle
Healing
0 5 10 15 mi
0 10 20 km

SAMARIA (and other regions between Galilee and Judea)

O Decapolis (Region of Ten Towns)
Many healings by Jesus (Matt. 15:29–31; Mark 7:31–37).

P Region between Galilee and Samaria
- Jesus was refused entry into a village (Luke 9:51–56).
- Ten lepers healed (Luke 17:11–19).

Q Sychar
Jesus's conversation with the Samaritan woman at the well (John 4:1–42).

R Ephraim (Ophrah)
Jesus entered into seclusion with the disciples (John 11:54).

S Region of Perea
- Teaching on marriage (Matt. 19:1–12).
- Possible location of healing of woman with infirmity (Luke 13:10–13).
- Possible location of healing of man with swollen limbs (Luke 14:1–6).
- Possible location of Jesus's discussion with the rich young ruler (Luke 18:18–30).

JUDEA

T Jericho
- Bartimaeus healed (Mark 10:46–52).
- Zacchaeus converted (Luke 19:1–10).

U Bethany
- Jesus raised Lazarus from the dead (John 11:1–44).
- Mary anointed Jesus (John 12:1–11).

V Jerusalem
- Jesus taken to temple as an infant and recognized as the Messiah (Luke 2:41–52).
- Jesus's discourse with Nicodemus (John 3:1–21).
- Healing at Pool of Bethesda (John 5:2–9).
- Woman caught in adultery and defended by Jesus (John 8:2–11).
- Attempted stoning of Jesus (John 8:12–59).
- Man blind from birth healed (John 9:1–12).
- Triumphal entry (Matt. 21:1–11).
- Temple cleansed (John 2:13–22).
- Last Supper (Luke 22:7–30).
- Trials and crucifixion (Matt. 26:57–27:50).
- Burial in the tomb (Luke 23:50–56).
- Jesus's resurrection appearances to Mary and the disciples (John 20:1–31).

W Emmaus
Jesus's resurrection appearances to two disciples (Luke 24:13–32).

X Mount of Olives
- Olivet Discourse (Matt 24:3–25:46).
- Jesus's prayer, agony, and arrest at Gethsemane (Matt 26:36–56).
- Jesus's ascension into heaven (Acts 1:6–12).

Y Bethlehem
Birthplace of Jesus (Luke 2:1–20).

Gadara
Nain
Caesarea
P
SAMARIA
O
DECAPOLIS
(TEN TOWNS)
Salim
Jordan River
Sebaste
(Samaria)
Q
Mount Ebal
Sychar
Mount Gerizim
Yarkon River
Jabbok River
S
PEREA
R
Ephraim
T
W
V
Jericho
Emmaus
Bethany?
(beyond the Jordan)
Jerusalem
Bethany
Mount of Olives
U
X
Bethlehem
Y
JUDEA
Dead
Sea
Miracle
Healing
0
5
10
15 mi
0
10
20 km

Where Jesus Walked

Jesus ministered almost entirely within the boundaries of ancient Israel, covering only about 120 miles (200 km). Wherever Jesus went, people followed; large crowds gathered to see and hear the miracle-worker and teacher. He healed the sick and the demon possessed, and he did other powerful miracles that proved the truth of who he was and what he said. John ends his gospel by telling readers that there were so many things Jesus did during his time on earth that "if they were all written down, I suppose the whole world could not contain the books that would be written" (John 21:25).

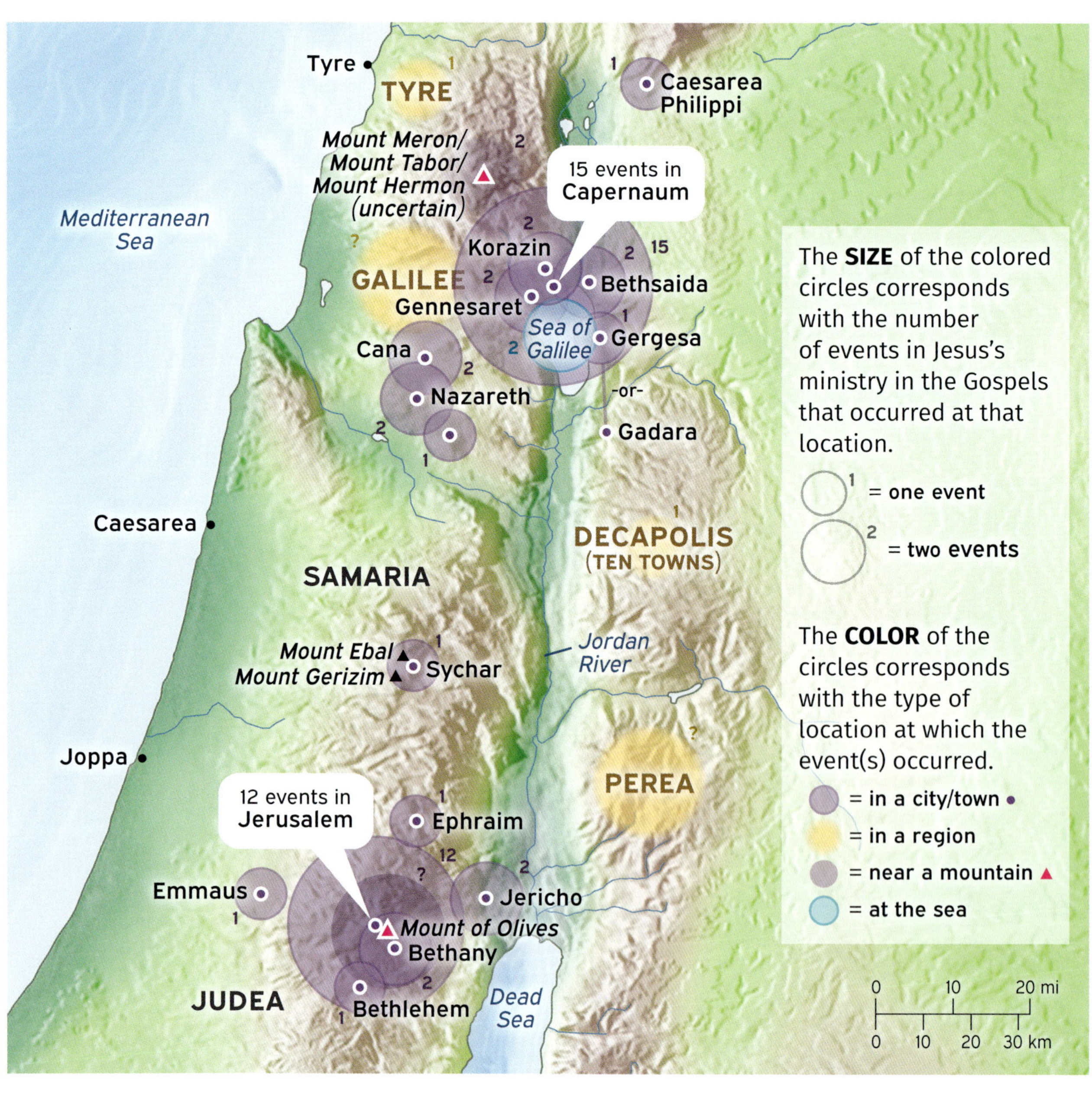

The Miracles of Jesus

The apostle John called the miracles that Jesus did *signs*. In a sense, they were like road signs pointing to something beyond them. Jesus's miracles pointed to a greater purpose: to show onlookers who Jesus really was—the Son of God. John noted that "the disciples saw Jesus do many other miraculous signs in addition to the ones recorded in this book" (John 20:30). There are still more miracles stories yet to be told.

The four Gospels record 37 miracles that Jesus performed during his ministry. These include:

- miracles in nature, like turning water into wine and calming a storm on the Sea of Galilee;
- healing men and women from illnesses and disabilities, such as giving sight to a man born blind and healing those with leprosy;
- raising people from the dead, like Lazarus and a widow's son; and
- freeing people from the power of evil spirits, like when casting out a multitude of demons from an afflicted man.

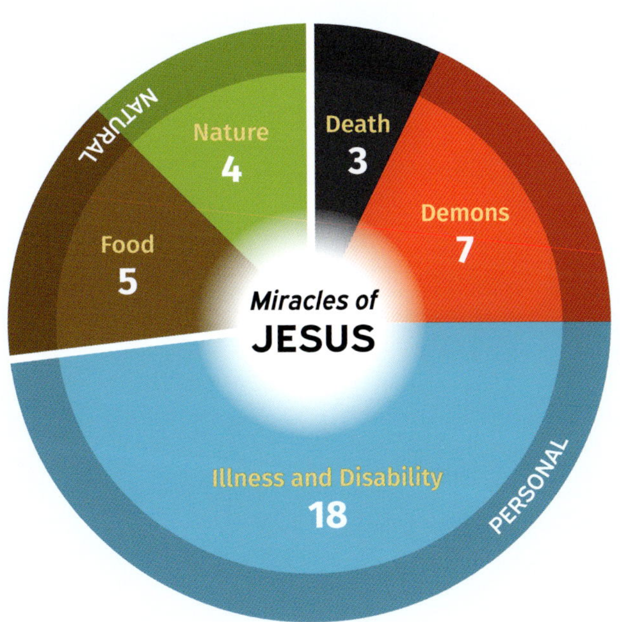

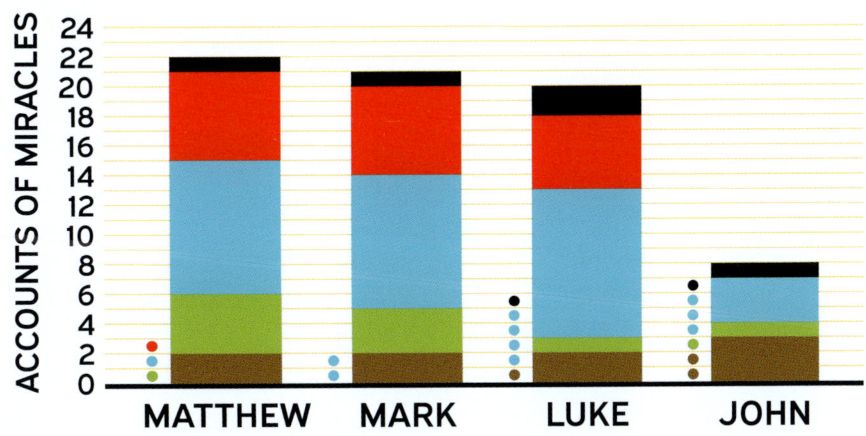

Dots indicate miracle accounts unique to that Gospel. Most accounts appear in more than one Gospel.

The **SEA OF GALILEE**, also called the Sea of Kinnereth or the Sea of Tiberias, is about 8 miles (13 km) wide. In the time of Jesus, it was a hub for the freshwater fishing industry, and its shores were populated with bustling cities. It was here that Jesus called his first disciples to follow him and become fishers of people (Luke 5:1–11).

The **JORDAN RIVER** begins at Mount Hermon and flows south through the Sea of Galilee and ends in the Dead Sea. Between the Sea of Galilee and the Dead Sea, the river stretches about 70 miles (110 km). In ancient times, it was an important source of fresh water, and it was much deeper and far more rapid that it is today.

The **DEAD SEA**, also called the Salt Sea, is named so because its intense saltiness and the surrounding dry, hot climate make it unsuitable for plant and animal life. The sea lies about 1,300 feet (400 m) below sea level, earth's lowest surface. In modern times, the sea has been rapidly shrinking, with water levels now dropping about 3 feet (1 m) every year.

Most of the ruins of the Capernaum synagogue date to about the fourth century AD and appear to have been constructed on the site of a first-century synagogue, most likely the one that Jesus taught in.

Capernaum Synagogue

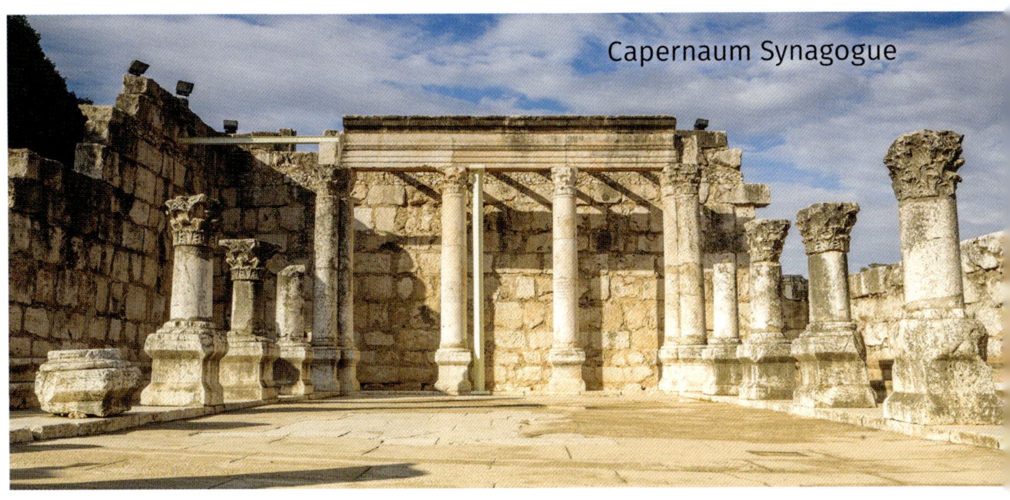

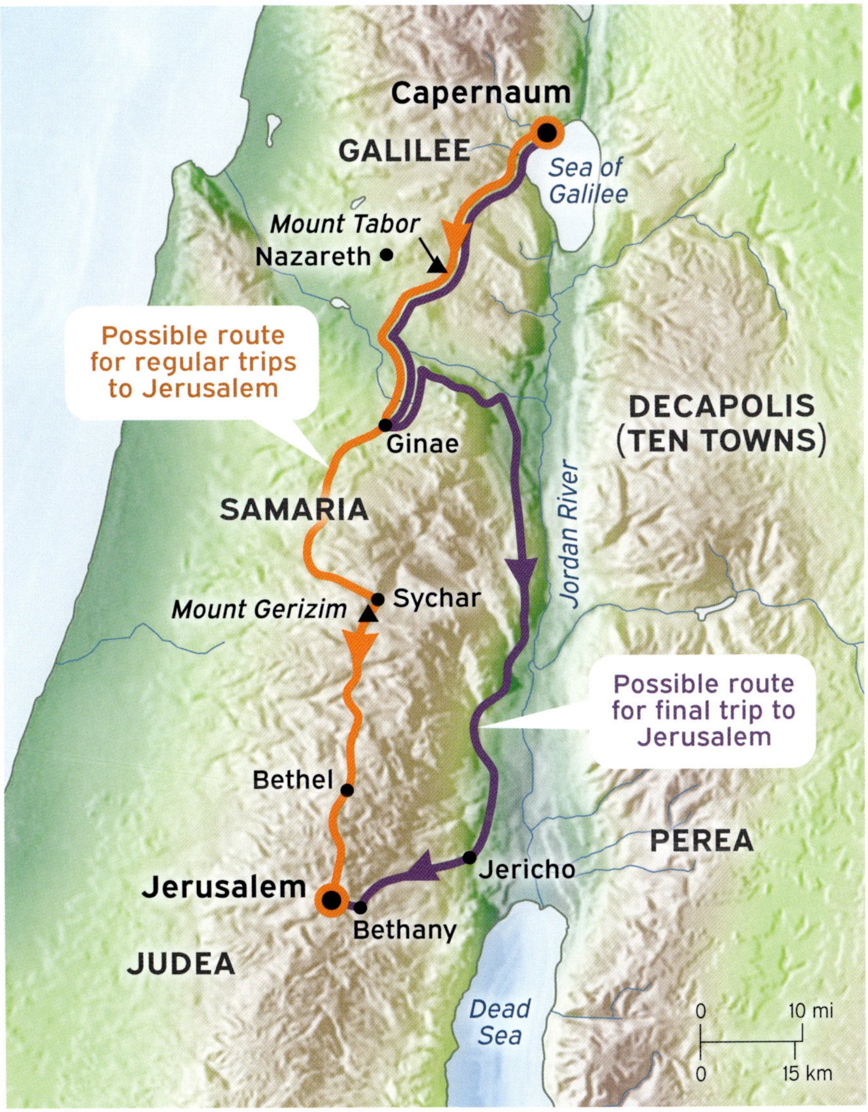

Traveling to Jerusalem

Jesus probably traveled from Galilee to Judea many times. There are two specific routes he may have taken: one through Samaria and the Judean hills and the other along the Jordan River.

Capernaum in Galilee was an important city by the Sea of Galilee with a well-known synagogue that Jesus taught in (John 6:59). Capernaum seems to have been Jesus's home base for his ministry in Galilee (Mark 2:1).

The village of **Bethany** in Judea was less than 2 miles (3 km) southeast of Jerusalem. This was the home of siblings Mary, Martha, and Lazarus, and was the place where Jesus stayed when he ministered in Jerusalem (Mark 11:11).

Jerusalem in the Time of Jesus

Jerusalem plays a key geographical role in the Gospels. At the temple, the infant Jesus was dedicated and recognized by Simeon and Anna as the Messiah. At age twelve, Jesus amazed the teachers at the temple. He frequently taught his followers in the temple courts, and his last week was centered in Jerusalem: he entered the city riding on a donkey, with crowds shouting "Hosanna," thus fulfilling prophecy; he prayed to his Father in the garden of Gethsemane; he stood trial in the palaces of religious and political leaders; and just outside the city walls, the Romans crucified him and placed his body in a tomb. But he would not be in the tomb for long.

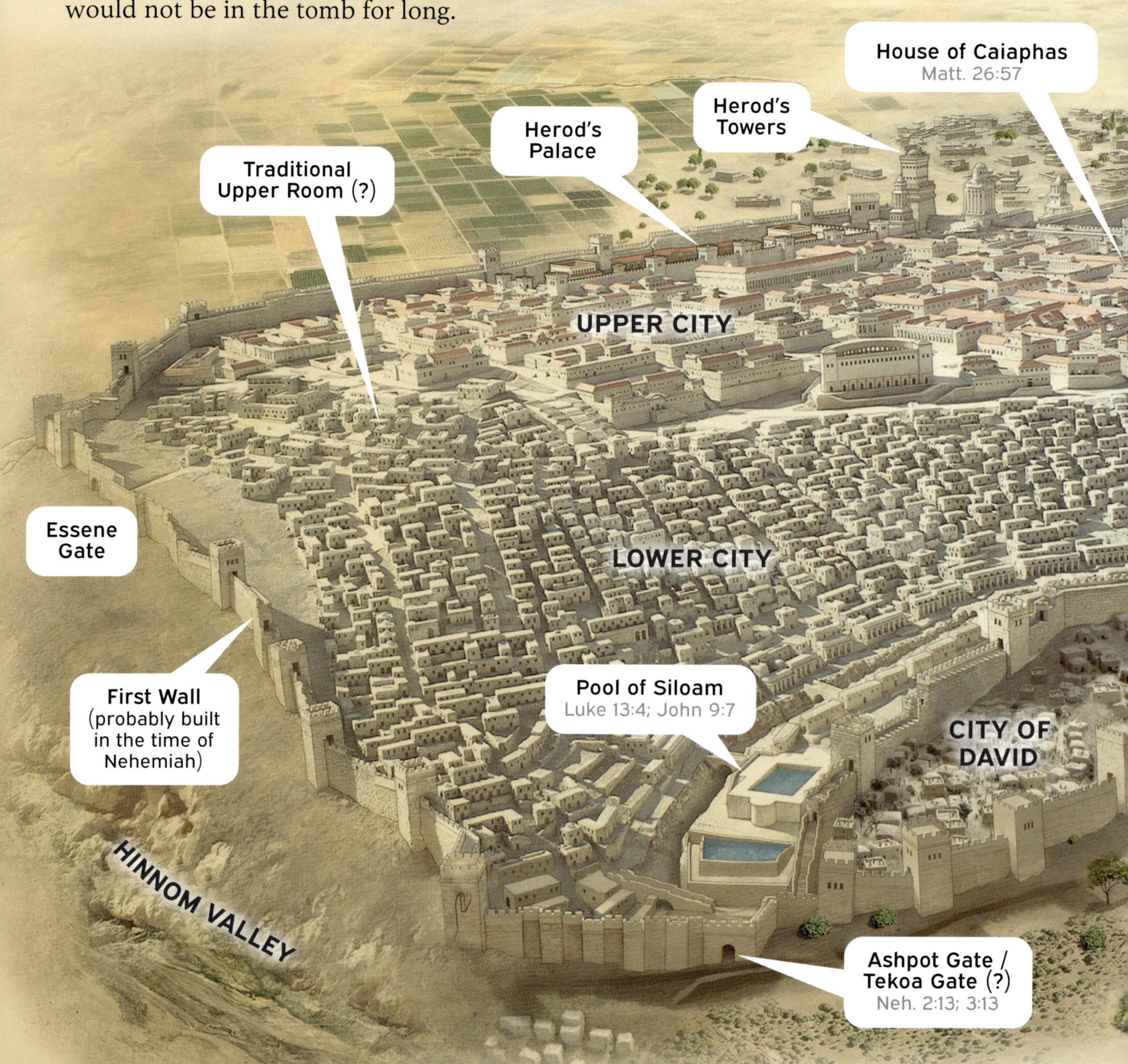

Herod the Great, who governed Judea from 37 to 4 BC, had built up the city extensively. His most prominent project was the rebuilding the temple complex. But in AD 70, about forty years after Jesus, the Roman general Titus destroyed the temple. Later, in AD 135, Emperor Hadrian razed Jerusalem completely.

Journey to the Cross

When Jesus went to Jerusalem to celebrate the Passover, he arrived knowing that he would "suffer many terrible things and ... be killed" (Mark 8:31). Seeing that the time was drawing near, Jesus shared a Passover meal with his disciples in an upper room. At this meal, he established the new covenant. Jesus would be the spotless Passover Lamb—his blood and body broken as a sacrifice to provide salvation. Arrested in the garden of Gethsemane, beaten, mocked, and ultimately crucified, the Son of God laid down his life for those he loved (John 10:17–18).

> **"Carrying the cross by himself, he went to the place called Place of the Skull (in Hebrew, *Golgotha*). There they nailed him to the cross."**
>
> JOHN 19:17–18

Church of the Holy Sepulchre

Gordon's Calvary

Where Was Golgotha?

Crucifixions were public executions that took place near major roadways. They were designed to shock and warn people to submit to local authorities. Jesus was crucified at *Golgotha*, "Place of the Skull," and it "was near the city" (John 19:17, 20). Most archaeologists agree that Golgotha was at the site of the present-day Church of the Holy Sepulchre. This traditional location is in the Christian Quarter of the old walled city of Jerusalem. An alternate site, called Gordon's Calvary (north of the Damascus Gate), is a small hill with tombs and a garden nearby. The rocky feature of the hill bears a resemblance to a skull, though it is unlikely it would have been there in the time of Jesus.

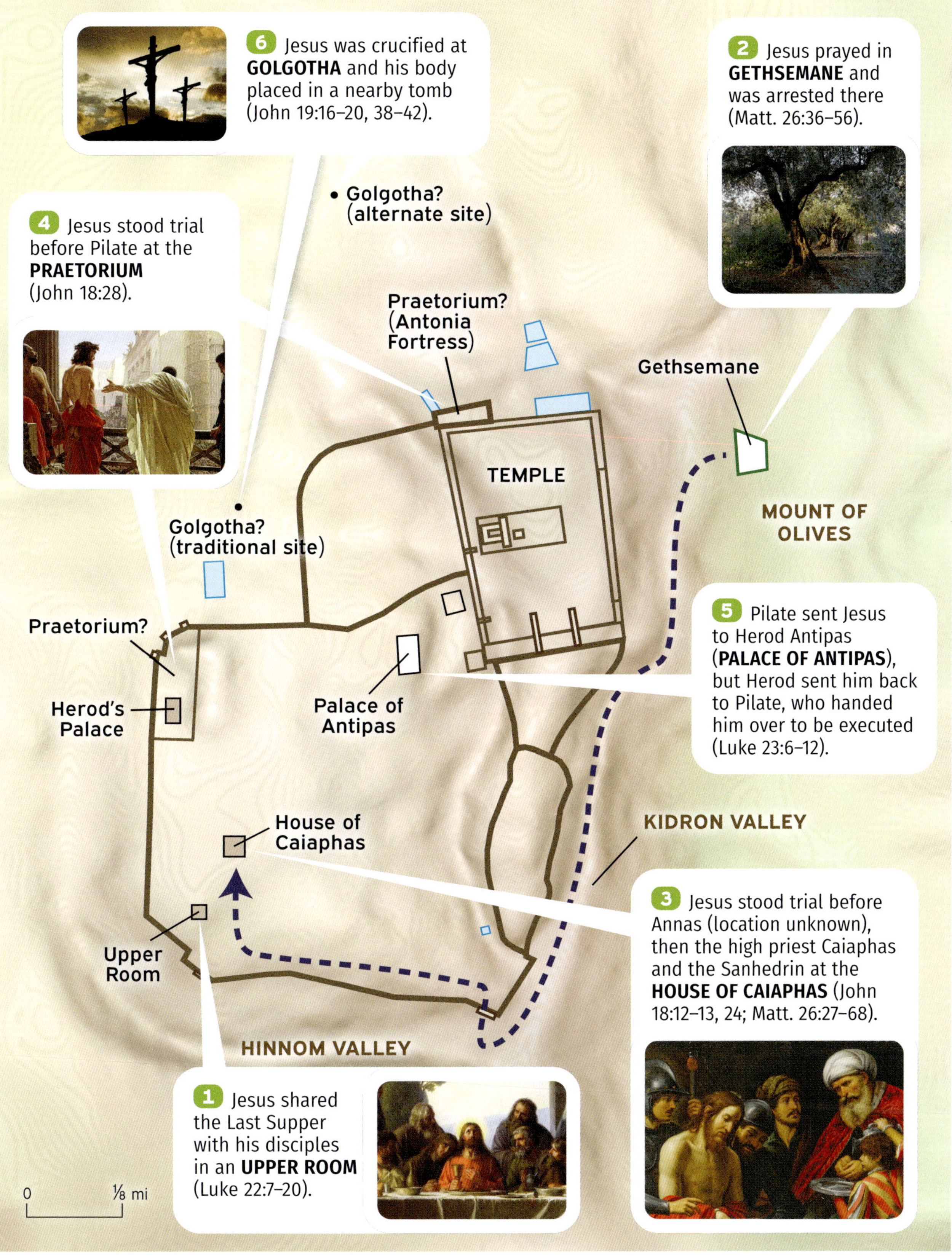
6 Jesus was crucified at GOLGOTHA and his body placed in a nearby tomb (John 19:16–20, 38–42).
2 Jesus prayed in GETHSEMANE and was arrested there (Matt. 26:36–56).
Golgotha? (alternate site)
4 Jesus stood trial before Pilate at the PRAETORIUM (John 18:28).
Praetorium? (Antonia Fortress)
Gethsemane
TEMPLE
MOUNT OF OLIVES
Golgotha? (traditional site)
5 Pilate sent Jesus to Herod Antipas (PALACE OF ANTIPAS), but Herod sent him back to Pilate, who handed him over to be executed (Luke 23:6–12).
Praetorium?
Herod's Palace
Palace of Antipas
House of Caiaphas
KIDRON VALLEY
3 Jesus stood trial before Annas (location unknown), then the high priest Caiaphas and the Sanhedrin at the HOUSE OF CAIAPHAS (John 18:12–13, 24; Matt. 26:27–68).
Upper Room
HINNOM VALLEY
1 Jesus shared the Last Supper with his disciples in an UPPER ROOM (Luke 22:7–20).
0
⅛ mi

The Resurrection

The body of Jesus was hastily laid in a tomb on "the day of preparation" for the Sabbath, that is, Friday afternoon just before the Sabbath began at sunset (Mark 15:42; Luke 23:54). After a day of Sabbath rest, "early on Sunday morning," Mary Magdalene and other women went to Jesus's tomb to complete the burial rite (Luke 24:1; John 20:1). To their amazement, the large, heavy stone covering the tomb had been rolled away and the body of Jesus was nowhere to be found.

> **"As they stood there puzzled, two men suddenly appeared to them, clothed in dazzling robes.... Then the men asked, 'Why are you looking among the dead for someone who is alive? He isn't here! He is risen from the dead!'"**
>
> LUKE 24:3–6

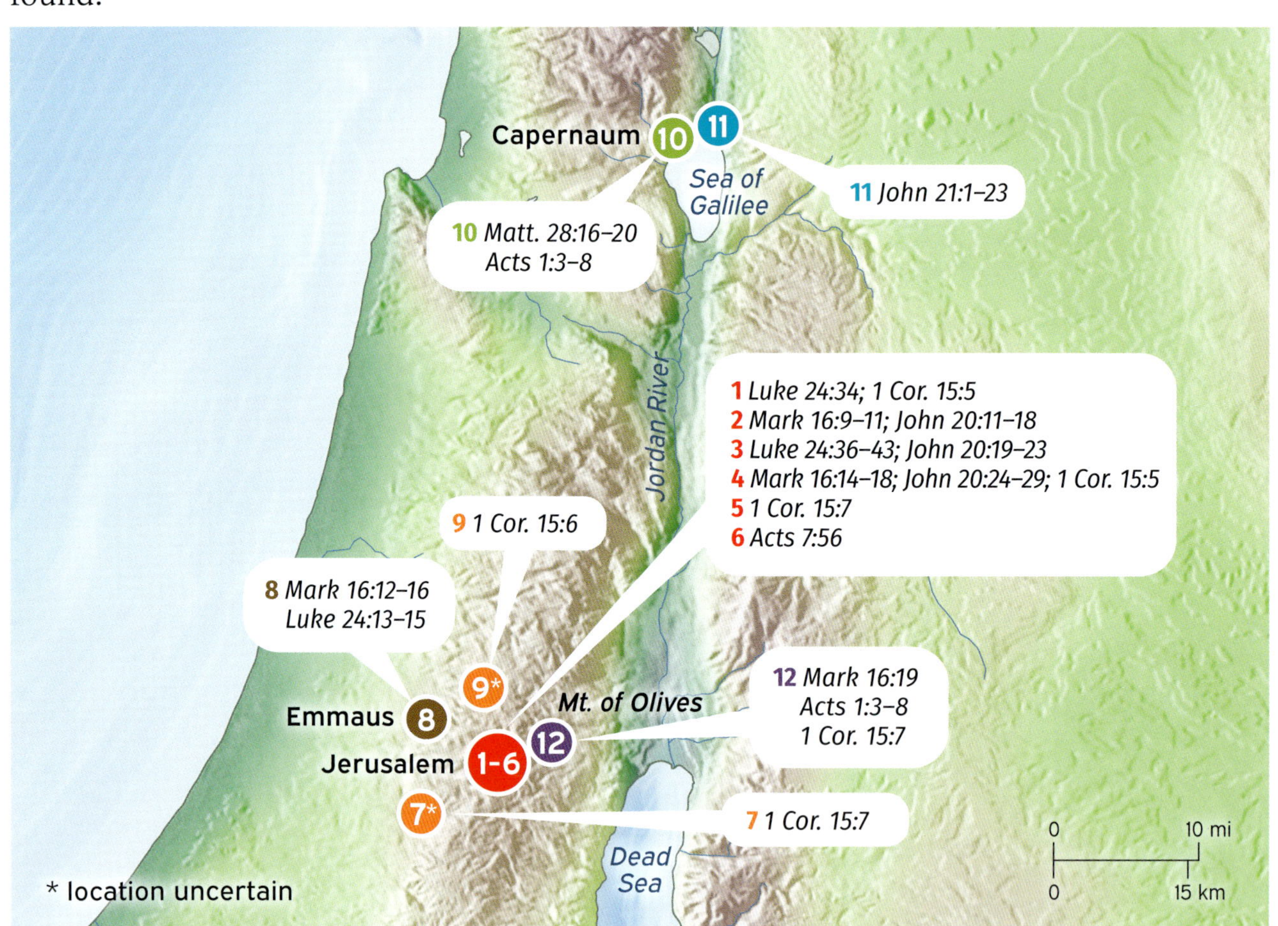

Appearances of Jesus

The Bible records twelve occasions when Jesus appeared to people after his resurrection. His appearances were not spectral sightings; they were encounters with the risen Christ, instances when he spoke with his followers, ate with them, taught them, and let them see and touch his crucifixion wounds to convince them that indeed, it was him, their Lord risen from the grave.

The Ascension

The ascension of Jesus Christ into heaven was a final commissioning service for his disciples (Acts 1:6–11). His ascension marked both the end of his earthly ministry (it was the last of his physical appearances) and the beginning of the powerful ministry of the Holy Spirit through the church (Luke 24:49). Christ was elevated to power and authority, seated at the right hand of God "in the heavenly realms" (Eph. 1:19–23). The ascension reminds believers in Jesus of his promise to return, and it assures them of their own future entrance into the presence of God, just as Jesus promised: "I am going to prepare a place for you. When everything is ready, I will come and get you, so that you will always be with me where I am" (John 14:2–3).

The Mount of Olives

The ascension took place east of Jerusalem on the Mount of Olives (Acts 1:12), traditionally on the peak of the ridge that rises about 250 feet (75 m) higher than the temple. Since King Solomon's time, the Mount of Olives had been used as a lookout point to protect the city. Today, the ridge is home to several churches, a large Jewish cemetery, houses, schools, and, of course, olive trees (though far fewer trees than in Jesus's day).

Mount of Olives

Church of St. Sava, Montenegro

THE CHURCH

Jesus established not so much a movement called Christianity or an institution called "the church," but a community of people who together make up the church—"one body in Christ" (Rom. 12:5 KJV). In the New Testament, this community is instructed to gather regularly and share the life of faith in Jesus together. Nearly all of the commands in the New Testament are in the plural, meaning they are to be obeyed by a community, not only by individuals.

The church began after Jesus's ascension into heaven, specifically at Pentecost when the Holy Spirit empowered believers who were gathered in Jerusalem. The book of Acts tells the story of how the church spread the good news (the gospel) of Jesus Christ from Jerusalem to Rome. Leaders like Peter, Philip, John, and Paul, along with countless other men and women, proclaimed the name of Jesus across the Mediterranean world. Through the narrative of the early church, we can see how prayer advances God's kingdom and the Holy Spirit energizes and equips God's people to carry out their mission, even in the face of intense persecution.

The epistles (letters) provided local congregations with guidance as they sought to live out their faith—guidance that is still valuable for Christians today. The book of Revelation makes it clear that this world will end, and a new world will begin. One day, Jesus will return, end this created order tainted by sin, and give the crown of life to his church for eternity (Rev. 21:1–7).

ACTS, THE EPISTLES, AND REVELATION

Acts continues the narrative of the Gospels and tells what happened to the followers of Jesus after his ascension. The Epistles are letters from Christian leaders (Paul, Peter, John, and others) to local churches, instructing them in the faith. Revelation is apocalyptic literature, with visions about good and evil and what will happen at the end of time when Jesus returns.

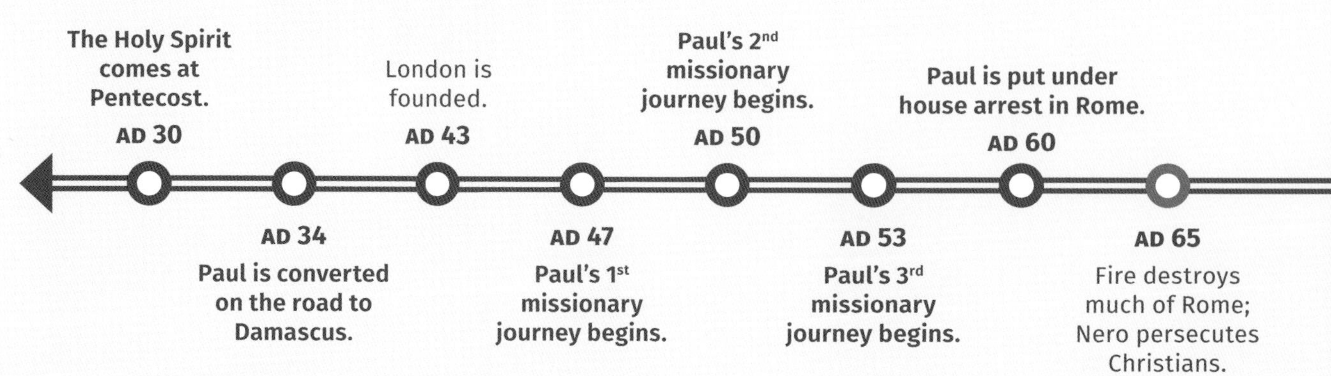

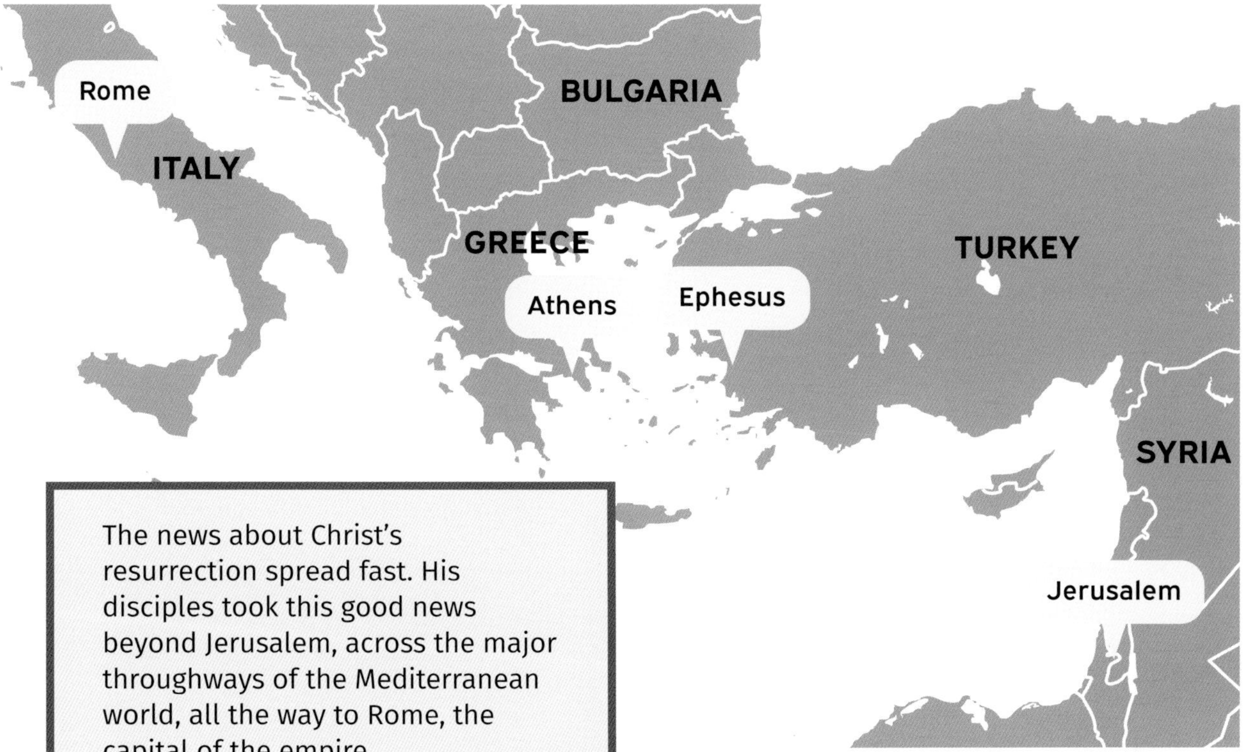

Rome
BULGARIA
ITALY
GREECE
TURKEY
Athens
Ephesus
SYRIA
Jerusalem

The news about Christ's resurrection spread fast. His disciples took this good news beyond Jerusalem, across the major throughways of the Mediterranean world, all the way to Rome, the capital of the empire.

- **AD 65** — Buddhism spreads to China.
- **AD 66–68** — **Paul and Peter are martyred.**
- **AD 70** — Romans destroy the Jerusalem temple.
- **AD 79** — Mount Vesuvius erupts, destroying Pompeii.
- **AD 81–96** — Domitian persecutes Christians.
- **AD 95** — **John is exiled on Patmos.**
- **AD 135** — Hadrian forces Jews to leave Jerusalem.
- **AD 313** — Constantine legalizes Christianity.

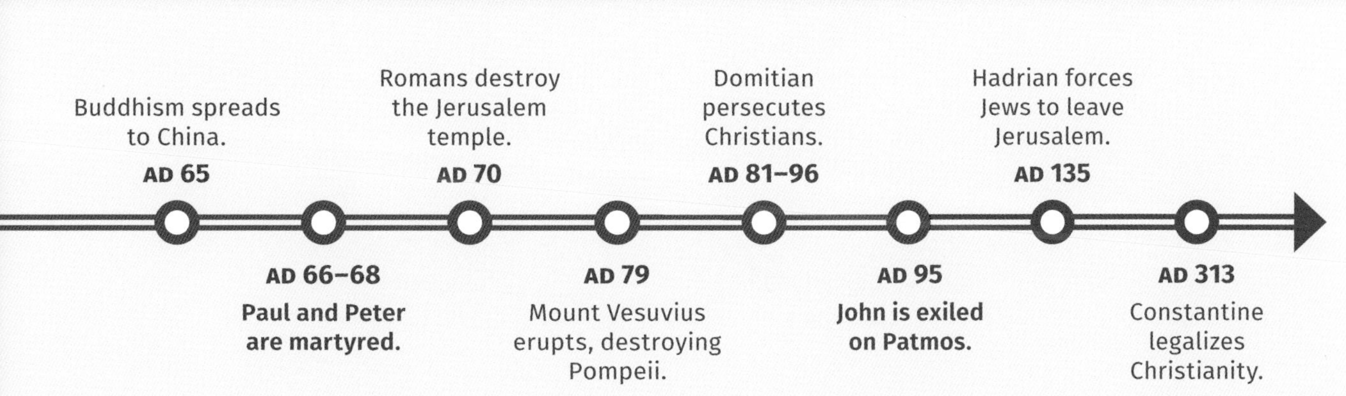

From Jerusalem to Rome

The narrative of the book of Acts shows how the gospel progressively spread farther and farther. The book of Acts begins with about 120 believers gathered together in Jerusalem (Acts 1:12, 15) and ends in Rome where the missionary Paul is under house arrest but still boldly sharing the gospel with all who would listen.

Where Acts Begins:

"You will receive power when the Holy Spirit comes upon you. And you will be my witnesses, telling people about me everywhere—in Jerusalem, throughout Judea, in Samaria, and to the ends of the earth."

ACTS 1:8

Where Acts Ends:

"For the next two years, Paul lived in Rome at his own expense. He welcomed all who visited him, boldly proclaiming the Kingdom of God and teaching about the Lord Jesus Christ."

ACTS 28:30–31

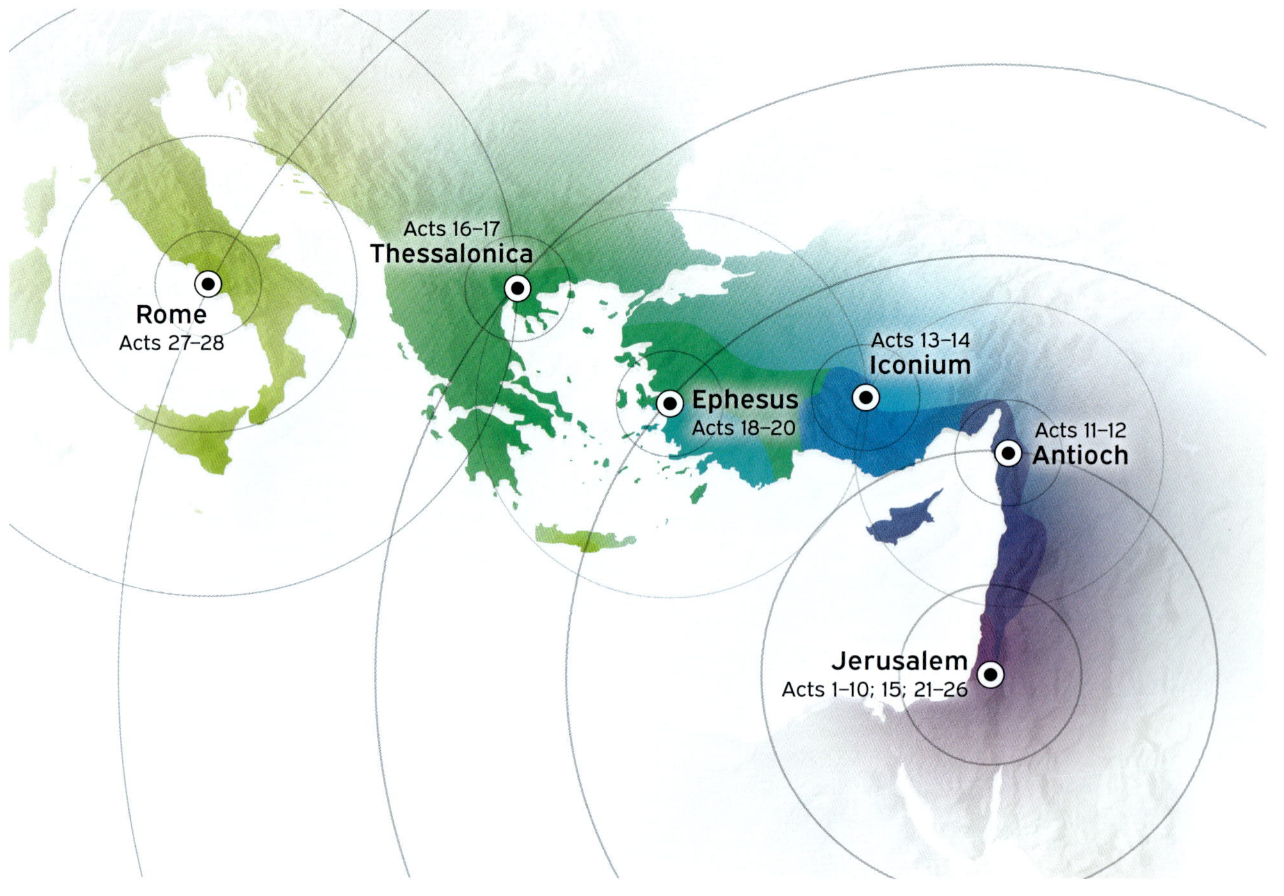

The Beginning of the Church

In Acts 2, people from all over the Roman and Parthian Empires arrived in Jerusalem for the Jewish festival of Pentecost. Jesus's followers were waiting in Jerusalem, just as Jesus had told them to do (Luke 24:49), when the Holy Spirit came upon them in power and enabled them to speak in other languages. They proclaimed in all the peoples' native languages the wonderful things God had done (Acts 2:11). The apostle Peter stepped forward and preached to the crowd. Three thousand people believed and were baptized (Acts 2:41)—and the church was born!

Nations at Pentecost (Acts 2:5–11)

- **Parthia**, the region stretching from the Tigris River eastward into India
- **Media**, in modern-day Iran
- **Cappadocia, Pontus, Asia, Phrygia,** and **Pamphylia**—all Roman provinces (modern-day Turkey)
- **Mesopotamia**, between the Tigris and Euphrates rivers (modern-day Iraq)
- **Elam**, near the Persian Gulf
- **Judea**, the Jewish homeland
- **Egypt**, with its large Jewish population, especially in Alexandria
- **Libya** and **Cyrene,** in northern Africa
- **Rome**, the imperial capital
- **Crete**, a large island near Greece
- **Arabia**, the region south and east of Jerusalem

PHILIP (Acts 8:4–8, 23–40)

Philip was a Greek-speaking Jewish Christian, who has come to be called "Philip the Evangelist" because of his Spirit-empowered witness for Christ.

1. Philip took the gospel north to **Samaria**, where many believed.
2. The Spirit directed Philip to go south toward **Gaza**. Along the way, he baptized an Ethiopian official.
3. The Spirit "snatched Philip away" to **Azotus**.
4. Philip went north to **Caesarea**, where he continued to live and preach the gospel.

PETER (Acts 9:32–11:18)

Peter, one of the original twelve disciples, became a leader among the apostles in Judea.

1. Sometime after meeting Saul in **Jerusalem** (Acts 9:26–28; Gal. 1:18), Peter left and began traveling "from place to place."
2. In **Lydda**, Peter healed a paralyzed man, Aeneas, in the name and power of Jesus.
3. In **Joppa**, Peter raised Tabitha (Dorcas) from the dead.
4. Peter went to **Caesarea** where the gentile Cornelius and his household were filled with the Spirit.
5. Peter returned to **Jerusalem**, reporting that gentiles had received the word of God.

SAUL (Acts 9:1–31)

Saul (Paul) was a violent opponent of Christianity whom God transformed into one of the early church's most successful missionaries.

1. In his zeal to stamp out Christianity, Saul traveled north toward **Damascus**, but along the way the risen Christ appeared to him. In Damascus, Saul was baptized as a believer.
2. Saul traveled to **Arabia** and back to Damascus (Gal. 1:17–18).
3. In **Damascus**, Saul escaped a plot against his life.
4. Saul fled to **Jerusalem**, where he met with the apostles.
5. Christians in Jerusalem took Saul to **Caesarea** to escape another death threat. He then sailed to **Tarsus**.

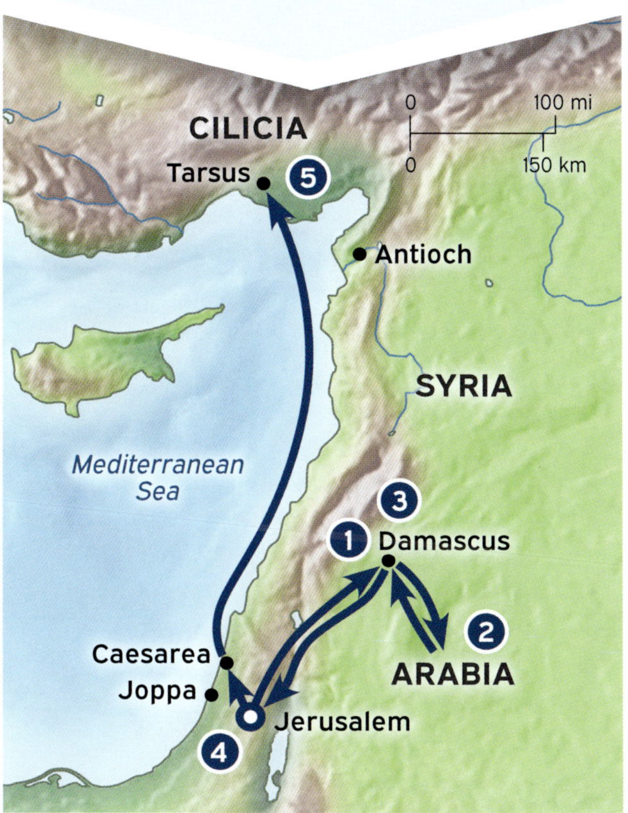

Who Was Paul?

Paul (or Saul, his Hebrew name) was born in Tarsus to Jewish parents who were Roman citizens. He was a tentmaker by trade but educated as a Pharisee. As a young man, his religious zeal led him to ruthlessly persecute Christians in Judea. But through a life-changing, personal encounter with the risen Christ on his way to Damascus, Paul dedicated the rest of his life to proclaiming Jesus as Savior and Lord (Gal. 1:13–16).

The book of Acts records his three major missionary journeys, plus his trip to Rome under Roman guard. Paul wrote thirteen of the New Testament epistles, which deal with a wide range of issues, including salvation, sin, church order, and what Christians believe about the person and glory of Christ.

After the story of Acts ends with Paul in Rome, Paul's later epistles indicate that he was able to travel again and continue his missionary work. According to tradition, Paul was martyred in Rome during Emperor Nero's persecution of Christians.

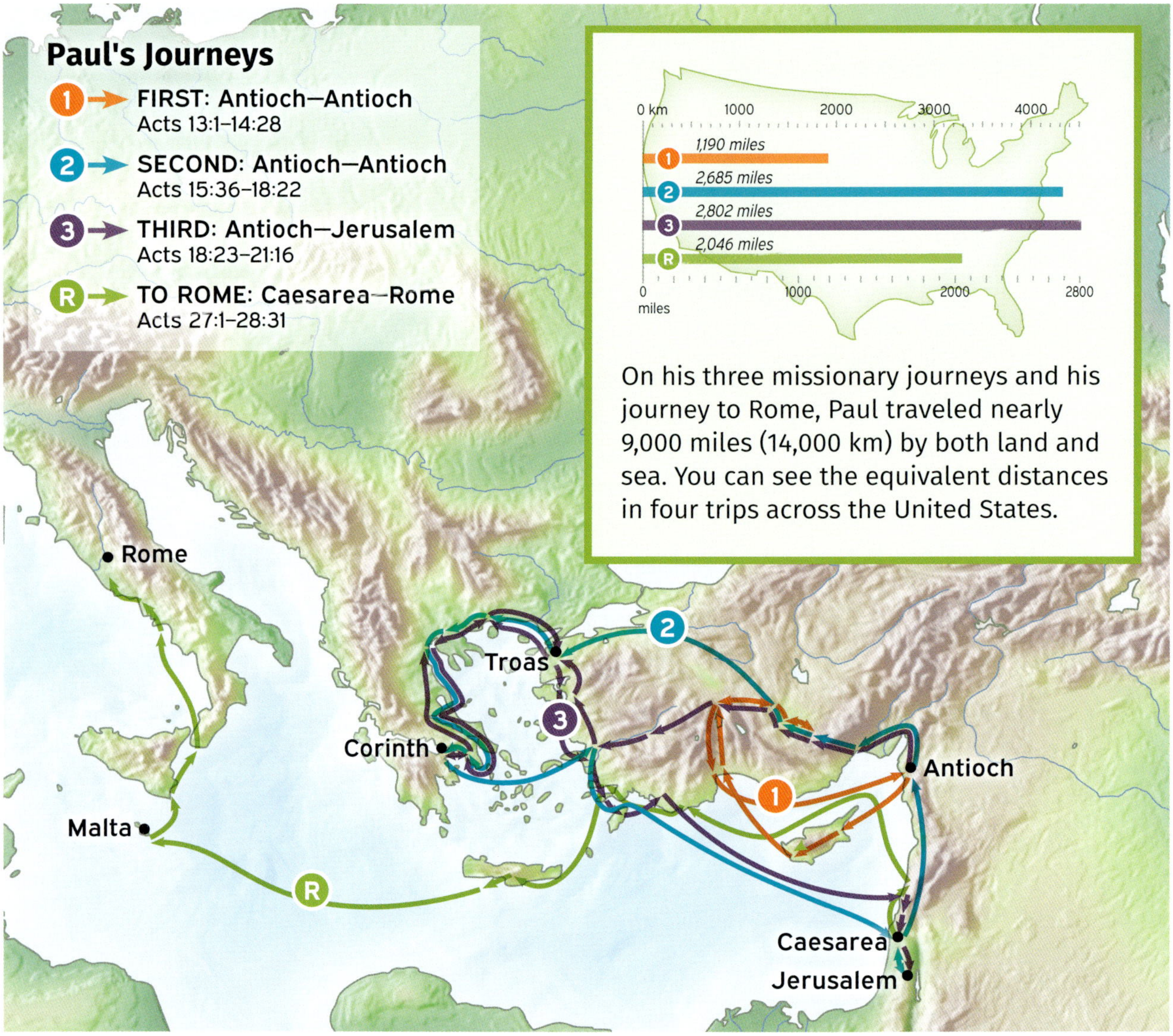

Paul's Journeys

1 FIRST: Antioch–Antioch
Acts 13:1–14:28

2 SECOND: Antioch–Antioch
Acts 15:36–18:22

3 THIRD: Antioch–Jerusalem
Acts 18:23–21:16

R TO ROME: Caesarea–Rome
Acts 27:1–28:31

0 km 1000 2000 3000 4000

1 1,190 miles
2 2,685 miles
3 2,802 miles
R 2,046 miles

0 miles 1000 2000 2800

On his three missionary journeys and his journey to Rome, Paul traveled nearly 9,000 miles (14,000 km) by both land and sea. You can see the equivalent distances in four trips across the United States.

Rome
Troas
Corinth
Malta
Antioch
Caesarea
Jerusalem

Antakya, Turkey (Antioch of Syria)

Antioch of Syria

Antioch of Syria was built by Emperor Seleucus around the year 300 BC. It became a busy cosmopolitan center of trade, religious ferment, and high levels of intellectual and political life. Jewish Christians fled to Antioch to escape fierce persecution in Jerusalem (Acts 11:19). The city was the heart of combined Jewish and gentile Christian living (Acts 15:1–35). Barnabas and Paul were active leaders of the Antioch church. Paul's three missionary journeys all began in Antioch.

Paul's Missionary Companions

1 BARNABAS

Barnabas was "a good man, full of the Holy Spirit and strong in faith" (Acts 11:24). True to his name, Barnabas ("Son of Encouragement"), he encouraged Paul in Tarsus to join the thriving Christian community in Antioch of Syria (Acts 4:36; 11:25–26). Commissioned in Antioch, they embarked on their first missionary journey, stopping first in Cyprus, Barnabas's homeland (Acts 13:1–4).

1 JOHN MARK

John Mark joined Barnabas (his cousin) and Paul as an assistant on their first missionary journey (Acts 13:5). For unknown reasons, he quit before the trip ended (Acts 13:13). This caused a disagreement between Paul and Barnabas, so Barnabas took John Mark on a missionary journey instead of joining Paul on his second journey (Acts 15:36–41). Later, John Mark appears to have assisted Peter (1 Peter 5:13) and also Paul in Rome (Col. 4:10; 2 Tim. 4:11).

2 SILAS

Silas went on Paul's second missionary journey (Acts 15:40). Silas remained faithful to their mission, even when they were beaten and imprisoned in Philippi and pursued by a mob in Thessalonica (Acts 16–17).

2 3 TIMOTHY

Timothy was one of Paul's most trusted helpers (2 Tim. 1:3–4). Timothy, who was both Jewish and Greek, joined Paul's missionary team when Paul passed through Timothy's hometown of Lystra (Acts 16:1–3). Some years later, Timothy was ministering to the Ephesian church when Paul wrote him two epistles encouraging the young pastor (1 Tim. 1:3; 2 Tim. 1:2).

2 3 R LUKE

Luke was a gentile, a doctor, and a loyal assistant to Paul. Luke began to accompany Paul on Paul's second missionary journey (Acts 16:10). Luke was also the author of the gospel of Luke and the book of Acts. He most likely wrote Acts while Paul was under house arrest in Rome, which is why the book ends there. Years later, Luke faithfully remained with Paul when Paul was in prison in Rome, awaiting execution (2 Tim. 4:11).

2 PRISCILLA AND AQUILA

Priscilla and Aquila were a Christian couple from Rome, but they were living in Corinth when they met Paul, and like Paul, they were tentmakers by trade (Acts 18:1–3). For a while, they joined Paul on his second missionary journey (Acts 18:18, 24–26). Later, it appears the couple returned to Rome where they led a house church (Rom. 16:3–5).

3 TITUS

Titus was a gentile Christian who served as Paul's assistant. He was often sent on special assignments, such as dealing with problems in the Corinthian church (2 Cor. 2:4, 9; 7:8–9) and organizing the church on the island of Crete (Titus 1:5). Though not mentioned in Acts, Titus worked with Paul in Ephesus during Paul's third missionary journey (2 Cor. 2:13) and most likely accompanied Paul on other journeys as well (Gal. 2:3; 2 Tim. 4:10).

ROME was the capital of the Roman Empire and the final destination of Paul's journeys in Acts.

CORINTH, a bustling commercial hub stood at the crossroads of Greece. Paul spent 18 months here on his second journey.

ATHENS, the leading city of classical Achaia, was still a center of learning when Paul stopped here on his second journey.

Paul's Journeys

- ① **First Journey**, AD 47–48, Acts 13:4–14:28
- *Return journey to Antioch*
- ② **Second Journey**, AD 50–52, Acts 15:36–18:22
- *Return journey to Antioch via Jerusalem*
- ③ **Third Journey**, AD 53–57, Acts 18:23–21:16
- *Return journey to Jerusalem*
- Ⓡ **Journey to Rome**, AD 59–60, Acts 27:1–28:31

PHILIPPI was a prominent Roman military city. It was Paul's first stop in Macedonia on his second journey.

ANTIOCH was the earliest and most important hub of Jewish-gentile Christianity. From Antioch, Paul and Barnabas were sent out on their first missionary journey.

CYPRUS was Barnabas's birthplace. He and Paul traveled through Cyprus on their first journey, and Barnabas later returned the island.

CAESAREA was a Roman administrative center. Paul was imprisoned here for two years before his journey to Rome.

Paul's First Missionary Journey

4 Many became believers in **ANTIOCH OF PISIDIA**, but Jewish leaders drove Paul and Barnabas out of the city (Acts 13:14–52).

3 From **PERGA**, John Mark left for Jerusalem (Acts 13:13).

5 After Paul healed a man in LYSTRA, the people thought he and Barnabas were gods. But soon a mob tried to stone Paul to death (Acts 14:8–20).
6 A plot to stone Paul and Barnabas forced them to flee ICONIUM (Acts 14:1–7).
7 Paul and Barnabas returned from DERBE to Antioch of Syria to report all that God had done (Acts 14:20–28).
1 In ANTIOCH OF SYRIA, the Holy Spirit appointed Paul and Barnabas to be missionaries (Acts 13:1–4).
2 Paul confronted the sorcerer Elymas in PAPHOS (Acts 13:5–12).
GALATIA
CILICIA
PAMPHYLIA
SYRIA
CYPRUS
Antioch
Iconium
Lystra
Derbe
Tarsus
Perga
Attalia
Antioch
Seleucia
Salamis
Paphos
Sidon
Tyre
Caesarea
Jerusalem

Paul's Second Missionary Journey

2 Timothy joined Paul's missionary team in LYSTRA (Acts 16:1–7).
CAPPADOCIA
PHRYGIA
1 In ANTIOCH OF SYRIA, Paul took Silas on his next journey, while Barnabas and John Mark went to Cyprus (Acts 15:36–41).
PISIDIA
GALATIA
Antioch
CILICIA
Iconium
Lystra
Tarsus
Derbe
Perga
Antioch
Attalia
PAMPHYLIA
SYRIA
Salamis
CYPRUS
Paphos
Damascus
Sidon
Tyre
8 Paul established a church in EPHESUS and left Priscilla and Aquila to tend to it (Acts 18:18–21).
Caesarea
9 Paul returned to Antioch by way of JERUSALEM (Acts 18:22).
Jerusalem

Paul's Third Missionary Journey

3 Paul encouraged churches in **MACEDONIA** and **GREECE** (Achaia) (Acts 20:1–3).

4 In **TROAS**, Paul revived a young man who fell from a third-story window (Acts 20:4–12).

5 In **MILETUS**, Paul told elders from Ephesus that he expected to be imprisoned in Jerusalem (Acts 20:13–38).

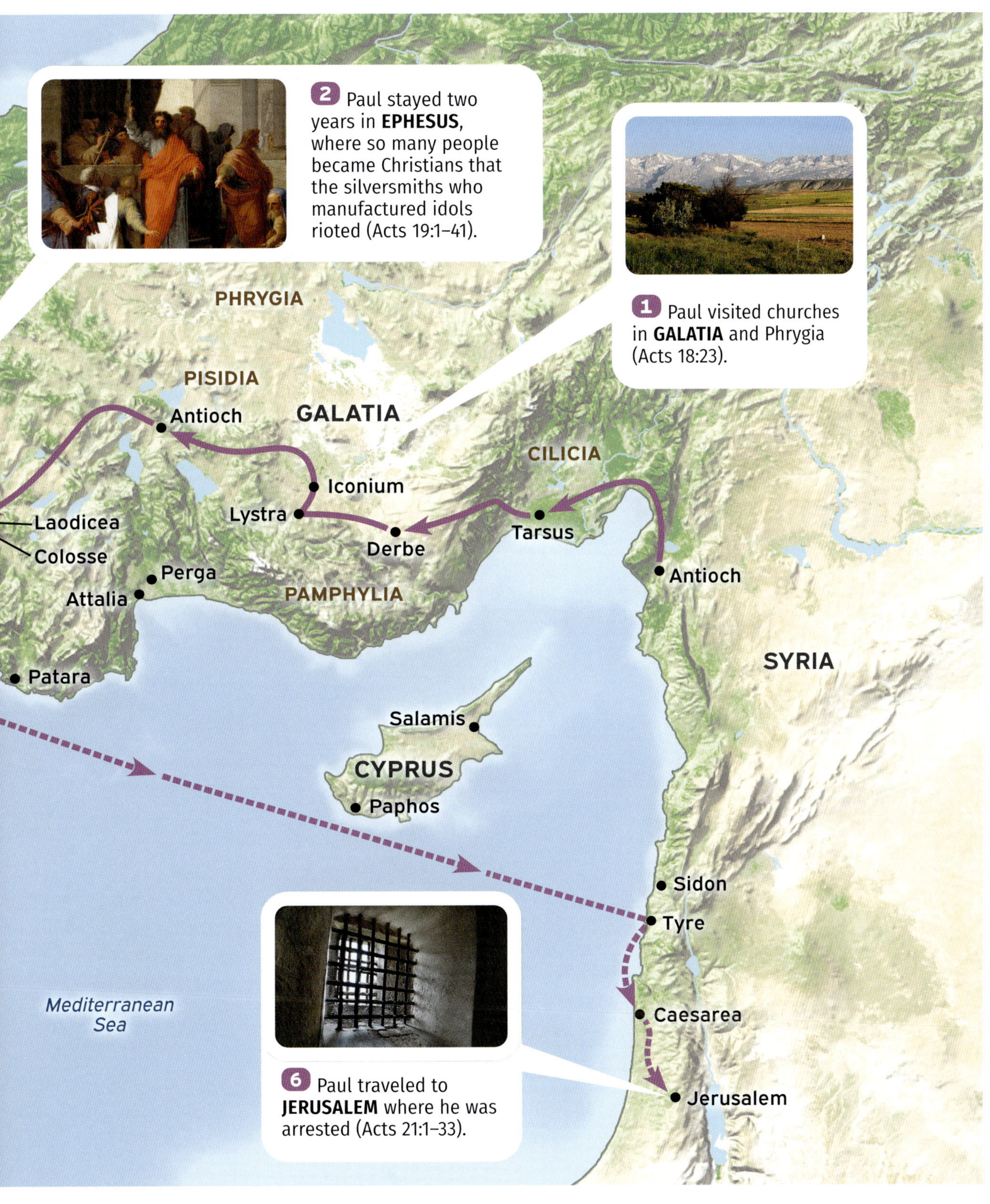
2 Paul stayed two years in **EPHESUS**, where so many people became Christians that the silversmiths who manufactured idols rioted (Acts 19:1–41).
1 Paul visited churches in **GALATIA** and Phrygia (Acts 18:23).
PHRYGIA
PISIDIA
Antioch
GALATIA
CILICIA
Iconium
Lystra
Derbe
Tarsus
Laodicea
Colosse
Perga
Attalia
PAMPHYLIA
Antioch
SYRIA
Patara
Salamis
CYPRUS
Paphos
Sidon
Tyre
Caesarea
Jerusalem
Mediterranean Sea
6 Paul traveled to **JERUSALEM** where he was arrested (Acts 21:1–33).

Paul's Journey to Rome

Black Sea
BITHYNIA AND PONTUS
THRACE
Philippi
Ancyra
CAPPADOCIA
Troas
ASIA MINOR
Aegean Sea
Pergamum
Thyatira
Antioch
GALATIA
Sardis
Smyrna
Philadelphia
Iconium
Laodicea
Tarsus
Ephesus
Lystra
Colosse
Derbe
Miletus
Antioch
Perga
SYRIA
Cnidus
Patara
Myra
Rhodes
CYPRUS
Paphos
CRETE
Fair Havens
Sidon
Tyre
Caesarea
Jerusalem
2 Their ship encountered difficult sailing, but they departed CRETE despite Paul's warnings (Acts 27:4–12).
1 From Jerusalem, Paul was taken to CAESAREA where he spent two years in prison before Governor Festus sent him to Rome (Acts 23:12–27:3).

Paul's Epistles

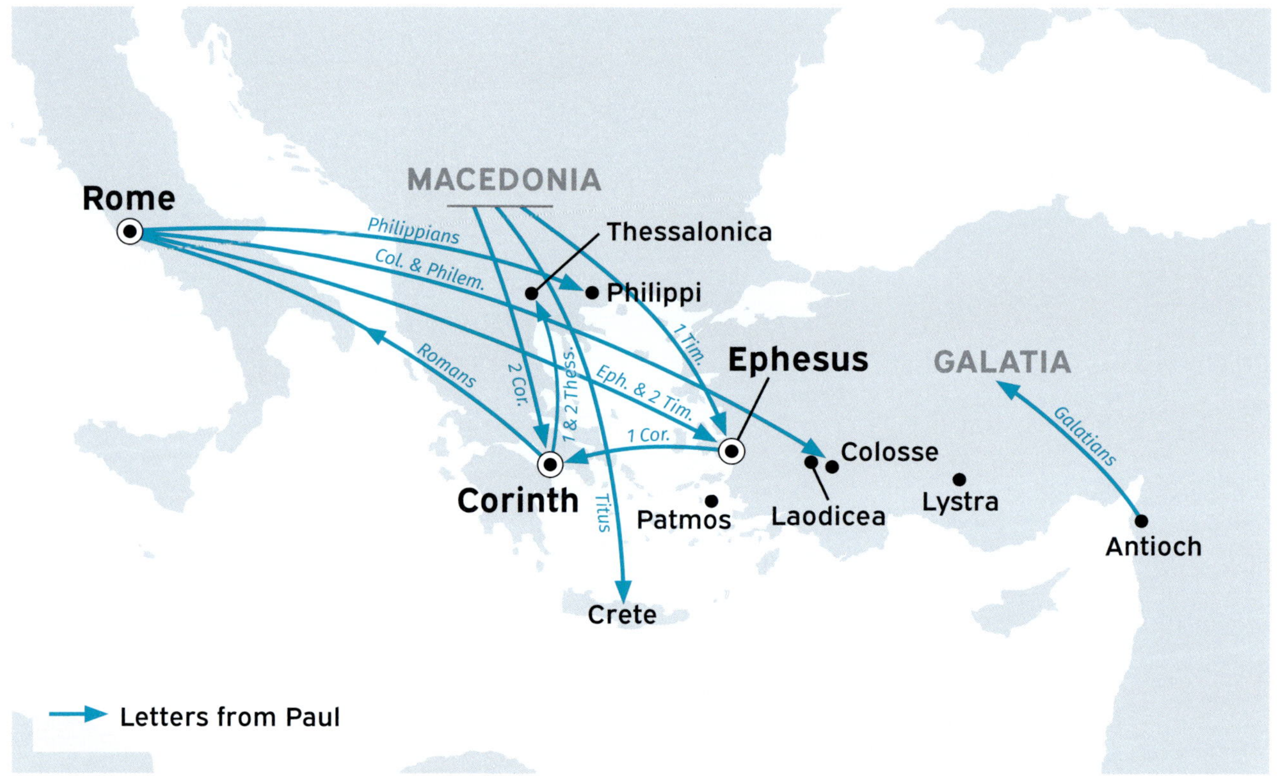

LETTER	DATE	AUTHOR	SENT FROM	SENT TO
Galatians	AD 48–49	Paul	Antioch?	Galatia
1 and 2 Thessalonians	AD 50–51	Paul	Corinth	Thessalonica
1 Corinthians	AD 53–56	Paul	Ephesus	Corinth
2 Corinthians	AD 56	Paul	Macedonia	Corinth
Romans	AD 57	Paul	Corinth?	Rome
Ephesians	AD 60–62	Paul	Rome	Ephesus
Philippians	AD 60–62	Paul	Rome	Philippi
Colossians and Philemon	AD 60–62	Paul	Rome	Colosse
1 Timothy	AD 63	Paul	Macedonia?	Ephesus
Titus	AD 63	Paul	Macedonia?	Crete
2 Timothy	AD 64–65	Paul	Rome	Ephesus

? = uncertain location. Dates and date ranges are estimates. Epistles listed by date written.

General Epistles and Revelation

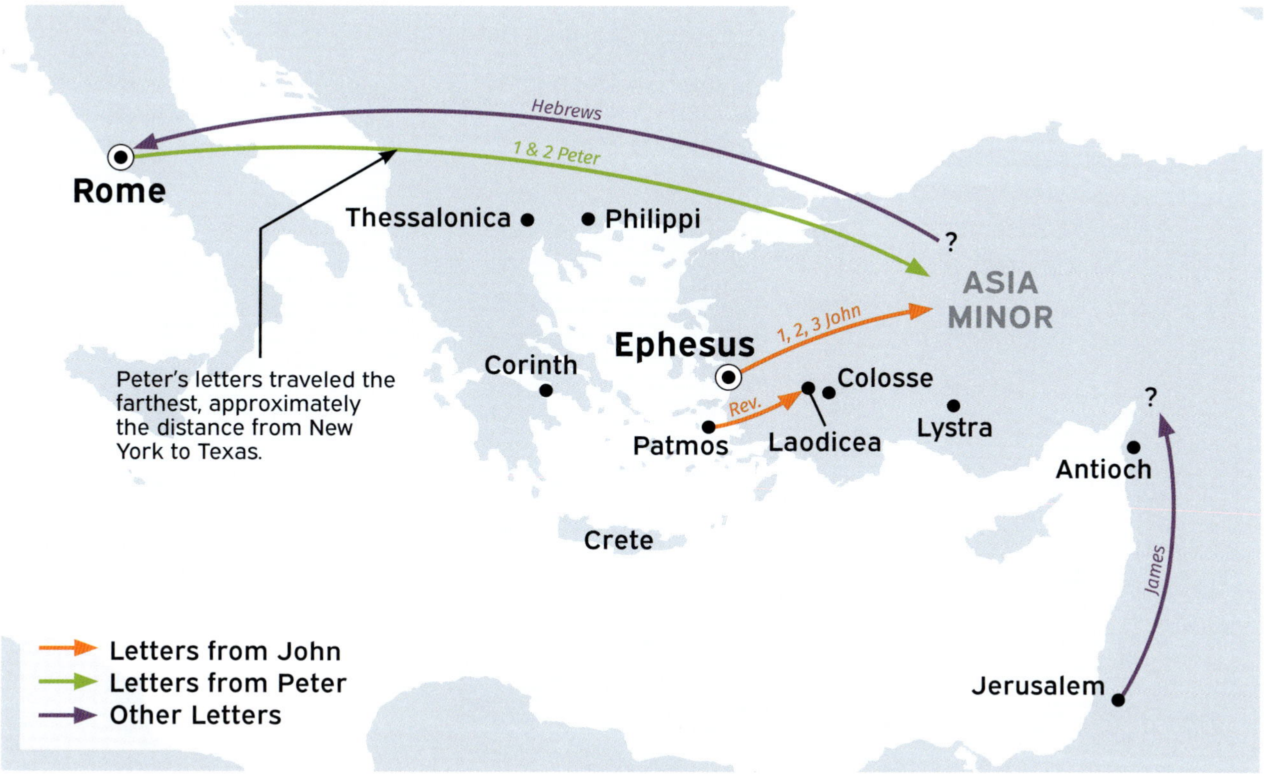

LETTER	DATE	AUTHOR	SENT FROM	SENT TO
James	AD 49	James the brother of Jesus	Jerusalem	Jewish Christians outside Judea
1 and 2 Peter	AD 64	Peter	Rome	Asia Minor
Hebrews	AD 60s	Unknown	Unknown	Rome?
Jude	AD 60–80s	Jude, possibly the brother of Jesus	Unknown	Unknown
1, 2, and 3 John	AD 85–95	John	Ephesus?	Seven churches in Asia Minor
Revelation	AD 95	John	Patmos	Asia Minor

? = uncertain location. Dates and date ranges are estimates. Epistles listed by date written.

Authors of the New Testament

The New Testament was written by about eight or nine different men:

- **MATTHEW**, a Jewish tax collector who became one of the 12 disciples
- **MARK** (John Mark), an assistant to Paul and to Peter
- **LUKE**, a gentile doctor and fellow traveler with Paul
- **JOHN**, one of the 12 disciples who ministered in Asia Minor late in life
- **PAUL**, a missionary and apostle to the gentile world
- **JAMES**, a brother of Jesus who became a leader in the Jerusalem church
- **PETER**, one of the 12 disciples and a leader among the apostles in Judea
- **JUDE**, possibly "Judas," the brother of Jesus mentioned in Matthew 13:55
- The author of Hebrews is unknown.

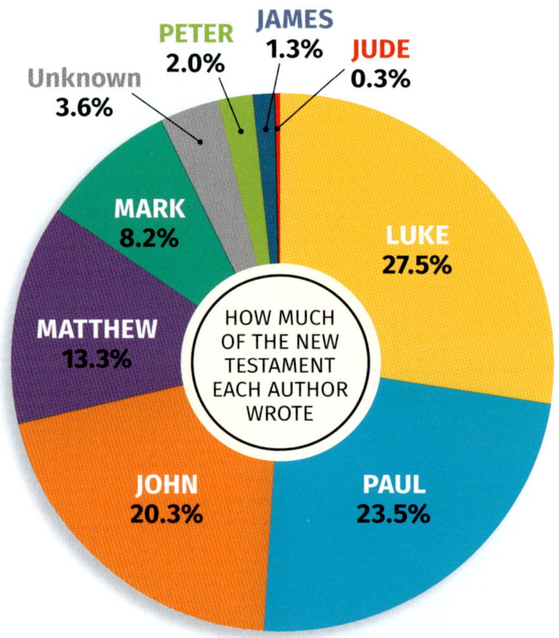

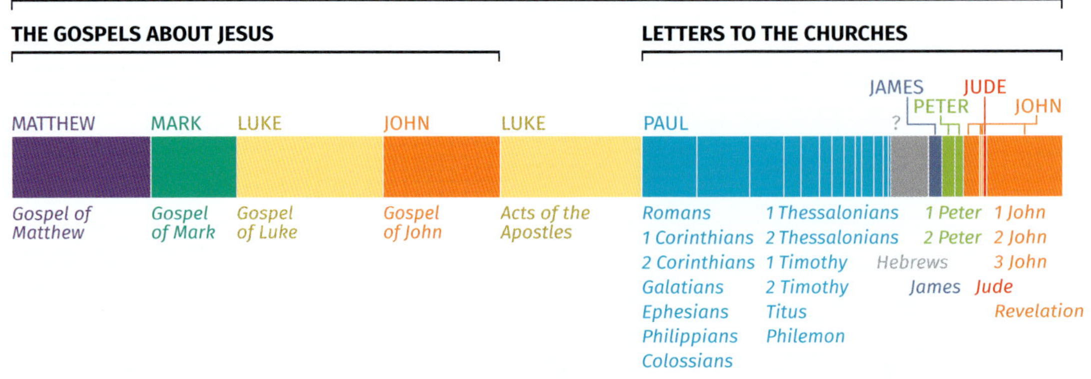

Peter, the Rock

Called to leave his fishing nets on the Sea of Galilee and follow Jesus, Peter would later walk on the sea's water with Jesus (Matt. 4:18–20; 14:22–32). Even though in Jesus's darkest hour in Jerusalem Peter denied knowing his Lord three times, Jesus restored him and commissioned him to "feed my sheep"—the church (John 21:1–17). After Jesus's ascension, Peter was filled with the Holy Spirit and became the spokesman for Christians in Jerusalem (Acts 2). After about three decades of preaching the gospel, Peter was imprisoned and crucified in Rome during Emperor Nero's persecution of Christians (AD 64–68). Peter is remembered as a reassuring example of Christ's forgiving grace and restoration, a follower of Jesus who was faithful to the end.

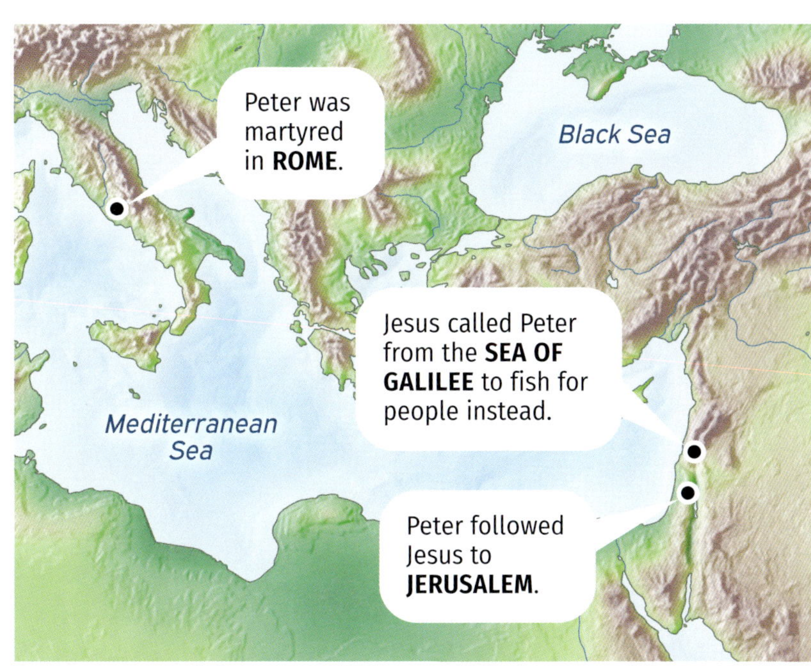

> **"Simon Peter answered, 'You are the Messiah, the Son of the living God.' Jesus replied, 'You are blessed, Simon son of John, because my Father in heaven has revealed this to you.... Now I say to you that you are Peter (which means 'rock'), and upon this rock I will build my church.'"**
>
> MATTHEW 16:16–18

Bethsaida in Galilee was Peter's hometown (John 1:44), but it seems he lived by the Sea of Galilee in Capernaum, with his wife, mother-in-law, and brother Andrew (Matt. 8:14–15; Mark 1:29–31). Shown here is a possible site of Peter's house in Capernaum; a modern pilgrimage church is built over the remains.

John, the Beloved Apostle

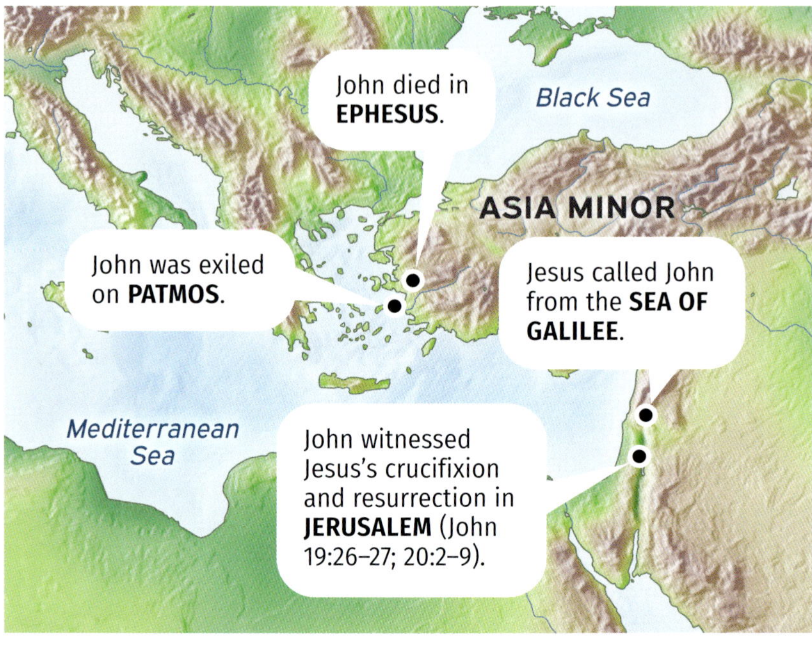

John was a fisherman on the Sea of Galilee who left everything to follow Jesus (Mark 1:19–20). John and his brother James, along with Peter, were among those closest to Jesus—his inner circle of disciples (Mark 5:37; 9:2). After Jesus's ascension, John and Peter ministered in Judea and worked miracles that confirmed the truth of the gospel they preached (Acts 3:1–11; 4:1–23). John lost his brother when James was martyred in Jerusalem by Herod Agrippa I (Acts 12:1–2). John spent his later years ministering in Asia Minor, and for a time he was exiled on the island of Patmos because of his testimony about Jesus (Rev. 1:9). It is believed that John died of natural causes in Ephesus at the end of the first century.

Church of St. John, Ephesus

"I [John] am writing to remind you, dear friends, that we should love one another.... Love means doing what God has commanded us, and he has commanded us to love one another."

2 JOHN 1:5–6

The Book of Revelation

The book of Revelation is an unfolding drama that stretches the imagination while bearing witness to God's supreme power. Written by John in an apocalyptic style reminiscent of the books of Daniel and Ezekiel, Revelation describes the plight of Christians, God's judgment on their persecutors, and the eternal promises for God's people. No matter how one interprets the details of the visions, the overarching message of the book is one of encouragement and hope in the face of persecution, knowing that evil ultimately will be punished and faithfulness rewarded.

Revelation's Old Testament Imagery

John's writings were steeped in the Hebrew Scriptures. The book of Revelation adopts imagery about judgment and salvation found in the Old Testament, especially from the prophets.

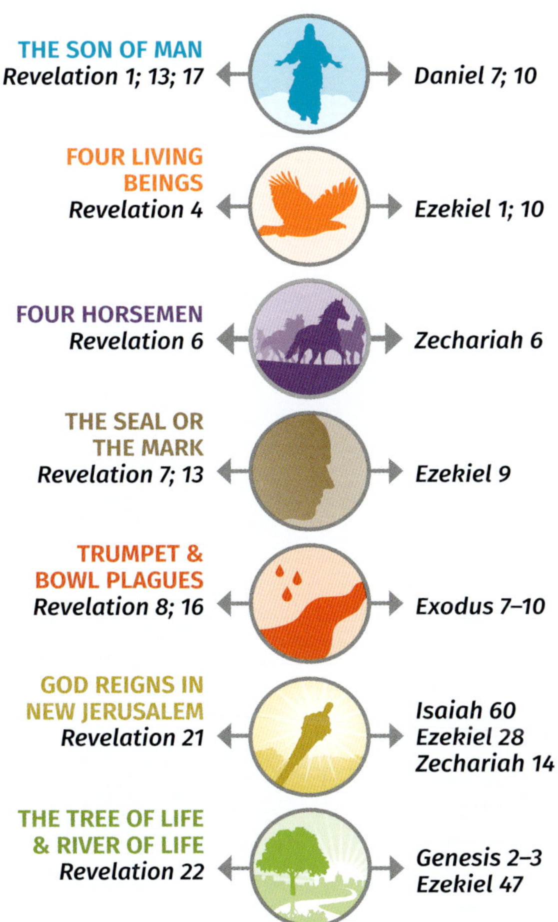

Patmos, Greece

The Island of Patmos

John's revelation takes place on the small island of Patmos in the Aegean Sea off the coast of Asia Minor (Rev. 1:9). In John's day, Patmos was a rocky, deserted place where the Romans sent prisoners. John was exiled on Patmos during Emperor Domitian's persecution of Christians in the AD 90s (though some scholars think it was during Nero's reign in the AD 60s). When the persecution abated, it appears that John was released from Patmos and lived out the rest of his days in Ephesus.

The Seven Churches of Revelation

The original recipients of Revelation were seven churches in the Roman province of Asia (Rev. 1:4). The cities of these seven churches were joined by a triangular road system, forming something like a mail route. The order of these cities addressed in Revelation is geographical and follows the route the courier probably took as he carried the writings of Revelation to be read in each church.

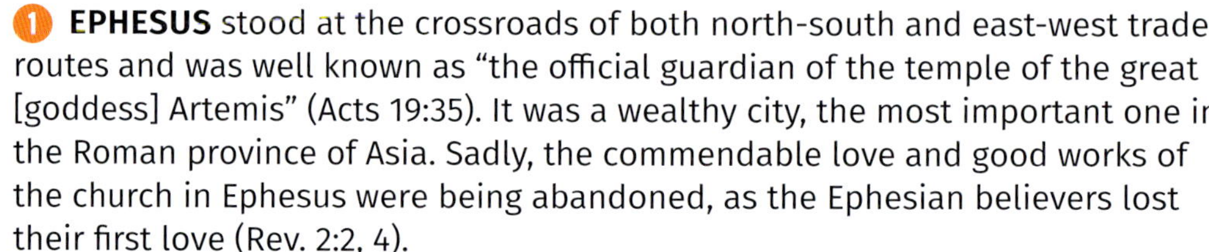

1 **EPHESUS** stood at the crossroads of both north-south and east-west trade routes and was well known as “the official guardian of the temple of the great [goddess] Artemis” (Acts 19:35). It was a wealthy city, the most important one in the Roman province of Asia. Sadly, the commendable love and good works of the church in Ephesus were being abandoned, as the Ephesian believers lost their first love (Rev. 2:2, 4).

2 **SMYRNA** was a small but thriving port just 35 miles (56 km) north of Ephesus. Founded as a Greek colony which later gave its allegiance to the Roman Empire, the city was filled with temples to various Greek and Roman gods. The church in Smyrna remained faithful to God though they faced intense satanic opposition.

3 **PERGAMUM** was the earliest capital of the Roman province of Asia. It contained a famous library, and its citizens developed the use of animal skins as writing materials. Christians in Pergamum were tempted to compromise their morality, and some were combining Christianity with paganism.

4 **THYATIRA** was an outpost city, known for its many trade guilds, including tanners, coppersmiths, potters, and dyers (the convert Lydia from Thyatira was “a merchant of expensive purple cloth;” Acts 16:14). The letter to the church in Thyatira confronts Christians who were mixing their faith with pagan practices and immorality.

5 **SARDIS** was nearly 50 miles (80 km) east of Smyrna on the southeast highway. It had a fortified acropolis, which perhaps gave the city’s inhabitants an overconfident sense of security. The message to the church in Sardis is to spiritually “Wake up!” or else they will face sudden judgment (Rev. 3:2).

6 **PHILADELPHIA** was situated in the foothills of the Timolus Mountains, open to fertile plains in the east. The city repeatedly experienced earthquakes, which left it weak and impoverished. The letter to the church of Philadelphia encourages those who seem to be weak and powerless to realize that their true strength is in Christ.

7 **LAODICEA,** about 40 miles (65 km) southeast of Philadelphia, was the economic and judicial center of a metropolitan region that included Colosse and Hierapolis. After a severe earthquake in AD 60, the people of Laodicea, being proudly self-sufficient, refused to accept aid from Rome and rebuilt their city themselves. The church in Laodicea was lukewarm, and they believed themselves to be rich, though they were spiritually quite poor.

Pergamum
Rev. 2:12–17
Thyatira
Rev. 2:18–29
Sardis
Rev. 3:1–6
Smyrna
Rev. 2:8–11
Philadelphia
Rev. 3:7–13
Laodicea
Rev. 3:14–22
Ephesus
Rev. 2:1–7
Miletus
Patmos
Rev. 1:9
John the apostle received the visions of Revelation while in exile.
Black Sea
The Seven Churches
ITALY
ASIA MINOR
GREECE
Mediterranean Sea
Roman roads connecting principal cities
0 25 mi
0 40 km